BRANDMAPS™

The Competitive Marketing Strategy Game

BRANDMAPS™

The Competitive Marketing Strategy Game

Third Edition

Randall G. Chapman

Mercer Management Consulting

Prentice Hall
Englewood Cliffs, New Jersey 07632

Library of Congress Cataloging-in-Publication Data

Chapman, Randall G.
    Brandmaps : the competitive marketing strategy game / Randall G.
Chapman. -- 3rd. ed.
      p. cm.
    Includes index.
    ISBN 0-13-177502-2
    1. BRANDMAPS.   2. Marketing--Computer simulation.   3. Product
management--Computer programs.   I. Title.
HF5415.125.C47   1994
658.8'0028'5369--dc20   93-5869
                                               CIP

Acquisitions editor: Sandra Steiner
Assistant editor: Wendy Goldner
Editorial assistant: Cathleen Profitko
Cover design: Wendy Alling Judy
Manufacturing buyer: Patrice Fraccio

 ©1994 by Prentice-Hall, Inc.
A Paramount Communications Company
Englewood Cliffs, New Jersey 07632

Printed in the United States of America

10 9 8 7 6 5 4 3 2

ISBN 0-13-177502-2

Prentice-Hall International (UK) Limited, London
Prentice-Hall of Australia Pty. Limited, Sydney
Prentice-Hall Canada Inc., Toronto
Prentice-Hall Hispanoamericana, S.A., Mexico
Prentice-Hall of India Private Limited, New Delhi
Prentice-Hall of Japan, Inc., Tokyo
Simon & Schuster Asia Pte. Ltd., Singapore
Editora Prentice-Hall do Brasil, Ltda.,Rio de Janeiro

CONTENTS

5 BRANDMAPS™ Marketing Research Studies   **51**

List of Exhibits

List of Forms

List of Tables

Preface and Acknowledgments

BRANDMAPS™ is a sophisticated marketing simulation game designed to be used on DOS personal computers. BRANDMAPS™ is designed to reflect the complexities, uncertainties, and challenges inherent in the marketing decision-making and analysis process. To the greatest extent possible, this game is designed to represent "reality" to the participants, rather than being just a "game." Nevertheless, it does represent an approximation to the real world, as do all marketing simulation games. Suggestions for ways in which BRANDMAPS™ might be enriched would be welcome.

This marketing simulation game's name, BRANDMAPS™, reflects its orientation: brand management of a number of individual brands within an organization's product line. As it is traditionally viewed, the brand management process involves on-going marketing, competitive, and financial analysis, as well as coordination of marketing programs and operations capabilities (capacity and inventory management, sales forecasting, and the like). These efforts lead to the development of marketing strategies which are implemented within short- and long-term marketing plans. All of these brand management elements — *M*arketing *A*nalysis, *P*lanning, and *S*trategy — arise in BRANDMAPS™.

The BRANDMAPS™ name is also consistent with the underlying structure of the game's simulated marketing environment. Just as positioning analysis and strategy are of crucial importance in understanding real competitive marketing situations, so it is in BRANDMAPS™. Within BRANDMAPS™, positioning issues arise continually. Sophisticated product design and positioning analysis tools (including concept testing, product preference testing, conjoint analysis, perceptual mapping, and test marketing) are important components of the BRANDMAPS™ environment.

For those who are familiar with the second edition of BRANDMAPS™, the following major participant-visible changes have been instituted in the third edition:

- The BRANDMAPS™ input program, used for changing decision variables and pre-ordering marketing research studies, has been split into two programs: B_DV.EXE (to change decision variables) and B_PREMRS.EXE (to pre-order marketing research studies). To improve access to these programs, a front-end driver, BRANDMAP.EXE, has been constructed. Students should use program BRANDMAP.EXE which provides convenient access to all participant-related BRANDMAPS™ disk-based input/output functions.

- BRANDMAPS™ may include between four and eight regional markets, chosen by the course instructor at the time BRANDMAPS™ is initialized. The number of market regions may not be changed after the game is initialized.

- Premium (in excess of 30% of current plant capacity) and negative (plant capacity sales) plant capacity orders are now possible.

- In addition to experience curve effects on production and labor costs, experience curve effects are now present in raw materials costs.

- Active dealer inventory behavior is now included within BRANDMAPS™. Dealers stock vaporware brands and sell from their inventory to meet final customer demand. Vaporware dealers are thoughtful, rational buyers. They may stockpile brands offered with a dealer rebate and then sell from their own local inventory first before re-ordering from the manufacturer.

- In addition to the standard product operating statement presentation style for reporting financial results, the following additional presentation styles now exist for brand-specific profit-and-loss statements: regional operating statement (all brands in each region), operating statement (previous and current quarter's data plus change rates for each active brand in each region), and historical operating statement (current and previous three quarters for each active brand in each region).

- A variety of changes and updates have been made to the BRANDMAPS™ marketing research studies. Most competitive monitoring studies have been reformatted to include current and four past-quarters data (if available in the BRANDMAPS™ historical archives). Conjoint analyses (one specific conjoint analysis design) may now be requested for all regions simultaneously. A major change in the procedures involved in ordering test marketing experiments has been implemented. The report formats for the conjoint and test marketing studies have been dramatically changed to improve interpretability.

- Due to technology limitations implemented in this third edition, the fifth vaporware raw material must always equal 5. Reformulations and marketing research studies involving vaporware raw materials must include a value of 5 for the fifth vaporware raw material.

- All BRANDMAPS™ brands have the formulation 30/30/30/5/5/5/5 at initialization (i.e., at quarter 1).

- Ten new marketing research studies have been added to BRANDMAPS™: "Regional Summary Analysis," "Marketing Research Ordering Statistics," "Marketing Support Spending Productivity Analysis," "Population Forecasts," "Per Capita Income Forecasts," "Consumer Price Index Forecasts," "Self-Reported Attribute Preferences," "Dealer Inventory Analysis - Own Brands," "Dealer Inventory Analysis - All Brands," and "Price Sensitivity Analysis."

- A variety of software enhancements improve the handling of multiple, simultaneous BRANDMAPS™ industries. From the student's point of view, it continues to appear as if only a single BRANDMAPS™ industry exists — the student's industry.

The original work on what ultimately evolved into BRANDMAPS™ began at Queen's University in the late 1970s. Since that time, more than 1,000 students at Queen's University, the University of Chicago, the University of Alberta, and Boston University have been involved in the author's marketing strategy courses where BRANDMAPS™ has been used. Since 1985, an additional 500 participants in executive development programs at the University of Chicago, the Banff School of Advanced Management (Banff, Alberta, Canada), the Boston University Management Development Program-Japan (Kobe, Japan), and the Boston University Executive MBA Program have been exposed to BRANDMAPS™. Their comments, suggestions, and reactions resulted in many useful and valuable improvements in BRANDMAPS™.

Shannon Gangl provided programming effort to assist in the original downsizing and conversion of the mainframe version of BRANDMAPS™ for the personal computer environment. She also played an important role in the development of BRANDMAPS™ through her participation in various executive development programs at the University of Chicago and the Banff School of Advanced Management. It is a pleasure to acknowledge her efforts.

Ruth Bolton's helpful comments and suggestions have been especially notable through all editions of BRANDMAPS™. She also provided the original suggestion for the name BRANDMAPS™.

Initial users of BRANDMAPS™ provided much helpful counsel with their questions, comments, and suggestions. The evolving development of BRANDMAPS™ has, to a major extent, being driven by users.

While retaining full responsibility for everything that is in and that is not in BRANDMAPS™, I would like to acknowledge the helpful early comments and suggestions of Richard Colombo (New York University), Alice Ford (Mercer University), John Ford (Old Dominion University), David Georgoff (Florida Atlantic University), Bruce MacNab (California State University — Hayward), Tom Madden (University of South Carolina), Paul McDevitt (Sangamon State University), Bill Mitchell (University of Texas — San Antonio), Stephen Paranka (Colorado State University), Doug Snetsinger (University of Toronto), Louis Volpp (California State University — Fresno), Jim Wiley (University of Alberta), Bennett Yim (Rice University), and Bob Young (University of San Francisco).

As the third edition of BRANDMAPS™ has unfolded in the last two years, comments and suggestions by Jerry Conover (Northern Arizona University), Gary Karns (Seattle Pacific University), Tom Kinnear (University of Michigan), Bob Kopp (Babson College), R. Krishnan (California Polytechnic State University — San Luis Obispo), Bruce MacNab (California State University — Hayward), Tom Madden (University of South Carolina), Chris Puto (University of Arizona), Allan Shocker (University of Minnesota), Dan Toy (California State University — Chico), Joe Urbany (University of South Carolina), Jim Wiley (University of Alberta), Ken Wilson (University of St. Thomas), Bennett Yim (Rice University), and John Zych (University of Scranton) have been particularly influential in shaping my thinking and the corresponding evolution of BRANDMAPS™.

Future revisions to BRANDMAPS™ will inevitably be based on users' suggestions and comments. Please do pass your suggestions and comments on to the author.

## Chapter 1

BRANDMAPS™ and Marketing Simulation Games

Introduction

BRANDMAPS™ is a marketing simulation exercise. Competing firms within a single industry make marketing decisions (price, product design, advertising, and so on) and a simulated marketplace responds to those decisions. Key features of marketing simulations include the introduction of explicit competition and continuity into the learning process. Participants make decisions in response to, and in light of, likely actions and reactions of competitors. Participants must live with the results and the consequences of their decisions. Market feedback (sales, revenues, market shares, and profits) provides various degrees of positive and negative reinforcement to enhance the learning experience. Rapid and continuous feedback serve as powerful devices to generate interest and motivate participants.

Establishing teams to handle the decision-making function in simulation games provides another valuable learning experience. Whether the team structure adopted is line or staff or some combination, the group decision-making experience is invariably interesting and educational. Another important feature of simulation games is their capability for compressing the time dimension. Such time compression enables teams to see the outcomes of their decisions without the long waiting period that occurs in real life.

Simulation exercises are normally very enjoyable activities for the participants. Participants generally find that their interest in the game increases with the passing of each simulated decision period. The game-related decision-making process becomes an adventure rather than the tedious chore that traditional assignments and cases may become.

Some Considerations in Simulation Game Design

In constructing marketing simulation games, game designers must cope with important trade-offs. All game developers have to resolve the inherent conflicts between realism and simplicity. Of course, all simulation games must have face validity if they are to be taken seriously by the participants. Based on extensive experience with BRANDMAPS™, participants do find it to be a challenging and realistic marketing exercise. Some of the principal marketing simulation game design considerations, and how they apply in BRANDMAPS™, are described in Table 1.

Table 1

SOME GENERAL MARKETING SIMULATION GAME DESIGN
CONSIDERATIONS AND HOW THEY APPLY IN BRANDMAPS™

Marketing Simulation Game Design Consideration	BRANDMAPS™ Application/Implementation
Whether to construct the game around a specific industry or product/service, or to deal with hypothetical scenarios.	BRANDMAPS™ is built around an unidentified durable good, vaporware, initially (at quarter 1) being sold for a few hundred dollars per unit. Vaporware is used in both industrial and consumer settings. For reference purposes, you might wish to think of vaporware as being some kind of electronic product, although viewing vaporware as a type of furniture, clothing, or mechanical product would not be fundamentally misleading.
Whether to use single or multiple products.	Firms in BRANDMAPS™ may market three different brands of vaporware. Brands of vaporware are distinguished by their physical composition of five underlying raw materials (Syntech, Plumbo, Glomp, Trimicro, and Fralange) plus Compatibility and Warranty. Firms control the composition of their vaporware brands, and can produce and market a wide range of possible formulations to attempt to meet customers' needs.
Whether to use single or multiple markets.	In BRANDMAPS™, there are four to eight regional markets. The market structure (number of regional markets) is specified by the course instructor when the game is initialized.
Whether the game should be designed for conflict and competition or require the competition against nature.	In BRANDMAPS™, a maximum of nine firms compete within an industry. To accommodate more than nine firms, parallel industries may be running simultaneously. However, such parallel industries are completely unrelated to each other.
Whether to encourage individual or group decision making.	Teams in BRANDMAPS™ are completely responsible for the management of their firms' activities. Teams may organize themselves in any way they wish to manage their affairs.
Whether to have an underlying market model that is deterministic or stochastic.	As in life, there are undoubtedly some random events in BRANDMAPS™. Remember the cynic who said, "Sometimes you get the elevator, sometimes you get the shaft." However, experience with BRANDMAPS™ indicates that careful and thoughtful analysis, planning, and strategizing will inevitably be successful in the long run.

Decision-Making Logistics in Computerized Simulation Exercises

BRANDMAPS™ is similar to other computerized simulation exercises with regard to the logistics associated with making decisions and receiving results. The general logistics in computerized simulation games involve three steps:

1	Teams meet and make decisions for the next decision period. Typically, some decision forms are used to record the decisions. These forms are ultimately passed on to a game administrator. The game administrator may be the course instructor. If not, the course instructor will identify the game administrator. The course instructor will also describe any other special procedures and requirements associated with submitting decisions.
2	The game administrator arranges to: (i) input all decisions to the game data base; (ii) run the game; (iii) generate the necessary financial and operating reports; and, (iv) assemble the reports for the teams.
3	The game administrator returns the financial and operating reports to the teams, prior to the next scheduled decision period.

The only additional consideration in BRANDMAPS™ is that requests for marketing research studies must be made prior to the next decision period. These marketing research requests must be included along with other decision change forms submitted to the game administrator. This simulates the real world where there is a time lag between ordering marketing research and receiving the marketing research results.

Management, Organization Design, and Teamwork in BRANDMAPS™

BRANDMAPS™ participants work in groups. Each group is assigned to manage a BRANDMAPS™ firm. Based on experience, deliberate and thoughtful management of the talents and resources of the individual group members — by the group members themselves — is the key to success in BRANDMAPS™.

A variety of line and staff functions exist within BRANDMAPS™. Firms must make decisions on how best to allocate their members' time to the necessary management tasks. As time passes, the initial allocation of group members to tasks may not be the best one in the light of new information and changing competitive circumstances. Teams should anticipate the need to periodically review their management structure and the allocation of their members' time to various BRANDMAPS™ tasks.

The key point here is that management of BRANDMAPS™ activities must be thought about regularly. Good management does not happen by chance. Experience indicates that poor (or completely absent) management is one of the major causes of poor performance in BRANDMAPS™.

A non-exhaustive enumeration of the types of tasks the BRANDMAPS™ firms must manage includes the following:

● Line Responsibilities:
Product Management of Each Brand in Each Region (Product Design, Pricing, Advertising, Research and Development, and Sales Force Decisions)
Sales Forecasting
Marketing Research (Competitive and Market-Monitoring)
Brand Planning and Budgeting
Brand Profit and Cost Control

- Staff Responsibilities:
    Plant Capacity Management
    Production and Finished Goods Inventory Management
    Marketing Research
- Corporate Responsibilities:
    Overall Firm Management
    Strategic Planning
    Design and Execution of Performance-Monitoring and Control Systems (By Product, By Region, Through Time)
    Cost and Information System Design and Maintenance
    Management of Archives
    Overall Budgeting and Planning Coordination.

Past BRANDMAPS™ firms have typically used some kind of matrix organizational structure. In such an organization arrangement, individual team members have both line (e.g., brand or regional management assignments) and staff (e.g., plant capacity management, database management and spreadsheet updating, etc.) responsibilities simultaneously.

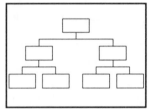

An area of management which must be carefully considered concerns whether a firm has a formally designated general manager. In the past, most smaller-sized teams (three to four members) have not adopted such an organizational structure. However, some larger-sized teams (six or more members) have opted for a formally-designed general manager position. Groups considering the implementation of a formally-designed general manager position are advised to talk at length about the roles and responsibilities associated with such a position.

With regard to responsibility allocations, the following piece of advice comes from a previous BRANDMAPS™ participant: *Don't Take Management Responsibilities Lightly: Friends are friends and business is business. Management is the key to this game. Without effective management, you are lost. Structure your management team as a business with formal authority and delegation of responsibilities.*

Based on experience, the following key questions about group functioning are of paramount importance within the BRANDMAPS™ exercise: How will the group be managed? Who will manage the group? How will the work be divided? How will coordination be achieved? How will work quality be ensured? How will conflicts among individuals be kept at a healthy level (not too high or low)? How often will group functioning be reviewed? Address these questions early and often within your group. Do not assume that these kinds of issues naturally take care of themselves. Regular discussions about the status of the group should be undertaken.

Some General Advice About BRANDMAPS™

Attitude and perspective are important when participating in a complicated marketing exercise like BRANDMAPS™. With regard to general attitude and perspective, the following piece of advice comes from a previous BRANDMAPS™ participant: *Don't treat this simulation as a game; treat it as real. This is the closest thing you can get to the real thing. Consider the profits as real and your time as a valuable commodity. Treat this game seriously; it is a chance to play the market without taking substantial financial and career risks, with the exception of personal pride!*

Some pieces of advice about how the BRANDMAPS™ marketplace operates are sprinkled throughout this manual. More generally, though, it is important to remember that you are in a competitive world. As one previous BRANDMAPS™ participant put it: *Do not underestimate your competition. Your performance is influenced by your competitors' actions. This marketplace is sensitive to changes and movements by your competitors!* It is important to remember that you may be able to learn about how the vaporware market works by watching closely your competitors' marketing initiatives, successes, and failures.

Desirable personal characteristics for a BRANDMAPS™ participant are described in the following "Help Wanted" advertisement constructed by a BRANDMAPS™ veteran:

HELP WANTED

Person to participate in an exciting and challenging commercial enterprise. This is a chance to run your own business with a small group of other talented, committed team players.

Ideal personal requirements:
- *intelligent*
- *learns quickly*
- *marketing, finance, and operations experience helpful*
- *rarely makes mistakes*
- *works well under pressure*
- *patient*
- *open-minded*
- *able to concisely voice and defend decisions*
- *uses time efficiently*
- *accepts criticism and rejection well*
- *sense of humor*
- *flexible and adaptable to changeable environments*
- *spreadsheet, data analysis, and word processing skills*

As this "Help Wanted" advertisement implies, many individual-level characteristics, skills, attitudes, and aptitudes are tapped within a BRANDMAPS™ exercise.

Welcome to BRANDMAPS™. Have fun and take it seriously. But, attempt to learn as you go along.

The BRANDMAPS™ Participant's Manual

The remainder of this BRANDMAPS™ participant's manual is organized into the following chapters:
- Chapter 2 provides an overview of the BRANDMAPS™ marketing simulation game.
- Chapter 3 includes a detailed description of all of the marketing decision variables (product design, pricing, and marketing support spending) in operation in BRANDMAPS™.
- Chapter 4 focuses on non-marketing decision variables and product-related costs. Capacity management and production ordering decisions receive detailed coverage in this chapter.
- BRANDMAPS™ marketing research capabilities are described in Chapter 5. There are 50 marketing research studies that BRANDMAPS™ firms may order.
- The various financial and operating reports that BRANDMAPS™ teams receive after each game run are described in Chapter 6.
- The BRANDMAPS™ decision change forms and marketing research pre-order request forms are contained in Chapter 7.

- Chapter 8 contains a summary of most BRANDMAPS™ cost data.

The course instructor may choose to include optional material described in Chapters 9-12 in your BRANDMAPS™ exercise:

- Chapter 9 is devoted to performance evaluation considerations in BRANDMAPS™. A particular quantitative performance evaluation mechanism for possible use in BRANDMAPS™ is described here.
- Marketing planning is discussed in Chapter 10. Firms may be required to develop formal written marketing plans within a BRANDMAPS™ exercise. Chapter 10 provides background, information, and suggestions that should be helpful in developing marketing plans.
- Chapter 11 provides details of budget-related matters in BRANDMAPS™. This chapter will be relevant if your course instructor chooses to use formal budgets within your BRANDMAPS™ exercise.
- Chapter 12 contains information about using the BRANDMAPS™ software (main program BRANDMAP.EXE and sub-programs B_DV.EXE and B_PREMRS.EXE) to change your decision variables and pre-order marketing research studies. This chapter will be relevant if your course instructor chooses to use the disk-based input/output option within your BRANDMAPS™ exercise.

Experience suggests that BRANDMAPS™ participants refer regularly to this manual throughout the BRANDMAPS™ marketing simulation exercise. Start off by skimming through the complete manual. Then, review Chapters 3-6 carefully and in detail. Browse through other parts of the manual as appropriate. Finally, don't feel shy about turning back to the manual on a regular basis. There is an incredible amount of detail to absorb in a relatively short period of time. No one gets it all right the first time! Take heart, though. Many others have successfully completed the BRANDMAPS™ experience. You can, too!

## Chapter 2

BRANDMAPS™ Overview

Introduction

BRANDMAPS™ is a multi-brand, multi-market marketing management simulation game. The game is cast within the context of an oligopolistic industry, with a maximum of nine firms competing in the industry. Each firm in the industry markets a variety of brands in the BRANDMAPS™ market regions. Firms are required to develop long-run strategies and short-term tactics, and to implement such tactics and strategies in the context of BRANDMAPS™.

BRANDMAPS™ is primarily a marketing game. Decisions required in BRANDMAPS™ are those which normally would fall within the realm of marketing decision making. Some apparently non-marketing decisions are required of teams because these decisions pertain to, or have major implications for, the marketing performance of the firm. For example, production ordering decisions are required of BRANDMAPS™ teams. This rather traditional manufacturing or operations decision is included within BRANDMAPS™ because it follows very naturally from the sales forecasting process that marketers must routinely undertake. Capacity planning decisions, expressed in terms of plant size additions (volume capacity), are also required of BRANDMAPS™ teams. Other functions such as accounting and finance are performed automatically within BRANDMAPS™. Of course, BRANDMAPS™ players must know how to interpret and analyze financial and operating statements.

BRANDMAPS™ focuses on the role of marketing planning, the development and implementation of marketing strategy, the role of financial analysis, the cost/benefit trade-offs associated with the use of marketing research information, sales forecasting, and the impacts of competitive dynamics, rivalry, and environmental forces within the context of the marketing management decision-making process. Teams develop and execute marketing strategies and plans within the marketing game.

BRANDMAPS™ is designed to help the participants strengthen their marketing analysis, decision making, and planning skills. BRANDMAPS™ provides a laboratory setting in which marketing plans and strategies are formulated and executed. A recurring theme emphasized in BRANDMAPS™ is the need to cope with competitive dynamics and uncertain environmental forces.

The major challenge facing each firm is to attempt to sort through the maze of possible marketing decisions in each quarter and to develop "reasonable" decisions, where "reasonable" is judged in terms of the firm's long-run goals and relative to the performance of other firms in the industry. One particularly interesting feature of BRANDMAPS™ is its extensive marketing research capabilities. Firms have the opportunity to purchase a wide range of marketing research studies. These studies should allow the members of a thoughtful firm to sort their way through the maze of the BRANDMAPS™ world in a satisfactory manner.

The key to success in BRANDMAPS™ is a carefully developed long-run strategy, with appropriate expertise being applied to sales forecasting, market monitoring, financial analysis, planning, and marketing decision making. Common sense and managerial acumen will be needed as well.

Perspective

BRANDMAPS™ is a competitive marketing strategy game. As such, participants focus continuously on issues associated with marketing analysis, strategy, and planning. However, the details associated with implementing and executing marketing strategies and plans are not a part of BRANDMAPS™. It follows that BRANDMAPS™ participants do not design/place specific advertising copy in media outlets, recruit/train/supervise sales representatives, order raw materials and schedule production runs, or conduct marketing research. These things are all implicitly taken care of by your firm's advertising agency, sales managers, plant management staff, and marketing research suppliers, respectively. In essence, BRANDMAPS™ participants receive information from various sources (internal company information systems and marketing research suppliers, in particular) and, on the basis of that information, make decisions and communicate these decisions via decision forms or by direct data entry with BRANDMAPS™ program BRANDMAP.EXE (and sub-programs B_DV.EXE and B_PREMRS.EXE). Others actually implement and execute your decisions.

The military metaphor immediately comes to mind to describe your situation in BRANDMAPS™. Your team members are the officers (managers) commanding your forces (products, plant capacity, financial resources, and marketing program elements). You are located at headquarters, which is some distance from the actual battle field (the marketplace). Based on regular reports from the field (financial and operating reports) and special reconnaissance that you request (marketing research), you analyze the situation, choose strategies (select marketing program elements), make decisions, and communicate those decisions to your field officers. The field officers actually implement your decisions. Just as you do not have to be on the actual battle field to direct a successful military campaign, you do not have to be in the actual marketplace to design a successful marketing program. However, you cannot be successful in either the military battle field or the commercial marketplace without information.

BRANDMAPS™ Terminology

Some terminology is used throughout this BRANDMAPS™ participant's manual:
- In BRANDMAPS™, the terms "product" and "brand" are used interchangedly.
- The terms "area" and "region" both refer to one of the markets in BRANDMAPS™. Thus, the terms "area" and "region" are used interchangedly throughout BRANDMAPS™.
- A "game period" is a quarter, with four "game periods" (quarters) in a BRANDMAPS™ year.

The Product Category

In BRANDMAPS™, the product category of interest is vaporware. Vaporware is an abstract product construct that is meant to represent a wide range of durable and capital goods. Vaporware brands are initially (when the game begins) sold for a few hundred dollars per unit. Vaporware has potential for use in both industrial and consumer settings. For reference purposes, you might wish to think of vaporware as being some kind of electronic or mechanical product, furniture, or possibly even clothing.

Vaporware brands are distinguished by their physical composition of five underlying raw materials (Syntech, Plumbo, Glomp, Trimicro, and Fralange) plus Compatibility and Warranty. Firms control the composition of their vaporware brands, and can produce and market a wide range of possible formulations to attempt to meet customers' needs.

BRANDMAPS™ focuses on an abstract product, vaporware, rather than any specific existing product category so that marketing decision-making and analysis skills are emphasized. BRANDMAPS™ players have to learn the marketing milieu within which vaporware functions, without reference to any particular existing product category. Ad hoc marketing rules of thumb that you might have learned in connection with the marketing of various products (such as spending a certain percentage of sales revenues on advertising) may or may not work well in BRANDMAPS™. Since BRANDMAPS™ uses an abstract product, you have to learn about vaporware by careful analysis, monitoring, experimentation, and the judicious use of marketing research studies. This "sink or swim" situation is just what you would have to cope with if you suddenly assumed marketing management responsibilities for some new product or service with which you were completely unfamiliar and for which there was no storehouse of brand, category, or industry knowledge, experience, expertise, or folklore. In any event, all teams are in the same situation.

Even though vaporware is an abstract product, the market for vaporware operates in a regular and sensible fashion, consistent with generally-accepted marketing and economic principles. For example, if you lower a brand's price (holding everything else constant), then its sales volume tends to increase. However, be forewarned: BRANDMAPS™ is based on a sophisticated model of a marketplace. For example, prices that are substantially below the industry norm may lead customers to doubt the quality level of the brand, thus possibly reducing demand. Further details about such sophisticated features of the BRANDMAPS™ world are sprinkled throughout this manual. Many things, however, have to be discovered within the play of the game.

Vaporware appeals widely to industrial and consumer buyers. Vaporware has been around for many years and would generally be considered to be in the mature phase of the product life cycle. Over the years, the physical characteristics and composition of vaporware has changed in response to changes in customer tastes and preferences, and to technological advancements.

Vaporware Brands

Each firm may market three different brands of vaporware. Here, the term "brand" corresponds to a particular vaporware formulation. A brand has a single formulation regardless of the number of market regions in which it is actively distributed.

The BRANDMAPS™ software actually contains four possible vaporware brands. However, normally only three brands are available in a BRANDMAPS™ exercise. Your course instructor will advise you whether and the conditions under which the fourth BRANDMAPS™ brand might become available during your BRANDMAPS™ exercise.

The Vaporware Industry

Your firm is one of the large companies in the vaporware industry. Each company in the vaporware industry is a large organization with many different product lines, one of which is vaporware. Due to various trade restrictions, tariff protection, and proprietary technology, competition from outside the vaporware industry is nonexistent.

Your Firm

Your company is divisionalized along product category lines, with each product group being a separate profit center. For various legal reasons, your vaporware division is a separately incorporated entity. Your stock trades on the stock exchange. Your corporate holding company currently controls about 50% of all of the outstanding stock of your vaporware division.

Your company and its vaporware division have both been profitable in the past. The general goals specified for your vaporware division include maintaining and improving the long-run profitability and market position of the vaporware division.

Within the vaporware division of your company, your management team has complete and total responsibility for all marketing-related functions. These responsibilities include such areas as pricing, advertising, product design, and sales force management. You also have the opportunity to purchase various pieces of marketing research information that may assist you in making sound marketing decisions and formulating appropriate marketing strategies. Personnel, accounting, and finance functions are performed at the corporate level (for which a corporate administrative overhead fee is levied against your vaporware division). Your vaporware division does not have to worry about these kinds of non-marketing activities.

Your company has a single plant which operates as a separate profit center and which produces vaporware brands for you. Current company policy dictates that you may buy vaporware only from your company's plant. This plant also purchases and stores raw materials for use in vaporware manufacturing. The plant has warehouse space in which finished goods are stored until shipped to dealers in the various market regions. Since your plant operates as a separate profit center within your company, it charges you directly for goods produced, raw materials purchased, and inventory carrying charges for finished goods. Among your other decisions, your team has to make capacity decisions with regard to possible additional investment in your plant. In the absence of such plant additions, normal levels of depreciation continuously reduce the capacity of your plant.

Market Demand Patterns

The demand for any vaporware brand depends on overall demand for the product category and the allocation of that demand into individual market shares of the competing brands. With regard to product category (industry) demand, seasonal forces do appear to exist in the vaporware marketplace. Historically, vaporware industry demand has varied up and down as much as 20%-30% from the low-demand winter quarter to the high-demand summer quarter. There has also been some variation in seasonal patterns across the market regions.

Market size (that is, population and GNP) and the decisions of the firms in the industry are thought to be major forces influencing overall industry demand for vaporware. For example, it has been noted in the past that heavy advertising by all firms in the industry tends to expand overall demand for the vaporware product class. Similarly, industry price levels influence overall industry demand for vaporware in the usual inverse fashion: higher industry price levels are associated with lower overall industry demand. As with all products, there are some customers who are relatively heavy users of vaporware, while others would never use vaporware even if it was free.

Market shares are influenced by the relative levels of the various marketing mix decision variables associated with each brand. Customers of vaporware seem to make implicit trade-offs among the brand offerings in terms of product design characteristics, price, and product quality. Customers are also influenced in varying degrees by firms' communications efforts in support of their brands. After all, an unknown brand is unlikely to have substantial sales! Sales force activities are directed at dealers who do seem to be influenced in varying degrees by the attention of a firm's sales force.

Experience suggests that customers' perceptions and beliefs about vaporware brands as well as actual marketing programs associated with vaporware brands influence brand choices. In particular, past research has shown that customers' perceptions of product performance and product convenience are major factors in the brand selection process.

The various BRANDMAPS™ market regions may respond differently to the available marketing variables at the disposal of the firms. What might work very well in one market region could be a disaster in another market region. Each market region may well have to be viewed as a separate market segment.

The BRANDMAPS™ Market Regions

Your BRANDMAPS™ industry consists of between four and eight regional markets, chosen by the course instructor at the time BRANDMAPS™ is initialized (i.e., at the time the initial results for quarter 1 are generated). Regional titles are displayed throughout the BRANDMAPS™ financial and marketing research reports.

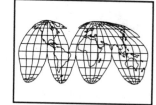

The available market regions in your BRANDMAPS™ industry are those established when the game is initialized. No new market regions may be added after initialization.

Execute Marketing Research Study #22 to obtain current information on aggregate market statistics and market region demographics (population, consumer price index, industry sales volume, etc.). See Marketing Research Studies #44, #45, and #46 for growth rate forecasts for market region demographics.

Currency Conventions in BRANDMAPS™

Although vaporware may be marketed internationally depending on the particular regional market configuration in your BRANDMAPS™ exercise, all currency transactions in BRANDMAPS™ are expressed in BRANDMAPS™ "dollar" terms. Of course, a BRANDMAPS™
"dollar" is not necessarily equivalent to any other well-known currency. Remember, there are U.S. dollars, Canadian dollars, Singapore dollars, Hong Kong dollars, New Zealand dollars, and Australian dollars, to cite just a few examples of dollar-based currencies. As appropriate, these currency values are translated into and from local currencies automatically within BRANDMAPS™. Thus, for all practical purposes, everything is denominated in BRANDMAPS™ "dollars" in all BRANDMAPS™ decision and reports. This currency convention facilitates BRANDMAPS™ decision making and BRANDMAPS™ report processing, since only a single currency is involved.

Marketing Research Information

The specific details of the available marketing research studies in BRANDMAPS™ are described in Chapter 5 of this BRANDMAPS™ participant's manual. You have many possible marketing research studies from which to choose. These studies help you analyze the markets that you face and the competitive activities of your rivals. These marketing research studies parallel the kinds of marketing research that can be purchased and that are often used (and abused!) by marketing analysts and decision makers in the real world.

All marketing research information in BRANDMAPS™ is supplied on an exclusive basis. That is, the marketing research information that you purchase is for your eyes only. There is no secondary resale market for marketing research information in the BRANDMAPS™ world. Evidence of secondary resales of marketing research information might well lead to a termination of access to the BRANDMAPS™ marketing research supplier for an offending firm.

You may only use information about the BRANDMAPS™ world that you purchase through the BRANDMAPS™ marketing research program or from the course instructor. Since the precise BRANDMAPS™ market is not identified, you are not able to use secondary sources to determine, for example, population or GNP growth rates of BRANDMAPS™ regions.

Team Organization and Functioning

The exact organization and allocation of responsibilities of your team depends on the particular abilities and interests of the individual team members. Through time, and as experience with BRANDMAPS™ is gained, reallocations of initial responsibilities may be appropriate.

Particular competitive situations and strategic initiatives may suggest the need for reallocations of short- or long-term responsibility assignments. The nature of the formal group operating structure that you adopt is not important as long as it provides for a workable and equitable assignment of responsibilities. BRANDMAPS™ teams often make a major mistake in not changing their organizational structure and work assignments as they move up the learning curve and as competitive situations dictate.

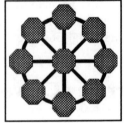

Based on experience, most teams in this marketing simulation game allocate responsibilities among team members in a brand- or product-management style of operation based on regional breakdowns. In such a management structure, specific individuals have responsibilities for managing the activities of all brands marketed in a specific region within BRANDMAPS™. This is done to capitalize on the potential regional diversity within BRANDMAPS™. This is, of course, in contrast to a traditional product-management style of operation where a single manager would be responsible for an individual brand in all the regions where it is marketed. BRANDMAPS™ teams will have to consider whether a product manager or a regional manager (or even a functional manager) style of organization makes the most sense to them. The interests and capabilities of the team members will be factors in the choice of organizational form.

A BRANDMAPS™ veteran provided the following rule for effective group management in the BRANDMAPS™ context: *The most important rule of*  *effective group management in BRANDMAPS™ is that all proposals presented to the group must include a report showing how the proposal will affect the firm's market position and financial performance. If you don't adhere to this rule, then the number of heated debates and the time it takes to resolve each one are certain to increase. Group members will offer proposals because their "management intuition" tells them it's the right thing or because they have received "divine inspiration from the BRANDMAPS™ deity." When a group member's support for a proposal is "I think it's what we should do," the rest of the group should immediately respond with "show us the numbers." This will serve to alleviate, to some extent, wishful thinking and replace it with fact-based marketing decision making.*

Disclosure of Information, Security, and Anti-Competitive Behavior

Information about your operating practices could be very valuable to your competitors. Protect yourself!

The normal laws governing anti-trust and anti-competitive behavior are in effect in BRANDMAPS™. Any peculiarities of BRANDMAPS™-specific laws are indicated within this documentation. For example, overt discussion of your marketing plans and policies with your industry competitors, either singly or in industry conferences, is illegal. Further, anti-competitive behavior such as price-fixing is also illegal.

The Starting Position Scenario: Quarter 1

At the beginning of quarter 1 of BRANDMAPS™, teams take over management responsibilities of an existing division. All of the previous division executives were at a Vaporware Industry Trade Association convention and they tragically perished in a flash explosion and fire at the convention hotel. Thus, there is no one to consult with about the division's affairs. Perhaps even more unfortunately, the previous management was not noted for their record-keeping abilities, so you also have no documentation about past activities and events in the division, in the markets in which your division operates, or about the industry as a whole (beyond the information contained in this manual).

You are, however, inheriting an on-going division with on-going decisions already in place. *Whether these current marketing decisions are good, bad, or mediocre is unknown.* You have to live with considerable uncertainty at the beginning of the BRANDMAPS™ exercise. You have a virtually unlimited mandate to spend money in support of marketing research efforts, marketing efforts in general, and new product introduction in particular. However, you are expected to learn quickly and to improve the long-run profitability of your division.

Firm Decision Variables

In each quarter, firms must make a range of decisions. These decisions may be grouped into three categories. First, *marketing decisions* along the full range of marketing mix decision variables (product design, price, dealer rebates, advertising, promotion, sales force management, and product quality levels) will form the primary focus of each team's attention. These decisions are described in Chapter 3. The second category of decisions may be described as *non-marketing decisions*. These decisions concern production ordering and plant capacity management. These decisions are described in Chapter 4. The third area of regular decision making involves *marketing research decisions*. Marketing research orders can be issued to your firm's marketing research supplier requesting specific marketing research studies to be conducted. Chapter 5 describes the marketing research studies which are available in BRANDMAPS™.

BRANDMAPS™ has a special continuous decision framework built into it. All decisions from the previous quarter carry-over intact into the present quarter, unless a firm issues orders to change a decision. All firm decisions in BRANDMAPS™ are, therefore, standing decisions and they continue to be in force until explicitly changed by a firm. Note, however, that the ordering of marketing research studies must be done in every quarter in which such studies are required.

You submit your decision change and marketing research requests at designated times. Your decision changes are entered into the BRANDMAPS™ game data base prior to the next game run. Your marketing research is conducted after the next game run; its results are returned to you along with the usual set of BRANDMAPS™ financial and operating statements.

## Chapter 3

Marketing Decision Variables

Introduction

In this chapter of the BRANDMAPS™ participant's manual, the full range of marketing decision variables currently in operation in BRANDMAPS™ is described in detail. These marketing variables are extensive, and they permit a wide variety of marketing programs to be initiated and sustained. A range of marketing program possibilities exists in BRANDMAPS™ to permit teams to seek out decisive sustainable differential advantage.

The BRANDMAPS™ marketing program variables include:
- product design
- price
- dealer rebates
- research and development activity
- advertising (amount, media copy content, and media mix allocation)
- promotion (amount and type)
- sales force management (size, allocation, and compensation program)
- sales forecasting.

Dollar spending allocations (via advertising, promotion, and sales force activities) are a major way in which each firm provides marketing support to its brands.

Product Design Decisions

Vaporware is composed of five basic raw materials: Syntech, Plumbo, Glomp, Trimicro, and Fralange. Three pounds of raw materials are required to make one unit of standard vaporware. The specific combinations of Syntech, Plumbo, Glomp, Trimicro, and Fralange to make vaporware are at the control of each firm. The specific mix of raw materials determines the type of vaporware manufactured and marketed. The composition of vaporware is determined by the percentage allocations (by weight) of the five basic raw materials that constitute vaporware. In standard vaporware, these percentages sum to 100% and, naturally, none of the percentages can be negative.

Vaporware may be composed of combinations of the five basic raw materials, with percentage compositions of at least 1% and no more than 99% for each of the five raw materials. Other technological limits — described below — must also be met.

Vaporware also may be manufactured with varying levels of Compatibility (vaporware product attribute #6) and Warranty (vaporware product attribute #7). The Compatibility and Warranty dimensions are both on "1" to "9" scales. A "1" on the Compatibility scale represents vaporware that has very little compatibility with other existing vaporware products, while a "9" describes vaporware that is highly industry-compatible with other existing vaporware products. The Warranty scale is expressed in months. For example, a score of "5" on the Warranty scale indicates that you offer a five-month Warranty on a vaporware brand. As described in Chapter 4, selection of Warranty and Compatibility levels can dramatically influence the costs associated with manufacturing vaporware brands.

In summary, vaporware brands are described by the seven product attributes (or characteristics) of:

Syntech composition (% of weight)
Plumbo composition (% of weight)
Glomp composition (% of weight)
Trimicro composition (% of weight)
Fralange composition (% of weight)
Compatibility score (1-9 scale)
Warranty score (1-9 scale).

Various vaporware brands are described by their particular configuration of these seven dimensions.

Within the vaporware industry, specific brands of vaporware are described by their mix of raw materials and their positioning on the Compatibility and Warranty dimensions. For example, a 40/20/40/67/5/3/7 vaporware brand is composed of 40% Syntech, 20% Plumbo, 40% Glomp, 67% Trimicro, and 5% Fralange with a positioning of "3" on the Compatibility dimension and a positioning of "7" on the Warranty dimension.

Note: The terms "formulation" and "composition" are used interchangeably within BRANDMAPS™ to denote the particular configuration of a vaporware brand on these seven underlying product dimensions.

A recent technological breakthrough has created the possibility of manufacturing vaporware brands whose weight differs from 3 pounds. Vaporware weighing between 1.5 pounds and 9.0 pounds is now technically feasible. A 9-pound vaporware brand would have percentage compositions on the first five vaporware brand attributes that sum to 300%.

Generally-accepted industry terminology breaks vaporware into categories, depending on weight:

Light Vaporware: Weight is less than 3 pounds
Standard Vaporware: Weight equals 3 pounds
Heavy Vaporware: Weight is greater than 3 pounds.

Non-standard vaporware (light or heavy) is described by a set of raw material weights (percentages) which do not sum to 100%. For example, light vaporware with a substantial concentration of Syntech might be 30/6/14/15/5/5/5, which would only weigh a total of 3(0.70) = 2.1 pounds, since the first five vaporware brand dimensions only sum to 70%.

Each BRANDMAPS™ firm may have a maximum of three different brands of vaporware at any point in time. Within BRANDMAPS™, these are described in terms of "firm#-brand#" notation. Thus, vaporware brand 3-2 is the terminology used to describe the second brand of firm #3.

A specific formulation of a vaporware brand is the same in all market regions. Thus, brand formulation is product-specific, not product- and market-specific. Therefore, the formulation of brand 4-1 (firm 4, brand 1) is the same in all BRANDMAPS™ market regions. It is not possible to have one formulation of brand 4-1 in BRANDMAPS™ region 1 and another formulation of brand 4-1 when it is marketed in BRANDMAPS™ region 3. The formulation of brand 4-1 is always the same in all market regions.

Vaporware Technology Constraints

Current vaporware technology constraints limit formulation possibilities. Specifically, the following two technological constraints exist in the vaporware industry:
- The raw material content of the first five vaporware product attributes must sum to between 50 and 300. This corresponds to 1.5 to 9.0 pounds of raw materials input.
- The fifth vaporware product attribute, Fralange, must equal exactly 5.

These two vaporware technology constraints together imply that the first four vaporware product attributes (Syntech, Plumbo, Glomp, and Trimicro) must sum to between 45 and 295.

Patent Laws in BRANDMAPS™

To protect manufacturers who have invested in research and development efforts to produce better and improved vaporware, patent laws adopted in all market regions where vaporware is sold prohibit the exact copying of any other existing vaporware brand. These patent laws were recently extended to cover the duplication of a brand by another brand of the same firm. This extension was made at the insistence of a number of vocal customer advocate groups and dealer associations, neither of whom liked the former vaporware industry pattern of some firms of having a number of virtually identical vaporware brands on the market simultaneously.

The patent laws are expressed in terms of the "closeness" of two formulations to each other. "Closeness" of two vaporware formulations is defined as the sum of the absolute differences along each of the seven dimensions which describe vaporware. An existing patent would be violated if this sum of the absolute differences is less than or equal to seven in comparison with any other brand.

As an example of the calculation of "closeness" between two formulations, consider the formulations 12/23/41/98/5/5/8 and 14/21/34/94/5/9/5:

Attribute	First Formulation	Second Formulation	Difference
1	12	14	2
2	23	21	2
3	41	34	7
4	98	94	4
5	5	5	0
6	5	9	4
7	8	5	3
"Closeness" of These Formulations			22

In the calculation of "closeness," note that "difference" is the absolute difference between formulations on an attribute-by-attribute basis. As may be noted, formulations 12/23/41/98/5/5/8 and 14/21/34/94/5/9/5 differ by a total "closeness" of 22.

To illustrate the operation of these patent laws, consider the following example. Suppose that your firm already had a brand with composition 38/20/20/44/5/5/5 and you attempted to introduce another brand formulation of 38/22/20/44/5/6/4. This would violate an existing patent (your own firm's on the 38/20/20/44/5/5/5 formulation) since the "closeness" of the two brands is only four, which is less than the minimum of seven required by the existing vaporware patent laws.

The complete patent law is actually more complicated than described above. The patent protection zone is actually as follows:

> It shall be considered a violation of this patent law if any brand of vaporware lies within the **protected zone**. The protected zone is defined by the closeness of any pair of vaporware formulations. **Closeness** is equal to the sum of the absolute differences of two brand formulations across the seven vaporware dimensions (Syntech, Plumbo, Glomp, Trimicro, Fralange, Compatibility, and Warranty). When a vaporware brand is initially reformulated, the protected zone shall be equal to a "closeness" of 25. After each subsequent quarter, the protected zone shall decrease by three units until the absolute minimum value of closeness of seven is reached (after six quarters since the reformulation of a brand).

Note that new formulations must be outside the protected patent zones of all existing vaporware brands. Since the minimum size of the "protected patent zone" is seven, new formulations must be at least a distance of eight from all other brands of vaporware. Of course, as described above, newly reformulated vaporware brands have a larger initial protected patent zone.

These recently enacted patent laws for the vaporware industry have a "grandfather" clause such that all existing patents are deemed to be in accordance with the patent law provisions, regardless of any existing patent infringement overlaps among the brand compositions of all existing vaporware. However, any reformulations of existing brands, or the introduction of new vaporware brands, have to adhere strictly to these patent laws.

In the past, there have been occasional attempts by individual vaporware firms and by some consumer and industry lobbying groups to have all patent protection dropped from the vaporware industry. The Vaporware Industry Trade Association has successfully fought these efforts in the past.

Reformulation Decisions

Firms have full discretion and control over the formulations of their brands, subject to patent law regulations and current vaporware technology. Through time, firms may wish to reformulate their brands, perhaps to adjust to changing customer preferences or to respond to changing costs of raw materials. A reformulation is defined as a change in any or all of a vaporware brand's seven attributes (Syntech, Plumbo, Glomp, Trimicro, Fralange, Compatibility, and Warranty). Thus, even a change as small as one unit on a single vaporware attribute is a complete reformulation.

Reformulations of existing vaporware brands should presumably only be undertaken after extensive product testing via the various BRANDMAPS™ marketing research capabilities. Given that preferences may vary across the market regions in BRANDMAPS™, it is easy to imagine that a firm might eventually develop a range of different vaporware brands, perhaps targeted to specific BRANDMAPS™ regions. Of course, it is also possible that specific preferences for product compositions do not really vary that much from region to region, so perhaps there is one all-purpose generic vaporware brand formulation that will be well received throughout the BRANDMAPS™ world.

Your research and development group and your plant manager have jointly concluded that costs of $500,000 are incurred for any reformulation of an existing brand of vaporware. These fixed costs cover the outlays associated with retooling existing plant equipment and the specific research and development efforts associated with perfecting any new product formulation.

As of quarter 1, each vaporware brand has the formulation 30/30/30/5/5/5/5. Brand #1 is actively distributed in all BRANDMAPS™ regions as of quarter 1. An introduction of currently-inactive brands into other BRANDMAPS™ market regions does not necessarily require a reformulation, if you are satisfied that their existing formulations are satisfactory for your purposes. Two marketing research studies (Marketing Research Studies #18 and #30) exist to determine whether any proposed vaporware formulation would violate existing patents. See Chapter 5 for details.

In BRANDMAPS™, reformulations are accomplished by submitting such requests along with all other decision variable change requests. See Chapter 7 for a description of the various BRANDMAPS™ decision variable change request forms. However, since patent protection considerations arise, each reformulation decision may be submitted along with several possible alternative reformulations, should the first one(s) not be available due to patent protection. Two alternative formulations may be submitted, along with the original reformulation. Three formulation variations are normally submitted for each reformulation request. Patent search requests are automatically ordered for each formulation request required to be executed.

Since any number of firms may submit reformulation requests simultaneously, the order of entry into the BRANDMAPS™ data base is of considerable importance. Early entry preserves the patent zone and subsequently-entered reformulations must not violate any existing patent, including reformulations done moments before your reformulation request! Reformulation queue position (and, therefore, order of entry into the BRANDMAPS™ data base) is based on bids submitted by each firm in connection with each requested reformulation. The highest reformulation bid is entered first. Lower reformulation bids follow in order of bid queue price.

Note that these bids are only for position in the reformulation queue. They do not guarantee that any proposed reformulation is actually legally patentable and available.

Bids of $0 are legal, but naturally such bids result in the associated reformulations being entered at the end of the queue. To avoid ties, it is suggested that odd numbers (such as $1,288 or $4 or $189,432 or $1,100,001 be used as bids) rather than rounded-off numbers (such as $1,000 or $10,000) be used for reformulation bids. The processing order of tied reformulation bids is resolved randomly.

If a reformulation request is unsuccessful, then the old formulation associated with a vaporware brand remains in effect.

Reformulation requests are unconditional. Other parts of a marketing program cannot be based on whether or not any specific reformulation request is successful. Thus, some delicate timing trade-offs may arise. For example, you may not wish to introduce a brand into a region unless a reformulation request is successful. Otherwise, you might be entering an old formulation which is totally unacceptable to customers in a market region. In such a case, the only sure way to proceed is to request the reformulation and not order the brand's introduction in the current quarter. Then, if the reformulation is successful, introduction may be effected in the following quarter. Of course, it is also possible to gamble on the success of the reformulation request, and go ahead and change the brand's marketing program. However, in considering such a course of action, you should review and weigh the possibility of, and the consequences associated with, an unsuccessful reformulation request.

When you try to reformulate a brand, the BRANDMAPS™ software first checks to see if any existing patent(s) would be violated by the reformulated brand. You are billed for this automatic execution of a patent search study (Marketing Research Study #18). If an existing patent or patents would be violated, you will not be allowed to reformulate the brand, although there is no penalty for trying.

The events associated with a reformulation follow a specific sequence. Reformulation bid processing occurs at the beginning of a quarter (i.e., at the beginning of a BRANDMAPS™ game run), before anything else happens. A successful reformulation occurs immediately. Bid prices are paid whether or not reformulations are successful. Bid prices are for reformulation queue position; they have nothing to do with the patentability of a particular reformulation.

When a reformulation bid "becomes active" (depending on where the bid stands in the reformulation queue), each existing patent is checked. This patent check involves looking at all brands' patents (except the brand being reformulated), including patents received just prior to this reformulation bid "being active" (for brands with higher reformulation bids). If the first reformulation try does not violate any existing patent, reformulation occurs. Otherwise, the second and third reformulation tries are checked successively.

- If the reformulation is successful, all inventory of the brand's prior formulation is immediately subject to a disposal sale. This means that the beginning inventory for a newly reformulated brand is zero in the current quarter.
- If the reformulation is unsuccessful, nothing else happens. Since the brand was not reformulated, its previous formulation stays in effect.

Since reformulations involve considerable work for your plant management, your research and development staff, your advertising agency, and your sales force, corporate policy limits reformulations in any quarter to a maximum of one.

When a vaporware brand is reformulated, a number of things happen. First, all inventory of the reformulated brand is immediately subject to a disposal sale. Only 75% of the value of the finished goods inventory of a reformulated brand is realized in such a disposal sale. The remaining 25% is recorded as an additional reformulation expense (Disposal Sales) and is so reported on the Divisional Profit and Loss Statement. The 75% disposal value is not actually recorded as sales. Rather, it is just a balance sheet transaction, with inventory assets being converted to cash. Thus, in addition to other direct costs of reformulation, the loss from disposal sales can be substantial. A usual strategy when contemplating a reformulation involves reducing inventory levels so that the losses from disposal sales are minimized. Inventory reduction methods include not ordering production for one or several quarters preceding a reformulation and also such tactics as changing the marketing mix variables to attempt to stimulate short-term increases in demand (for example, by using promotion or price).

Second, experience has been gained by your research and development group in product quality improvements is completely lost when a reformulation occurs. Among other consequences, this may translate into some short-term problems in quality control and quality assurance. This may lead customers to have some initial doubts as to the quality of your newly reformulated brand.

Third, any experience curve effects on production costs are lost upon reformulation. Experience accumulates for the new formulation from a starting point of zero. See Chapter 4 for information on experience curve effects.

Fourth, the general level of brand loyalty and goodwill associated with brands tends to carry-over after reformulations. No doubt some customers are lost after any reformulation, but the numbers have never been thought to be particularly large. However, it must be expected that the carry-over of customer and dealer brand loyalty to the newly reformulated brand depends on the similarity of the old brand composition to the new. Large changes in a brand's composition may lead brand-loyal customers to reconsider their brand preferences and assess whether a newly reformulated brand still meets their needs. Of course, if a reformulated brand is substantially more preferred than its old formulation, then presumably many new customers will be attracted to the reformulated brand.

Reminder: Reformulations must satisfy existing vaporware technology constraints. Technologically-infeasible reformulation requests are not processed and the previous formulation of a vaporware brand remains in effect.

Research and Development Decisions

Firms may choose to allocate funds to their research and development groups to aid in brand quality improvements. Although there are no absolute minimums in this regard, it is generally thought that at least

$10,000 per quarter should be allocated to research and development in support of each brand that a firm is actively marketing. Additional funds allow for further research and development staff to be deployed to support product quality improvement efforts.

Product quality improvements tend to require sustained effort on the part of your research and development group over an extended time frame. Thus, it should be expected that a continual flow of funds tends to work much better than occasional large expenditure levels. Experience suggests that vaporware brands are only rarely successful for long if expenditures on research and development are low.

The value of research and development efforts have never really been clearly established in the vaporware industry. There is no generally agreed upon yardstick with which to measure the effectiveness of research and development efforts. However, many industry analysts maintain that the impact of research and development expenditures and activities is ultimately felt on the quality perceptions that customers hold for vaporware brands.

There are limits on research and development spending changes from one quarter to the next for each brand. Specifically, research and development spending support may not increase by more than $250,000 for each brand from the previous quarter's research and development spending level. Thus, a larger research and development budget increase, for example, would have to be phased in over several quarters. Research and development spending may be reduced to any amount, including $0, at any time. Note that if research and development spending support is $0 in any quarter, then the maximum possible research and development spending level in the following quarter is $250,000.

Product Preference and Product Quality

In BRANDMAPS™, a product's formulation influences the preference that customers have for it (*product preference*). Research and development spending, in the main, is ultimately translated in *product quality* perceptions. *Product preference* and *product quality* are two different and unrelated constructs in BRANDMAPS™.

To illustrate the differences, consider the choice of a restaurant for a special dining-out occasion. Here, "product preference" would depend on such things as food selection, service, ambience, and the like. "Product quality" would refer to the actual quality of the food, given the particular food selection and specialization. In this context, a restaurant specializing in seafood might score very high on "product quality" (if it has good seafood) but very low on "product preference" for someone with an aversion to seafood. Alternatively, a fine sports car might score highly on "product preference" for someone who values such aspects of automobiles, but very low on "product quality" if it is unreliable transportation.

In summary, product preference and product quality are different things, and high performance on one does not necessarily imply corresponding excellence on the other.

New Product Development and Introduction

The introduction of a new vaporware brand in BRANDMAPS™ should presumably be preceded by product testing research. A range of marketing research studies are available to assist you in these new product development endeavors. See Chapter 5 for details.

New products may be created within BRANDMAPS™. Brands must be explicitly introduced into BRANDMAPS™ regions. Actual introduction into the marketplace occurs immediately.

Brands may be actively distributed in one or more of the BRANDMAPS™ market regions. There is no need to have complete distribution of vaporware brands in all BRANDMAPS™ market regions.

It is possible to delay actual brand introduction to permit pre-launch marketing support efforts to be initiated prior to actual launch. Thus, you may decide to allocate marketing support expenditures to advertising, sales force, and research and development prior to actually launching a brand. Any such marketing support spending occurs immediately after you authorize it. Such pre-launch marketing efforts may speed the introduction process by making dealers and customers aware of the existence of the impending launch. Of course, such activities may also come to the attention of alert competitors.

Brands may be dropped from active distribution in any or all regions. Such brand deletion decisions are implemented immediately. After a brand is dropped from active distribution, it is also necessary to ensure that the advertising and promotion support spending levels are changed to zero and that any sales force time allocation for the deleted brand is reallocated to other active brands.

Dropping a brand from active distribution does not, in itself, alter the marketing support activities associated with it.

New product development activity should be viewed as an integral component of each BRANDMAPS™ firm's marketing strategy. The actual out-of-pocket costs of introducing a new product may be only a very small component of the total new product development costs. The major costs of new product development activity are undoubtedly incurred in the marketing research efforts related to designing a product that will be well-received by customers.

To introduce a vaporware brand into any of the BRANDMAPS™ regions costs $400,000. These are fixed setup costs incurred to convince dealers of the merits of stocking your particular brand of vaporware. The costs are charged on the introducing firm's operating statements in the quarter in which actual brand introduction occurs.

Introductions and reformulations are completely separate and independent decisions. In BRANDMAPS™, an "introduction" refers to the decision to actively distribute a brand in a region or regions; "reformulation" refers to changing a brand's formulation. After a reformulation, a brand does not have to be re-introduced into markets in which it is already being actively distributed. However, a brand reformulated and specifically targeted for one or more regions in which it is not yet actively distributed must be formally introduced into the targeted markets.

A brand may be reformulated without being introduced. This might be done if there is great concern that a reformulation request might not be successful. In such a case, a firm might not wish to launch a brand with its old formulation, if the requested reformulation is not available. Thus, by submitting a reformulation request and then waiting to ensure that the reformulation is successful (prior to introducing the reformulated brand in the subsequent quarter), a firm may avoid such risks. There is, of course, an opportunity cost associated with waiting a quarter prior to launching what might be a successful product.

An existing brand may be introduced into one or more markets without being reformulated. The brand would be introduced with its current formulation. Presumably, such a decision would be based on some marketing research which indicates the potential attractiveness of the existing formulation to customers in the targeted region(s).

Distribution Considerations

Vaporware is sold widely by various dealers and sales agents (for the industrial segment) and in various dealer outlets (for the consumer segment), including general purpose types of stores (that is, department stores) and specialty stores. In the vaporware industry, such dealers, sales agents, and dealer outlets are collectively referred to as "dealers." Dealers purchase vaporware directly from the various competing firms in the vaporware industry. Exclusive dealership arrangements do not exist in the vaporware industry.

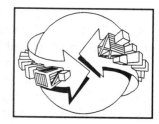

A recent event of note in the industry concerns the delisting of small market share vaporware brands by dealers in some BRANDMAPS™ market regions. Delisting means that dealers refuse to stock a brand. This action followed after many dealers noted a proliferation of many small market share brands, products that took up valuable space while yielding little financial return to dealers. The solution to this problem has involved fairly drastic measures, at least that is the way they have been described by vaporware industry experts. Specifically, dealers have begun to consider delisting any brand that does not average a market share of about at least 2% over any four successive quarters. Since distribution of vaporware by any other channel mechanism is impossible, this effectively means that the offending vaporware brand is banned from the marketplace. Based on prior actual experience, dealers send clear warning signals a quarter or two before delisting is likely to be seriously considered.

Dealers' stocking decisions (and the amount of space, resources, and effort allocated to the vaporware product category and to any particular vaporware brand) are thought to be based largely on return-on-investment kinds of criteria. That is, dealers generally desire to stock and support products that have a high markup potential, a large volume, and no need for special handling. All vaporware brands satisfy the "no special handling" criterion without any problems. High markup would be associated with the higher-priced brands (since dealers use a fairly standard cost-plus pricing strategy), while actual volume or turnover would depend on customer acceptance (that is, market share). Dealer rebates, described later in this chapter, represent another approach to improving dealers' financial returns from stocking specific vaporware brands.

Sales force efforts are thought to be of value in encouraging dealers to stock and support vaporware brands. BRANDMAPS™ firms may direct their sales forces to allocate their efforts among various brands. Thus, for example, it is possible to direct the sales force to emphasize support of a new product being introduced into a market region, to attempt to ensure that it receives adequate distribution coverage. When a firm has more than one brand being actively distributed in a market region, the firm may specify how the sales force is to allocate its available selling time in support of its brands. These time allocations are expressed in percentage terms.

Dealer Inventory Activity

Exclusive dealership arrangements do not exist in the vaporware industry. Rather, dealers typically represent and stock vaporware brands of multiple manufacturers. The term "stock" includes a wide spectrum of vaporware brand dealing activity, from a mere listing in a readily available catalog from which customers may order through to active representation with vaporware units available for immediate sale from a dealer's local inventory.

Vaporware brands are sold outright by manufacturers to dealers. Since transportation takes some time from manufacturers to dealers, dealers must keep an amount of inventory on hand to service immediate customer orders. Vaporware dealers are thoughtful, rational buyers. They may stockpile brands offered with a dealer rebate and then sell from their own local inventory first before re-ordering from the manufacturer.

When a vaporware brand is reformulated, dealers respond by immediately selling-off all existing inventory of the "old" brand. "Old" and "new" brand formulations never exist simultaneously in

BRANDMAPS™. By custom and contract, vaporware manufacturers reimburse dealers partially for the losses associated with these sell-offs. The payment to dealers is 5% of current dealer inventories times current manufacturer price. For example, with 5,512 units in dealer inventory, a reformulation of a brand with a manufacturer price of $521 would result in a reformulation payment to dealers of (0.05)(5,512)($521) = $143,588. These dealer payments are recorded as part of Disposal Sales. These sell-offs increase initial sales to some extent for newly reformulated brands. After the dealer sell-off of "old" inventory, dealers have no inventory of a newly reformulated brand so initial sales of a reformulated brand also reflect dealers' needs to create an appropriate inventory level.

Marketing Research Studies #48 and #49 provide estimates of current dealer inventories (at the end of the just-completed quarter) of a firm's own brands and all firms' brands, respectively.

Pricing Decisions

BRANDMAPS™ firms control the list price of brands. The list price is the manufacturer's price for vaporware. List prices may vary for each vaporware brand in each of the market regions.

Vaporware is sold through dealers in each market region. Dealers markup vaporware manufacturers' prices to arrive at dealer prices. Dealer prices are the prices at which dealers sell vaporware to final customers. Markup rates should be expected to vary by market region.

Experience in the vaporware market has shown that demand is sensitive to price in the usual fashion: customers prefer lower priced vaporware brands, holding all other relevant factors constant. For market shares, customer choice of any particular brand of vaporware is partially based on the brand's price relative to the prices of competing brands of vaporware. Frequent price changes seem to upset dealers, sometimes causing some to discontinue selling such vaporware brands.

While there seems to be some degree of brand loyalty toward vaporware brands, price changes tend to upset such loyalty and cause formerly brand-loyal customers to look around and consider purchasing other brands. A vaporware brand price that is far below the industry norm runs the risk of having customers wonder about the quality of the low priced brand. Given natural aversion to risk on the part of customers, such concerns might lead to reductions in purchases of such a super low priced vaporware brand. Particularly high priced vaporware, even for highly desirable product formulations and even for brands that are supported with massive marketing effort (advertising, promotion, and sales force activities), are not likely to be well received by customers.

The obvious impact of price on final customers is noted above. There is another, perhaps equally important, indirect effect of pricing decisions in the vaporware industry. Dealers' margins are influenced directly by firms' prices. Since vaporware dealers follow cost-plus markup pricing rules, higher costs (manufacturers' prices) translate into more financial return (margin) per unit of vaporware sold. Of course, dealers' total profitability depends on unit margins times volume (plus dealer rebates, if any). Thus, high prices affect dealers positively and final customers negatively.

There are limits on how much a vaporware brand price may change from one quarter to the next. Specifically, prices may not increase by more than $1,000 from the previous quarter's prices. Prices may be reduced by any amount at any time, as long as a manufacturer list price of at least $100 is charged. Thus, a larger price increase, for example, would have to be phased in over several quarters. Note that a brand not actively distributed (marketed) in a quarter may have any price in the $100-$9,999 range in the following quarter.

Prices are expressed in even-dollar amounts only in BRANDMAPS™; cents are not used.

Prices of inactive brands are irrelevant in BRANDMAPS™. Thus, there is no need to have a price of $0 for inactive brands. An active brand being dropped from a market may have its price left at the former value since an inactive brand has no sales.

Reminder: Firms do not necessarily have to charge the same price in each BRANDMAPS™ market region in which a brand is distributed.

Dealer Rebates

Rebates may be offered to dealers to encourage them to stock and emphasize specific vaporware brands. Such rebates are a way of temporarily increasing dealer margins, and consequently making specific brands more attractive to dealers. Rebates offered quarter after quarter may be treated by dealers as being permanent, and their subsequent withdrawal may not be well received by dealers. Thus, dealer rebates are typically used by vaporware firms in a "pulsing" fashion — a rebate offered one quarter is followed with no rebate for the next several quarters.

Dealer rebates may not exceed 20% (expressed in $ per unit terms) of the current manufacturer list price for a vaporware brand in any region. Rebates are expressed in $ per unit terms. Rebates are expressed in even-dollar amounts only in BRANDMAPS™; cents are not used. Firms do not have to offer the same dealer rebate in each BRANDMAPS™ market region in which a brand is distributed.

The custom of vaporware dealers is to absorb all of the value of the rebates directly, in the form of increased margin. Thus, none of the dealer rebate is passed on to final customers directly.

Promotion Decisions

Firms may choose to allocate funds to sales promotion activities to support any brand in any market region. Sales promotion efforts may be directed to ten different kinds of activities, and a range of pairwise combinations of the ten, as described below. Thus, decisions on dollar amounts of promotional effort, as well as promotional type, are required in BRANDMAPS™.

Promotional activities are managed by firms' regional sales managers in the various BRANDMAPS™ market regions. Since any individual promotional effort costs at least $25,000 to design and implement in a region, the first $25,000 of promotional budgets in any quarter goes toward fixed setup costs. As described below, this setup cost is higher for pairwise combinations of the ten basic promotional types. Dollar amounts over this minimum are then available for use in executing promotional activities.

Table 2 contains a list of the ten basic promotional possibilities available in BRANDMAPS™. These promotional efforts may be directed to dealers, a firm's sales force, or to customers. Examples of promotional activities routinely conducted in the vaporware industry include special dealer volume discounts, customer rebates, special display activities at dealers' premises, special

educational and training programs for dealers' sales representatives, trade show presentations and participation, special trade-in and exchange conditions, and the like. Of course, promotional activities directed at dealers presumably also influence customers, although indirectly. Also, some promotional activities involve a firm's sales force. These take the form of special sales contests and similar short-term incentive programs.

In addition to the ten basic promotional types, seventy-two pairwise combinations of promotional

Table 2

BASIC PROMOTIONAL TYPES AVAILABLE IN BRANDMAPS™

Promotional Type	Promotional Activity
Directed To Dealers:	
1	Trade Show Participation
2	Special Dealer Display Activities
3	Special Dealer Training
4	Special Dealer Volume Discounts
5	Special Trade-In and Exchange Program
Directed To Sales Force:	
6	Sales Contests — Cash Prizes
7	Sales Contests — Merchandise and Travel Prizes
8	Special Sales Representative Training
Directed To Customers:	
9	Customer Rebates
Regional Sales Manager's Discretion:	
10	Promotional Funds Used at the Regional Sales Manager's Discretion (Which Normally Means Some Combination of Promotional Types 1-5)

types are possible. Only a single promotional activity (or a valid pairwise combination, as described below) may be executed for any vaporware brand in any BRANDMAPS™ market region in any quarter. However, multiple promotions associated with multiple brands may be run in a region simultaneously, as long as only a single promotion (or valid pairwise combination) is associated with each active vaporware brand in the region.

A two-digit promotional type code results in the promotional budget being split between two promotional types. That is, promotional type #IJ (for I=1,2,...,9 and J=1,2,...,9, with I and J not equal) results in an allocation of the promotional budget according to the formula 65% to promotional type #I and 35% to promotional type #J. For example, the specification of promotional type #52 results in 65% of the specified promotional budget being allocated to promotional type #5 and 35% to promotional type #2. See Table 3 for a complete specification of all valid pairwise promotional types in BRANDMAPS™.

Since promotional types #12 to #98 involve pairwise promotions (requiring the development of two coordinated promotions), there are fixed costs of $75,000 associated with such efforts. That is, for pairwise promotions, the first $75,000 of any promotion is used in fixed setup costs and only amounts above $75,000 are available for actual promotion spending.

Vaporware industry experts believe that, if used at all, promotions should be varied from quarter to quarter. Repeatedly executing the same promotional type (either individually or in pairwise combination with another promotional type) quarter after quarter is thought to lead to reduced effectiveness of that promotion.

Table 3

PAIRWISE COMBINATION PROMOTIONAL TYPES IN BRANDMAPS™

Prom. Type	65% Allocation To Prom. Type	35% Allocation To Prom. Type	Prom. Type	65% Allocation to Prom. Type	35% Allocation To Prom. Type
11	Invalid	Invalid	56	5	6
12	1	2	57	5	7
13	1	3	58	5	8
14	1	4	59	5	9
15	1	5			
16	1	6	61	6	1
17	1	7	62	6	2
18	1	8	63	6	3
19	1	9	64	6	4
			65	6	5
21	2	1	66	Invalid	Invalid
22	Invalid	Invalid	67	6	7
23	2	3	68	6	8
24	2	4	69	6	9
25	2	5			
26	2	6	71	7	1
27	2	7	72	7	2
28	2	8	73	7	3
29	2	9	74	7	4
			75	7	5
31	3	1	76	7	6
32	3	2	77	Invalid	Invalid
33	Invalid	Invalid	78	7	8
34	3	4	79	7	9
35	3	5			
36	3	6	81	8	1
37	3	7	82	8	2
38	3	8	83	8	3
39	3	9	84	8	4
			85	8	5
41	4	1	86	8	6
42	4	2	87	8	7
43	4	3	88	Invalid	Invalid
44	Invalid	Invalid	89	8	9
45	4	5			
46	4	6	91	9	1
47	4	7	92	9	2
48	4	8	93	9	3
49	4	9	94	9	4
			95	9	5
51	5	1	96	9	6
52	5	2	97	9	7
53	5	3	98	9	8
54	5	4	99	Invalid	Invalid
55	Invalid	Invalid			

Industry experts believe that promotional activities have some impact on dealers and customers. However, the effects of such sales promotion efforts seem to be felt only in the quarter in which they are used, with little residual carry-over into subsequent quarters. In the past, promotional efforts have been used to give a brand a shot-in-the-arm, particularly in the case of new product introductions into BRANDMAPS™ regions. They have also been used as a competitive countermeasure against new product introductions, although a still-pending anti-trust suit regarding the unnatural and predatory use of such promotional expenditures has dampened the enthusiasm of some industry participants for using promotions in such a way.

There is considerable continuing debate in the vaporware industry about how promotional budget dollars should be used. Some believe that firms should be promoting aggressively at all times. Others believe that firms should only use promotion selectively, and then with a major effort. Still others believe that only certain kinds of promotions are effective at all. The majority of industry experts, however, believe that promotions of various kinds are likely to have positive effects on dealers and customers. Nevertheless, the actual profitability of promotional efforts is unknown.

There are limits on how much promotion may change from one quarter to the next. Specifically, promotion spending support for any vaporware brand in any market region may not increase by more than $5,000,000 from the previous quarter's promotion spending level. A larger promotion budget increase would have to be phased in over several quarters. Promotion spending on a vaporware brand in any market region may be reduced to any amount, including $0, at any time. Note that if promotion spending support for a brand in any market region is $0 in any quarter, then the maximum possible promotion spending level for the brand in that market region in the following quarter is $5,000,000.

Promotional type is only relevant when a non-zero promotion budget allocation is in effect. So, with a promotion budget allocation of zero, promotional type is irrelevant.

Sales Force Decisions

Your division maintains a separate sales force in each of the BRANDMAPS™ market regions. Sales force activities do not influence customers directly. Rather, they influence the behavior of dealers. Most reputable vaporware industry experts believe that sales force efforts can have a substantial influence on channel members' behavior.

BRANDMAPS™ firms make three specific sales force management decisions in each market region in which vaporware brands are actively distributed: sales force compensation levels (salary and commission), sales force size, and sales force time allocation among the firm's brands. By making these various sales force management decisions, a firm is establishing policies that are executed by the regional sales manager in each BRANDMAPS™ region. Thus, the sales force size is really an allocated level of sales representatives, and the regional sales manager establishes appropriate hiring policies to maintain that level.

BRANDMAPS™ firms may establish different sales force compensation levels (salary and commission) in each of the market regions, if they choose. It has been observed that sales force motivation (and, therefore, effort and effectiveness) seems to be positively affected by salary levels. High-paying firms tend to attract more able sales representatives, who tend to be more effective in performing the sales task.

Since sales representatives tend to be quite sensitive about changes in the sales force compensation arrangements, firms should be somewhat careful about changing compensation levels too frequently. The vaporware industry norm in this regard seems to involve salary adjustments about once or, at most, twice a year.

A problem has recently arisen within the vaporware industry regarding sales force compensation. In particular, some firms have established salary policies that involve widely differing compensation levels for their various sales forces across the regions in which they are actively marketing vaporware. While cost-of-living considerations and competitive market forces might well lead a firm to have a sales force compensation policy with some variation from one region to another, levels which are substantially different from region to region are likely to lead to morale problems across all of a firm's regional sales forces, not just in the regions where compensation levels are particularly low. Such morale problems, were they actually to exist, would likely translate into lower performance, higher turnover, and other manifestations that would impede the selling effort. Thus, extreme compensation ranges may run the risk of being harmful to the performance level of a firm's sales force. Deviations in a firm's compensation levels across the BRANDMAPS™ market regions of 10%-20% are not thought to be extreme. However, deviations of more than 50% would probably be viewed as quite extreme.

Attempts to lower sales force compensation levels (especially salaries) are viewed with substantial disfavor by sales representatives, as might be expected. Recognizing this, your firm has a general policy of not lowering sales force salaries. If a team really wants to lower sales force salaries in any market region, they generally have to leave the salaries at a constant level and let inflation lower them (perhaps slowly!) in real terms through time. If a team feels that it is critical to make a substantial decrease in sales force salaries immediately, they have to obtain special approval from the course instructor.

Within BRANDMAPS™, salaries are expressed in terms of dollars per month. Thus, a $24,000 per year salary would be specified as a $2,000 salary per month within BRANDMAPS™. Commissions are based on sales revenues. Sales commissions are limited to the range 1%-9% in integer amounts. Sales Overhead is based on total sales force compensation (salaries plus commissions).

Firms are free to vary the size of their sales force complements in each of the market regions. However, there are certain costs associated with hiring new sales representatives and in firing existing sales representatives. The cost of hiring a new sales representative is equal to one month's salary. This represents the costs associated with recruiting, screening, and hiring. Reducing the current sales force in a BRANDMAPS™ market region requires a lump-sum settlement equal to two months' salary. It has been observed in the past that newly hired sales representatives tend not to be as effective as existing sales representatives for the first quarter or so. Part of this reduced effectiveness is attributable to your firm's standard sales training program which each new representative completes.

Transferring sales representatives from one market region to another is equivalent to firing the representatives in the originating marketing region and then hiring them in the destination market region. Thus, there are no cost savings associated with transferring sales representatives from one market region to another market region.

Firms may direct their sales managers in each market region to allocate the efforts of their available sales representatives to support each vaporware brand in active distribution. These time allocations are expressed in percentage terms. Firms with only a single brand in an area will, of course, have 100% of their sales force's time allocated to that brand. With two brands in an area, any combination of time allocation percentages (such as 50% and 50%, or 10% and 90%) is possible so long as they sum to 100% across the three vaporware brands. Experience seems to suggest that efforts at pushing products through the channel of distribution have had some success.

Within BRANDMAPS™, teams control sales force size (the number of sales representatives) and sales force time allocations across brands. BRANDMAPS™ calculates sales force effort as being equal to the product of sales force size and time allocation percentage. For example, a sales force size of 200 representatives in a market region and a 50% time allocation to a particular brand in the region would result in a sales force effort of (200)(0.50) = 100, which is interpreted as the equivalent of 100 sales representatives being used to support the brand in the market region.

Each sales representative incurs standard expenses in connection with the sales task. These expenses involve both direct and indirect components. Direct expenses generated are in terms of fringe benefits (health insurance, government taxes of various kinds, and so on) and travel costs (automobile costs and per diem expenses while away from home). Indirect costs to support the sales representative include periodic sales training activities, sales management overhead, office support, and the like. In total, these expenses are equal to the compensation (salary and commission) level of a sales representative. Thus, if you have a monthly sales force salary level of $2,500 and 0% commission in a BRANDMAPS™ market region, a further $2,500 of sales force expenses per month is also incurred to support the sales representative. Your division is automatically billed for the direct and indirect costs associated with maintaining sales representatives in each of the market regions in which you choose to have an active sales force. These sales expenses are recorded as Sales Overhead.

While it is not required that you maintain a sales force in each of the BRANDMAPS™ market regions, you may not do very well in securing and maintaining distribution coverage for your brands if they are not supported by appropriate sales force efforts.

There are limits on how much sales force size and sales force salary may change from one quarter to the next. Specifically, sales force size may not increase by more than fifty from the previous quarter's sales force size level; any level of sales force size reduction may be effected at any time. In particular, sales force size may be reduced to zero at any time. Sales force salary may not change by more than $500 from the previous quarter's sales force salary level. Sales force salaries may not decrease, without special permission from the course instructor. Larger sales force size or sales force salary increases would have to be phased in over several quarters. Note that if sales force size is zero in any quarter, then the maximum possible sales force size in the following quarter is 50.

Advertising Decisions

Firms make decisions on the amount of money to be allocated to customer advertising in support of each vaporware brand in each BRANDMAPS™ market region. Associated with this advertising expenditure decision are media content and media mix allocation decisions.

In BRANDMAPS™, media content means copy emphasis, such as an emphasis on price or product availability or guarantees. Media content may vary from market region to market region and from brand to brand. For example, it would be possible to use one content in support of one brand and another content in support of a second brand, even if both brands were being marketed in the same BRANDMAPS™ market region. Also, the same brand may have different media contents across the various BRANDMAPS™ market regions in which it is distributed.

In addition to specifying a total advertising spending amount and the media content emphasis of the advertising message, five different media types are available. Total advertising spending may be allocated across the media direct marketing, magazines, newspapers, radio, and television. Your firm's advertising agency is responsible for spending your advertising funds according to your media mix allocation.

Media mix allocations are based on five-digit codes. Each digit in the five-digit code must be between 1 and 9. The first digit refers to the first media type, direct marketing; the second digit refers to the second media type, magazines; etc.

The total advertising spending amount is allocated proportionally to the sum of the digits in the media mix allocation code. Three examples are shown below.

Example #1: A media mix allocation of 11111 (or 22222 or 33333 or ...) results in overall advertising spending being equally divided among the five media types.

Example #2: A media mix allocation heavily weighted toward the first two media types (direct marketing and magazines) and with minimum weightings on the other three media types (newspapers, radio, and television) would be 99111. A 99111 media mix allocation results in the following allocation proportions of total advertising spending:

Media Type #1, Direct Marketing	9/21
Media Type #2, Magazines	9/21
Media Type #3, Newspapers	1/21
Media Type #4, Radio	1/21
Media Type #5, Television	1/21

since 9+9+1+1+1=21.

Example #3: A media mix allocation heavily weighted toward the first and last media types (direct marketing and television), with a mid-level weighting on the third media type (newspapers), and with minimum weightings on the second and fourth media types (magazines and radio) would be 91519. A 91519 media mix allocation results in the following allocation proportions of total advertising spending:

Media Type #1, Direct Marketing	9/25
Media Type #2, Magazines	1/25
Media Type #3, Newspapers	5/25
Media Type #4, Radio	1/25
Media Type #5, Television	9/25

since 9+1+5+1+9=25.

In making advertising decisions, BRANDMAPS™ firms are really just providing direction to their advertising agencies. The advertising agencies create copy and place it in designated media. When you change the media content associated with the advertising of one of your vaporware brands in some BRANDMAPS™ market regions, your advertising agency has to channel some of the advertising expenditures toward the actual creation of the new copy. Thus, a reduced amount of the overall advertising budget is available for actual placement in any quarter in which a media copy change is implemented. Media content changes should probably not be made in every quarter.

There are six basic media contents available in BRANDMAPS™: price, quality, uses, benefits, availability (frequency with which dealers stock products), and performance guarantees.

Any pairwise combination of two of these six basic media contents may be used, generating an additional fifteen possible media contents. Thus, there are a total of twenty-one (6+15) possible different media contents or combinations of contents that firms may choose in BRANDMAPS™. These media contents may be thought of as different kinds of advertising copy emphases. The complete set of twenty-one different media contents are enumerated in Table 4.

Within BRANDMAPS™, the effectiveness of media contents tends to vary from one market region to another. The effectiveness of media content naturally depends partially upon the brand with which it is associated. For example, even though a price message might have some level of effectiveness in general, if a price message is tied to a brand whose price is among the highest in a market, it is reasonable to expect that the specific effectiveness of such a message would be substantially reduced (in comparison with the general level of effectiveness of price messages in the BRANDMAPS™ region). The impact of advertising on customers is thought to have fairly substantial carry-over effects beyond the original quarter of the expenditure.

There are limits on how much advertising may change from one quarter to the next. Specifically, advertising spending support for any vaporware brand in any BRANDMAPS™ market region may not increase by more than $3,000,000 from the previous quarter's advertising spending level. A larger advertising budget increase would have to be phased in over several quarters. Advertising spending may be reduced to any amount, including $0, at any time. If advertising spending support is $0 in any quarter, then the maximum possible advertising spending level in the following quarter is $3,000,000.

Table 4

BRANDMAPS™ MEDIA CONTENTS

Media Content Code	Media Content
1	Price
2	Product Quality
3	Product Uses
4	Product Benefits
5	Product Availability
6	Product Performance Guarantees
7	Price and Product Quality
8	Price and Product Uses
9	Price and Product Benefits
10	Price and Product Availability
11	Price and Product Performance Guarantees
12	Product Quality and Product Uses
13	Product Quality and Product Benefits
14	Product Quality and Product Availability
15	Product Quality and Product Performance Guarantees
16	Product Uses and Product Benefits
17	Product Uses and Product Availability
18	Product Uses and Product Performance Guarantees
19	Product Benefits and Product Availability
20	Product Benefits and Product Performance Guarantees
21	Product Availability and Product Performance Guarantees

Sales Forecasting Decisions

Although not usually categorized as a marketing mix decision variable, sales forecasting decisions are inevitably required of all practicing marketing managers. Good sales forecasting requires a careful balancing between inventory levels and stock-outs, both of which are costly. Sales forecasting prowess also represents an important signal as to a BRANDMAPS™ team's basic understanding of the marketplace in which it competes.

Sales volume forecasts for every active brand in every region are required in each quarter. As with all BRANDMAPS™ decision variables, sales forecasts are considered permanent, until they are changed. If you are satisfied with the previous quarter's sales forecast value, then no action is required. However, since sales volumes are influenced by both your marketing program and by those of your rivals, sales forecasts are likely to be the most frequently changed BRANDMAPS™ decision variable. This probably means sales volume forecasts will be updated every quarter for every brand in every region.

Sales forecasting accuracy is one of the mechanisms by which a team's performance may be evaluated. Sales forecasting accuracy is one of the components of Operating Efficiency, described in

Chapter 9. Also, a separate Sales Forecasting Score exists in BRANDMAPS™. It is reported when Marketing Research Study #16 is requested.

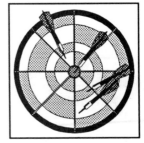

Within BRANDMAPS™, sales forecasts are evaluated on the basis of how close they are to the actual sales volume realization in each quarter. The evaluation mechanism is as follows: a sales volume forecast within 1% of actual sales volume receives 100 points; a sales volume forecast within 2% of actual sales volume receives 99 points; and so on down to a sales volume forecast within 99% of actual sales volume which yields 1 point. Sales forecasts which vary by more than 100% above or below actual sales volumes receive no points. The evaluation for each team is then based on the average sales forecasting points achieved per forecast.

Sales volume forecasting accuracy influences the overhead costs (Administrative Overhead) associated with each product in each market region in which it is active. This situation reflects the implicit and explicit costs associated with poor sales forecasts. Sales volume forecasts represent important inputs into manpower planning, facilities planning, production scheduling, and cash management processes. Errors in such forecasts have costly consequences.

Regional fixed costs equal the base fixed costs only if the corresponding sales volume forecast has an accuracy score of 100. With a sales volume forecasting accuracy score of 0, fixed costs are double the base costs. Values of sales forecasting accuracy between 100 and 0 linearly increase fixed costs from their base value to twice their base value. For example, a sales volume forecasting accuracy score of 78 would result in fixed costs being equal to 1.22 times the base costs.

Sales forecasts are only "scored" (that is, counted in the Sales Forecasting Accuracy Score) when the associated vaporware brand market share in a quarter is at least 2.5% in a BRANDMAPS™ region. This is meant to alleviate the sales forecasting problems associated with new product launches, which may be very unpredictable.

Two marketing research studies (Marketing Research Study #31 and #32) provide some assistance to those making sales volume forecasting decisions. However, potential users of these marketing research studies are cautioned that these sales volume forecasts are simply extrapolative in nature. They assume that the direction and pattern of current marketing efforts of all firms, both your firm and all competitors, remain the same in the next quarter. These sales volume forecasts do take seasonality into account. For more details about these marketing research studies, see Chapter 5.

Reminder: Sales volume forecasts do not automatically affect production orders. Sales volume forecasts and production orders are separate and independent elements in BRANDMAPS™. Changes in sales volume forecasts have no direct influence on changes in production orders. Firms must make production orders independently of sales forecasts, and record both sales volume forecasts and production orders on the appropriate BRANDMAPS™ decision variables change forms.

BRANDMAPS™ Marketing Decision Variable Change Limits

As described earlier in this chapter, BRANDMAPS™ marketing decision variables have built-in limitations related to how much they may change from one quarter to the next. For reference purposes, these limitations are summarized in Table 5.

Table 5

MAXIMUM CHANGES POSSIBLE IN BRANDMAPS™ MARKETING DECISION VARIABLES

Decision Variable	Maximum Permissible Increase From One Quarter To The Next
Advertising	$3,000,000, but advertising may be reduced to any amount below its current level (including $0) at any time.
Dealer Rebates	No limit, but dealer rebates may not exceed 20% (in $ per unit terms) of the current manufacturer list price associated with a brand.
Price	$1,000, but price may be reduced to any amount below its current level at any time, as long as the price is not less than $100. (Note: A brand not actively distributed in a BRANDMAPS™ market region in a quarter may have any price in the $100-$9,999 range in the following quarter.)
Promotion	$5,000,000, but promotion may be reduced to any amount below its current level (including $0) at any time.
Research and Development	$250,000, but research and development may be reduced to any amount (including $0) at any time.
Sales Force Salary	$500. (Note: Sales force salary decreases are not possible, without special permission.)
Sales Force Size	50, but sales force size may be reduced to any level (including zero) at any time.

Chapter 4

Non-Marketing
Decision Variables

Introduction

Non-marketing decision variables are described in this chapter of the BRANDMAPS™ manual. These non-marketing decisions include finished goods inventory management and capacity management activities. In addition, a number of cost-related parameters and matters in BRANDMAPS™ are discussed.

Capacity Management

In BRANDMAPS™, teams must manage the capacity of their plant. Plant capacity depreciates each quarter, one part of the depreciation being related to actual plant usage (variable depreciation) and another part being independent of usage (fixed depreciation). The actual BRANDMAPS™ decision variable for plant capacity is "plant capacity additions." BRANDMAPS™ teams control the absolute level of plant capacity via the plant capacity additions that are added to existing capacity.

The production of a unit of vaporware requires a unit of plant capacity. In the long run, the key to success in BRANDMAPS™ plant capacity management is to have a plant capacity about equal to current sales volume. Of course, a firm's marketing program may be used to influence its sales volume. A short-term mismatch between capacity and sales volume can be corrected with plant capacity additions and with temporary adjustments in marketing efforts.

Plant capacity may be used for any vaporware brand. Plant capacity is not associated with particular brands and each vaporware brand does not have its own plant capacity. Rather, all brands draw upon the available plant capacity.

Each quarter, regardless of production levels, 3% of the available plant capacity depreciates (that is, becomes inoperative). Even if no production is ordered in a quarter, 3% of the plant still depreciates. This fixed rate of depreciation is charged directly to a firm's DIVISIONAL OPERATING STATEMENT as Depreciation.

In addition to the fixed depreciation component, a variable amount of the plant depreciates each quarter, depending linearly on production volume. If the production volume in a quarter is 100% of capacity, then an additional 12% of the plant depreciates. Thus, a plant operating at only 50% of capacity in a quarter has a variable depreciation rate of $(0.50)(12\%) = 6\%$. Production levels which exceed a plant's capacity results in overtime runs, which has variable depreciation rates based on the excess of production over capacity. See Table 6 for the details of the variable depreciation costs in effect for various levels of excess capacity. For accounting purposes, this variable depreciation is added directly into cost of goods sold.

Table 6

VARIABLE DEPRECIATION COST PREMIUMS FOR EXCESS PLANT CAPACITY USAGE

Production Level As a % of Capacity		Variable Cost Depreciation Premium	Variable Depreciation Cost
Minimum	Maximum		
0%	100%	None	BVDR*U
100%	110%	50%	BVDR+[(BVDR*1.50)(U-1.00)]
110%	125%	100%	[1.15*BVDR]+[(BVDR*2.00)(U-1.10)]
125%	150%	200%	[1.45*BVDR]+[(BVDR*3.00)(U-1.25)]
150%+		300%	[2.20*BVDR]+[(BVDR*4.00)(U-1.50)]

Notes: BVDR is the basic variable depreciation rate, currently 0.12. U is the current quarter capacity utilization, which equals current quarter production volume of all brands (regular and emergency) divided by current production quantity. If current production capacity is less than 100,000 units, then a value of current production capacity of 100,000 units is assumed for the purposes of calculating variable depreciation.

Based on the premiums reported in Table 6, it may be noted that a firm operating at 130% of its current production capacity (that is, at 30% over capacity) has a variable depreciation rate equal to
$$[1.45*0.12]+[(0.12*3.0)(1.30-1.25)] = 0.192.$$
Thus, 19.2% of the plant capacity would be used up in the quarter as variable depreciation. Of course, a further 3% of plant capacity would be lost through fixed depreciation.

As this simple example illustrates, running over capacity is hardly advisable for long periods of time. Firms' marketing programs have to be designed and implemented in light of capacity constraint considerations. For example, a firm might increase price or cut back on marketing support to keep demand down until such time as production capacity can be increased to service the current potential demand level. Likewise, firms in a temporary capacity shortage situation might consider raising prices to drive demand (and sales) down. In general, close coordination between marketing and operations (production and capacity management) aspects of the business is required within BRANDMAPS™.

Firms may add to existing plant capacity through capacity expansion. Each unit of capacity currently costs $750. Any non-zero plant capacity order in a BRANDMAPS™ quarter absorbs an additional fixed cost of $250,000. Thus, an order of 20,000 units of plant capacity costs a total of $750(20,000)+$250,000 = $15,250,000. In ordering plant capacity, the minimum capacity that may be ordered (if a non-zero amount is ordered) in a quarter is 5,000 units. The maximum plant capacity that may be ordered in any quarter without paying premium plant capacity order rates is equal to 30% of the current plant capacity (excluding plant capacity on order).

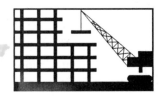

Plant capacity additions do not become available for use until the end of two quarters after ordering. Thus, plant capacity additions are not available for use until the start of the third quarter after they are originally ordered. The full cost of a plant capacity addition is payable upon initiation of the order. The balance sheet records the current status of plant capacity, and any pending orders of plant capacity additions, in the following fashion:

```
CURRENT PLANT                          [CAPACITY = 300,000]   $225,250,000
PLANT ON ORDER FOR 1 QUARTER HENCE  [CAPACITY = 100,000]       75,250,000
             [TOTAL CURRENT & PENDING PLANT CAPACITY = 400,000]
```

To illustrate the timing of the ordering and receipt of plant capacity additions, consider the following example. Suppose that the next quarter is quarter 9. Then, an order for 100,000 units of additional plant capacity (made along with all other decisions submitted for quarter 9) appears on the "Plant On Order For 1 Quarter Hence" line of the balance sheet in quarter 9, and is added to the "Current Plant" at the end of quarter 10. However, the 100,000 units of plant capacity is not actually available for use until the beginning of quarter 11.

To illustrate the plant capacity depreciation process, consider the following examples. Suppose that the current plant capacity is 300,000 units (valued, in this example, at $225,250,000). Suppose further that an order for additional plant capacity of 100,000 units (valued, in this example, at $75,250,000) is pending one quarter hence.

Suppose that the current quarter total production volume across all brands is equal to 150,000 units. Then:

- Fixed depreciation would reduce the current plant capacity by 3% (9,000 units, valued at $6,757,500).

- Since total production is 50.0% (150,000/300,000) of current plant capacity, variable depreciation would be (0.12)(0.50) = 0.06. This represents an additional 18,000 units of plant capacity charged to variable depreciation (valued at $13,515,000).

- End-of-quarter capacity *prior to the addition of new capacity* is 300,000 - 9,000 - 18,000 = 273,000 (valued at $225,250,000 - $6,757,500 - $13,515,000 = $204,977,500).

- End-of-quarter capacity *after the addition of new capacity* is 273,000 + 100,000 = 373,000 units (valued at $204,977,500 + $75,250,000 = $280,227,500). These are the values (current capacity of 373,000 units, valued at $280,227,500) that will be displayed on the firm's balance sheet after the next quarter.

Suppose, instead, that the current quarter total production volume across all brands is equal to 450,000 units. This level of production volume is equal to 150% of the current capacity level. Then:

- Fixed depreciation would reduce the current plant capacity by 3% (9,000 units, valued at $6,757,500).

- Since total production is 150% (450,000/300,000) of current plant capacity, variable depreciation would be

$$[0.12*1.45]+[(0.12*3.0)(1.5-1.25)] = 0.264,$$

  which represents an additional 79,200 units of plant capacity charged to variable depreciation (valued at $59,466,000).

- End-of-quarter capacity *prior to the addition of new capacity* is 300,000 - 9,000 - 79,200 = 211,800 (valued at $225,250,000 - $6,757,500 - $59,466,000 = $159,026,500).

- End-of-quarter capacity *after the addition of new capacity* is 211,800 + 100,000 = 311,800 units (valued at $159,026,500 + $75,250,000 = $234,276,500). These are the values (current capacity of 311,800 units, valued a $234,276,500) that will be displayed on the firm's balance sheet after the next quarter.

Plant capacity order refers to the new (incremental) plant capacity that is ordered. Plant capacity size is not controlled directly. Rather, the rate at which new plant capacity is added is at the firm's control.

In quarter 1, plant capacity orders are set (by the BRANDMAPS™ software) at a default value of 0. This means that no new plant capacity is being ordered as the game begins.

Once you place a new plant capacity order, that amount of new plant capacity is ordered in every subsequent quarter until you change the plant capacity order value. For example, if you specify a plant capacity order of 30,000 units, then that amount of new plant capacity is ordered every quarter until the new plant capacity order value is explicitly changed to some other value. Thus, if you wish to make a one-time plant capacity order of 30,000 units (for one quarter only) and then order no additional new plant capacity in subsequent quarters, be sure to reset your plant capacity order variable to 0 after the next quarter.

Plant capacity strategy should be designed to minimize costs associated with over- and under-utilization of capacity. In the long run, firms should strive to match their plant capacity with their production volume. A firm's marketing mix decision variables may be used to temporarily reduce demand and thereby production volume requirements pending additions to capacity by the normal ordering route. For example, as noted earlier, an increase in price may reduce demand somewhat and alleviate the need for expensive over-capacity production runs.

Firms with excess capacity above and beyond their current production needs (and, presumably, above and beyond any desired capacity safety cushion) have several courses of action. First, attempts may be made to sell the excess capacity to some other firm or firms in the vaporware industry through private negotiations or at a public auction. In such a case, the course instructor would have to arrange for the actual transfer of the plant capacity units, presuming that the buying and selling firms have already agreed upon a transfer price for a specified number of plant capacity units. Second, the excess capacity can be held with depreciation ultimately reducing the excess capacity to acceptable levels. Third, a negative plant capacity order may be executed. See the following section for details about negative plant capacity orders.

In general, plant capacity decisions involve adding new plant capacity regularly (typically, every quarter) to offset the depreciation of the existing plant capacity. This depreciation, of course, arises from two sources: *fixed* (unrelated to actual usage) and *variable* (based on actual usage of the plant for regular and emergency production orders). As may be noted from the examples reported in this section, operating at significant levels of over-capacity reduces plant capacity very rapidly, due to the over-capacity premiums. Over-capacity plant usage can also result in substantial increases in variable costs, since the variable depreciation component is included in the total variable costs associated with vaporware brands.

Plant capacity orders refer to how much additional plant capacity is to be ordered. To stop ordering any additional plant capacity, a plant capacity order of zero units must be made. Firms do not influence the total plant capacity directly. Rather, total plant capacity is influenced indirectly by the amount of new plant capacity that is ordered. Such new plant capacity ordered eventually (after two quarters) is added to the then current total plant capacity.

> *Reminder: Plant capacity order refers to the new (incremental) plant capacity that is ordered. Plant capacity size is not controlled directly in BRANDMAPS™. Rather, the rate at which new plant capacity is added is at the firm's control.*

Special Aspects of Capacity Ordering

Three special aspects of BRANDMAPS™ plant capacity ordering are described below: emergency plant capacity orders, premium plant capacity orders (beyond the normal maximum of 30% of existing plant capacity), and plant capacity sales.

Emergency Plant Capacity Orders

An emergency plant capacity order mechanism is built into BRANDMAPS™. If your plant capacity becomes less than 50% of your total production (regular and emergency production for all brands) in a quarter, an automatic plant capacity diversion operation is executed. This diversion operation involves permanently shifting some of your firm's operating capacity for non-vaporware products to vaporware production. This emergency plant capacity is available for usage immediately (that is, in the current quarter), but such a plant capacity diversion has a 100% premium over normal plant capacity expansion costs associated with it. This plant capacity diversion is executed automatically by BRANDMAPS™ whenever circumstances warrant. The purpose of this feature in BRANDMAPS™ is to avoid situations where a firm runs out of plant capacity. Due to the associated 100% premiums, relying on this automatic diversion feature is, however, a very costly way to manage plant capacity!

An emergency plant capacity order is executed automatically by the BRANDMAPS™ software when total production (regular production plus emergency production for all brands) during a quarter is greater than twice the next quarter's available plant capacity. Note that next quarter's available plant capacity is the current quarter's beginning plant capacity less depreciation during the current quarter plus regular plant capacity additions (plant capacity orders) at the end of the current quarter.

For example, if current quarter production orders are 500,000 units and this quarter's plant capacity, after accounting for depreciation and normal plant capacity orders, is 200,000 units, then an emergency plant capacity order of 50,000 units would be executed automatically by the BRANDMAPS™ software. Next quarter's available plant capacity (shown on the balance sheet for this quarter) would be equal to 200,000+50,000.

Given the situation described in the example above, the following notice (assumed to be for firm #1) would appear in the SPECIAL NOTES, REMINDERS, AND WARNING MESSAGES sub-section of the FINANCIAL AND OPERATING STATEMENT MESSAGES page in the BRANDMAPS™ financial and operating statement results:

```
Emergency plant capacity order executed for firm 1:
  Current quarter total production orders are   500,000 units.
  Without an emergency plant capacity order, next quarter available
    plant capacity would be only   200,000 units, which is less than 50%
    of current quarter total production orders.
  Emergency plant capacity order executed for    50,000 units.
  Next quarter available plant capacity (current plant capacity as
    recorded on these financial statements) is   250,000 units.
```

Premium Plant Capacity Ordering

You are only permitted to order a maximum of 30% of your existing plant capacity in any quarter at the regular price of $750 per unit. However, BRANDMAPS™ permits new plant capacity orders to exceed the 30%-maximum, albeit at a premium cost.

Plant capacity orders between 30% and 60% of current plant capacity are possible at a 50% premium over regular plant capacity costs. For example (assuming that plant capacity ordering costs $750 per unit), with current capacity of 150,000 units:
- a maximum of 45,000 units of new plant capacity could be ordered at the regular price of $750 per unit
- an additional 45,000 units of new plant capacity (above the initial 45,000 units) could be ordered at $1,125 per unit (a 50% premium over the regular $750 per unit cost)
- if all 90,000 units of new plant capacity were ordered, the average cost would be $937.50 per unit (45,000 units at $750 per unit and 45,000 units at $1,125 per unit).

Negative Plant Capacity Orders (Plant Capacity Sales)

Plant capacity orders are used in BRANDMAPS™ to add capacity to a vaporware firm's existing plant. Such plant capacity order additions offset the regular depreciation of plant capacity that results from production orders. In their normal usage, plant capacity orders are positive numbers.

Negative plant capacity orders are also possible in BRANDMAPS™. Negative plant capacity orders correspond to a sale or disposal of existing plant capacity, presumably because much too much plant capacity exists to meet current and near-future sales requirements. Negative plant capacity orders to -50,000 units are possible.

Negative plant capacity orders yield 75% of the current cost of new plant capacity. (The other 25% of the value of the negative plant capacity order is recorded as a "Consulting Fee.") For example, if plant capacity order additions currently cost $750 per unit, then a plant capacity disposal sale order only realizes $562.50 per unit of capacity sold. Negative plant capacity orders are processed at the end of the quarter so such to-be-sold plant capacity is still available for use for the quarter following the plant capacity disposal sale order. Of course, this implies that your firm continues to pay depreciation on the plant capacity disposal sale order for another quarter.

Production Ordering Decisions

Your plant processes orders from your management team for production of your various vaporware brands. Production is available to meet the demand for vaporware brands in the current quarter. That is, if you order production of 100,000 units of a specific vaporware brand, these 100,000 units are available for sale immediately during the current quarter.

As orders for vaporware brands arrive from dealers in the various BRANDMAPS™ market regions, your plant automatically attempts to fill them from the finished goods inventory on hand at the start of a quarter plus the regular production volume ordered for completion during the quarter. If sales exceed the sum of finished goods inventory available for sale at the beginning of the quarter plus the regular production volume order, your plant has to execute an emergency run of such stocked-out vaporware to meet the excess of demand over available supply. Emergency production is completed within the current quarter, so it is available for sale to meet current quarter orders from dealers. Such an emergency order of production is automatically executed by your plant management as the need arises.

Unit costs on emergency order production are 25% above standard production costs. This 25% premium for emergency order production is based on the total variable cost of producing a brand. This includes raw materials, production, labor, packaging, variable depreciation, and Compatibility and Warranty premiums. Your plant charges your division for these emergency production order premiums by increasing the unit cost by 25% for all vaporware produced on an emergency basis. This emergency production order premium is necessitated by the required use of overtime and the opportunity costs associated with diverting production activities and efforts from the many other products produced by your plant for the other divisions of your firm.

When emergency production actually occurs, the following message appears in the EMERGENCY PRODUCTION ACTIVITY sub-section of the FINANCIAL AND OPERATING STATEMENT MESSAGES page in the BRANDMAPS™ financial and operating statement results:

```
EMERGENCY PRODUCTION ACTIVITY
    Product 1-1 has emergency production of   3,314 units, which is 100.0%
    of total product 1-1 production this quarter.
```

In addition, the following message appears in the SPECIAL NOTES, REMINDERS, AND WARNING MESSAGES sub-section of the FINANCIAL AND OPERATING STATEMENT MESSAGES page in the BRANDMAPS™ financial and operating statement results:

```
SPECIAL NOTES, REMINDERS, AND WARNING MESSAGES
    Product 1-1, region 2, has unfilled sales orders of   6,886 units:
        With total potential sales volume of    7,651 units (SALES (Units)
        plus UNFILLED SALES) and an emergency production limit of  10%, a
        maximum of        765 units of emergency production are possible for
        sale in this market region.
    Product 1-1, region 3, has unfilled sales orders of  21,389 units:
        With total potential sales volume of   23,765 units (SALES (Units)
        plus UNFILLED SALES) and an emergency production limit of  10%, a
        maximum of      2,376 units of emergency production are possible for
        sale in this market region.
    Product 1-1, region 4, has unfilled sales orders of   1,564 units:
        With total potential sales volume of    1,737 units (SALES (Units)
        plus UNFILLED SALES) and an emergency production limit of  10%, a
        maximum of        173 units of emergency production are possible for
        sale in this market region.
```

You may control the amount of emergency production for each vaporware brand by establishing emergency production limits. Values of emergency production limits may be set between 0% and 50% (in integer amounts). An emergency production limit of 0% would mean that no emergency production would occur for a particular brand. With an emergency production limit of 0%, sales could not exceed beginning inventory plus regular production during the quarter. With an emergency production limit of 42%, up to 42% of total potential sales could be met through emergency production orders. One of the operating reports documents total potential sales, unfilled orders, and actual sales for all vaporware brands of a firm.

BRANDMAPS™ firms often use emergency production limits to control overcapacity usage situations, especially for newly reformulated brands and for new brands introduced into BRANDMAPS™ market regions. By setting relatively low emergency production limits (say, in the 0% to 10% range), capacity usage may be controlled and sales may be predicted with greater accuracy. Of course, lost sales may result, with a host of implicit opportunity costs associated with such unfilled orders.

If demand for a brand exceeds beginning inventory plus regular production plus the maximum amount of emergency production permitted, then a stockout occurs. Some of the stocked out sales presumably will involve customers and dealers who will wait another quarter and return to purchase the stocked out brand at that time. Other customers do not wait and choose to purchase some other available (non-stocked out) brand. Still other customers who encounter a stockout situation may choose not to purchase any vaporware brand at this time. It should be expected that stockouts have some customer and dealer badwill associated with them. That is, brands that stockout may be viewed less positively by customers and dealers in the future.

It is possible to order production that exceeds your current plant capacity. Such orders are executed, although the variable depreciation premiums associated with over-capacity usage are in effect. These premiums are described earlier in this chapter. It is generally much more expensive to run into emergency production order premiums than it is to order modest amounts of production above your current capacity level.

Note that your production ordering decisions are of the "standing order" variety. That is, they continue to be in effect in each subsequent quarter until you explicitly change them.

All emergency production ordering premiums are charged separately on the firm's DIVISIONAL OPERATING STATEMENT. See the line item "Emergency Premiums (Production)" on the DIVISIONAL OPERATING STATEMENT.

To illustrate the production and inventory processes in BRANDMAPS™, consider the following examples. Suppose that the inventory of a brand at the end of the last quarter was 100,000 units. Thus, this is the beginning inventory at the start of the next quarter. Suppose that the production order for the next quarter is 150,000 units. Then, a total of 250,000 units are available for sale during the next quarter.

Suppose that demand (sales volume) during the quarter is 200,000 units. Then, inventory at the end of the next quarter would be equal to 100,000 + 150,000 - 200,000 = 50,000 units.

Suppose that demand (sales) during the quarter is 300,000 units. Then, an emergency production order of 50,000 units would be executed automatically by your plant to cover the inventory shortage (assuming that the emergency production limit for the brand is at least equal to 17%, or 50,000/300,000 expressed in percentage terms). Thus, inventory at the end of the next quarter would be equal to 100,000 + 150,000 + 50,000 - 300,000 = 0 units. (If the emergency production limit had been 10%, then only 30,000 units of emergency production would have been produced, resulting in unfilled orders of 20,000 units.) Any time emergency production is required, ending inventory will be equal to zero units.

Suppose that the brand has been reformulated. Also, suppose that demand (sales) during the quarter is 200,000 units. With a reformulation, the inventory of 100,000 units would be subject to a disposal sale, thus resulting in a zero inventory position at the start of the next quarter. The 150,000 units of regular production would be added to this zero inventory level, resulting in 150,000 units available for sale. Since demand is 200,000 units, there would be an emergency production run of 50,000 units needed to satisfy current demand (assuming that the emergency production limit is at least equal to 25%).

Fixed charges exist for production orders. The current charges for each regular and emergency order are $100,000 per production order. These fixed charges are reported on the DIVISIONAL OPERATING STATEMENT under the line item "Production Orders (Fixed Costs)."

Inventory (storage) costs accrue from finished goods being stored at your plant's warehouse. By agreement between your division and the plant, the inventory charges are on the basis of the average dollar value of the inventories on hand. This is based on the average of the beginning and the ending inventory levels in any quarter. For finished goods, the charge is 5% of the average dollar value of inventories. This level of inventory charge includes full warehouse charges (space usage, insurance, and so on), plus a factor for spoilage. With this inventory charging mechanism, inventory charges are only $0 at the end of a game quarter if the current and previous quarters' inventory levels were both equal to zero.

Productions orders for any vaporware brand may not increase by more than 100,000 units from the corresponding value in the previous quarter. Production orders may decrease by any amount (including to 0 units) at any time. This limitation means that a production order for a brand of 0 units in one quarter may be followed by a maximum production order of 100,000 units for that brand in the next quarter.

Product-Related Costs

Your plant charges your vaporware operating division for the costs associated with manufacturing vaporware brands. The cost of goods sold (per unit) may be expressed, approximately, in the following terms:

$$COGS = RMCOST + LCOST + PRCOST + PDCOST + PKCOST$$

where:

COGS is total cost of goods sold ($ per unit) at the plant, not including cost adjustment premiums for vaporware brands with Compatibility and Warranty levels above the minimum level

RMCOST is raw materials cost ($ per unit)

LCOST is labor cost ($ per unit)

PRCOST is production costs ($ per unit)

PDCOST is variable cost ($ per unit) of plant depreciation attributable to a specific vaporware brand

PKCOST is packaging cost ($ per unit).

The cost-adjustment premiums associated with vaporware brands with non-minimum Compatibility and Warranty levels are described below.

PDCOST is based on plant capacity utilization. It reflects the variable depreciation of capacity associated with the processing of production orders. The amount of PDCOST allocated to any vaporware brand in any quarter is based on a weighted average of the total production ordered in the quarter across all of your brands, where the weights are the production orders of the vaporware brands. As described earlier, variable depreciation cost is currently 12% (assuming that a firm is operating at or less than current capacity). With a $750 per unit capacity charge, this amounts to $90 per unit in variable depreciation charges.

The current costs of the other components of COGS are as follows: LCOST is $30.00 per unit, PRCOST is $60.00 per unit, and PKCOST is $10.00 per unit. These costs are generally negotiated with your plant on a yearly basis. Since your plant operates as a separate profit center, it negotiates fixed cost contracts with your plant. These costs are in effect until the end of the next game year. In the recent past, these costs have increased roughly with the inflation rate.

The LCOST and PRCOST values described above are base values. They increase if the (regular) production volume order for a brand changes from one quarter to the next. These production smoothing cost adjustments increase the base labor and production costs, reflecting the various costs associated with changing production volume levels. The production smoothing adjustments are as follows: each 1% change in regular production volume from one quarter to the next increases base labor costs by 0.50% (to a maximum adjustment in base labor costs of 100%) and increases base production costs by 0.25% (to a maximum adjustment in base production costs of 100%). Emergency production orders are costed at the base labor and production rates, since they are subject to separate penalty cost premiums.

In combination with the cost premiums associated with Compatibility and Warranty levels, these production smoothing cost adjustments can add significantly to vaporware variable costs. The management of these smoothing adjustment costs require a close coordination between marketing programs and operations activities. In particular, holding steady production levels from quarter to quarter (even in the face of inventory buildups or shortfalls) and adjusting marketing programs to stimulate or suppress sales, to some extent, may be necessary to control these costs.

Reminder: Productions orders for any vaporware brand may not increase by more than 100,000 units from the corresponding value in the previous quarter. This limitation means that a brand production order of 0 units in one quarter may be followed by a maximum production order of 100,000 units for that brand in the next quarter. This 100,000 production order increase maximum must also be taken into account in your smoothing cost and inventory management efforts.

The current raw materials cost per pound for each of the five basic raw materials in vaporware are as follows: Syntech, $25.00; Plumbo, $35.00; Glomp, $15.00; Trimicro, $10.00; and Fralange, $5.00. Your plant normally negotiates yearly contracts with several suppliers of these raw materials, so these raw materials costs normally do not change throughout a BRANDMAPS™ year. However, yearly costs adjustments should be expected in these raw material costs.

The purchasing agent at your plant has well-established working relationships with all major suppliers. Since the raw materials ingredients are essentially commodities with only a single grade being available, raw materials prices posted by suppliers tend to be virtually identical to each other. Your purchasing agent typically splits purchases about equally among the major raw materials suppliers, so as not to be overly dependent on any single supplier.

Raw materials prices have generally increased about equally with changes in the consumer price index. However, this is not true for Plumbo, which is a petroleum derivative. Plumbo's costs have increased as much as 25% in some recent years, although with the current world oil situation some instability in the price of Plumbo is anticipated.

Given the above information, the total raw materials costs, RMCOST, associated with each unit of vaporware can be expressed in the following terms:

$$RMCOST = 3*(25.00*WS + 35.00*WP + 15.00*WG + 10.00*WT + 5.00*WF)$$

where WS, WP, WG, WT, and WF are the proportions of the vaporware brand compositions of Syntech, Plumbo, Glomp, Trimicro, and Fralange, respectively.

The cost-of-goods-sold figure described earlier is based on vaporware with Compatibility and Warranty levels both equal to 1. Compatibility and Warranty levels above 1 affect total costs as follows. Each increment above the values of 1 for Compatibility and Warranty adds a premium of 1.0% and 1.2% of costs, respectively, times the square of the amount of the product attribute value above 1 to the overall costs associated with a vaporware brand. These costs are compounded (that is, multiplied).

To illustrate the variable cost impact of the sixth and seventh vaporware product attributes, consider first a 30/30/35/10/5/1/1 vaporware brand. Such a brand of vaporware would cost $73.50 per unit in raw materials. This total cost per unit is derived as follows:

$$3[\$25.00(0.30) + \$35.00(0.30) + \$15.00(0.35) + \$10.00(0.10) + \$5.00(0.05)] = \$73.50.$$

In addition, other manufacturing costs (production, labor, packaging, and variable depreciation) would amount to an additional $60+$30+$10+$90 = $190, assuming that the firm is operating at full capacity and that no production smoothing cost adjustments are necessary. Thus, excluding Compatibility and Warranty adjustments, the total per unit manufacturing costs for a 30/30/35/10/5/1/1 vaporware brand would amount to $263.50. Note that there are no extra cost impacts of Compatibility and Warranty levels in this case, since they are both equal to their minimum value, 1.

Alternatively, the vaporware brand 30/30/35/10/5/5/6 would also cost $263.50 in terms of basic manufacturing costs, but the impacts of the Compatibility of 5 and the Warranty of 6 are substantial. The total per unit cost, including the Compatibility and Warranty cost adjustment premiums, would be: 263.50*[1+0.010(5-1)(5-1)]*[1+0.012(6-1)(6-1)]= (263.50)*(1.16)*(1.30) = $397.36. As may be noted, high levels of Compatibility and Warranty have a substantial influence on costs. The maximum levels of Compatibility and Warranty, 9 in each case, would have a cost impact of

$$[1+0.010(9-1)(9-1)][1+0.012(9-1)(9-1)] = [1.64][1.77] = 2.90$$

on a vaporware brand. This represents a 190% cost premium impact, above and beyond all other manufacturing costs, to achieve the maximum levels of Compatibility and Warranty. Obviously, high levels of Compatibility and Warranty have a material influence on variable costs.

Cost adjustment premiums associated with all possible combinations of Compatibility and Warranty are shown in Table 7.

Table 7

COST PREMIUMS FOR VARIOUS COMPATIBILITY AND WARRANTY LEVELS

		Compatibility								
		1	2	3	4	5	6	7	8	9
	1	1.000	1.010	1.040	1.090	1.160	1.250	1.360	1.490	1.650
	2	1.012	1.022	1.052	1.103	1.174	1.265	1.376	1.508	1.660
	3	1.048	1.058	1.090	1.142	1.216	1.310	1.425	1.562	1.719
	4	1.108	1.119	1.152	1.208	1.285	1.385	1.507	1.651	1.817
Warranty	5	1.192	1.204	1.240	1.299	1.383	1.490	1.621	1.776	1.955
	6	1.300	1.313	1.352	1.417	1.508	1.625	1.768	1.937	2.132
	7	1.432	1.446	1.489	1.561	1.661	1.790	1.948	2.134	2.348
	8	1.588	1.604	1.652	1.731	1.842	1.985	2.160	2.366	2.604
	9	1.768	1.786	1.839	1.927	2.051	2.210	2.404	2.634	2.900

Notes:
(1) These cost adjustment premiums are applied to the total cost of a vaporware brand, including raw materials, production, labor, packaging, and variable depreciation costs.
(2) Example: A vaporware brand with a total cost of $450 per unit, and Compatibility and Warranty levels of 3 and 7, respectively, would have overall cost of $450*1.489 = $670.05, after including the cost premiums adjustments associated with these Compatibility and Warranty levels.

Experience Curve Effects and Product Costs

Based on recent technological advancements in the manufacture of vaporware, your plant now believes that it is possible to realize the benefits of experience curve effects. These experience curve effects lower the variable costs associated with vaporware manufacturing. Experience curve effects operate at the level of individual brands and result in reduced unit costs associated with labor, production, and raw materials costs (but not on variable plant depreciation or packaging costs). Since raw material, production, and labor costs account for the majority of vaporware product costs, experience curve effects have the potential — if large enough — to materially reduce variable costs.

Experience (cumulative production volume) accumulates only for a specific brand formulation. A reformulation of a brand's composition results in all production experience on that brand being lost. The PRODUCTION COST ANALYSIS REPORT in the regular financial and operating statements may be consulted for some information on current costs and levels of cumulative production experience.

Only regular production accumulates in the experience curve effect. Emergency production is not included in the accumulation of production experience, although all regular and emergency production volume are costed on the basis of experience curve effects.

Experience curve effects are felt only after some minimum cumulative production experience (volume) has been achieved with a specific brand formulation. Experience curve adjustments on the base labor, production, and raw materials costs occur only for the cumulative production experience in excess of this minimum. The precise values of the minimum level and the shape of the cost savings with cumulative experience are not known with certainty. Only experience will reveal their possible magnitudes.

Cumulative production experience curve effects only accrue to an existing formulation of a brand. All experience-based cost savings are lost upon a reformulation. Thus, cost savings accrue to brands whose formulations remain constant through time. Of course, buyers' preferences may change through time, leading buyers to prefer different formulations.

Transportation and Shipping Costs

By arrangement with the various dealers in the BRANDMAPS™ market regions, your firm pays for the transportation and shipping costs associated with having vaporware orders delivered to the dealers. The current total transportation and shipping costs vary by BRANDMAPS™ market region and reflect the distance from your plant to the market region. Transportation and shipping charges are for each unit of vaporware, regardless of formulation and weight.

The specific transportation and shipping costs associated with the BRANDMAPS™ market regions are reported in the SPECIAL BRANDMAPS NOTICES section on the last page of your firm's financial and operating results reports.

In the past, transportation and shipping costs have increased through time approximately at the rate of inflation.

General Overhead Charges

Corporate overhead is charged on a "per active brand per quarter" basis. This charge appears as "Corporate Overhead" on the DIVISIONAL OPERATING STATEMENT. The current charge is $100,000 per active brand per quarter. In addition, "Administrative Overhead" of $50,000 per quarter are charged to your division for each BRANDMAPS™ region in which each brand is in active distribution. This base amount of $50,000 is predicated on a sales volume forecasting accuracy of 100. As described in Chapter 3, inaccuracies in sales volume forecasts can double this base "Administrative Overhead" value.

Note that this adjustment in "Administrative Overhead" cost is made for all active brands, even for those with market shares of less than 2.5% in a BRANDMAPS™ market region. Although sales forecast accuracy scores are not counted for small market share brands (that is, those with a market share in a BRANDMAPS™ market region of less than 2.5%), sales forecasting accuracy does affect the "Administrative Overhead" cost for all brands, regardless of their market shares.

Taxation

The corporate tax rate in the vaporware industry is currently 50%. This tax rate is levied on the total income (operating and non-operating income) of your division.

If your division has negative income in any quarter, the application of this tax results in negative tax being due. Such negative tax is a tax credit that is used to offset future tax obligations. All payments of taxes and applications of tax credits to future tax obligations are handled automatically by the BRANDMAPS™ software.

Banking Arrangements

Provisions exist in BRANDMAPS™ for automatic lines of credit (bank loans) to be extended and for investments of excess cash in short-term marketable securities to occur as the occasion arises.

When the game first runs, any existing bank loans are paid off and any existing marketable securities are sold off. After the game runs, cash on hand is examined. If cash is less than 5% of the quarter's sales revenues, an immediate loan is taken out to raise current cash on hand to this level. If cash is more than 8% of the quarter's sales revenues, then the excess is immediately invested in short-term (one quarter) marketable securities. Thus, a firm never has both a loan and a short-term investment in marketable securities simultaneously. These operations are performed automatically within BRANDMAPS™.

The normal cost of short-term loans is currently 3% per quarter, which is the current prime rate of interest in the BRANDMAPS™ world. This 3% interest rate is applicable if outstanding loans do not exceed 20% of net assets. Net assets are equal to total assets less outstanding loans, if any. (Net assets are also equal to common stock plus retained earnings.)

For firms whose outstanding bank loans in any quarter exceed 20% of net assets, higher interest rate charges are payable. These interest premiums reflect the risk situation associated with relatively highly levered firms. The complete current interest rate schedule for outstanding loans in the vaporware industry is as follows:

Interest Rate	Relationship Between Loans and Net Assets
3%	If Loans/Net Assets ≤ 0.20
4%	If 0.20 < Loans/Net Assets ≤ 0.30
5%	If 0.30 < Loans/Net Assets ≤ 0.40
6%	If 0.40 < Loans/Net Assets ≤ 0.50
9%	If Loans/Net Assets > 0.50

This interest-rate schedule is based on a normal interest rate of 3%. If the prime rate applicable to the vaporware industry changes, all of the other interest rates in this schedule would be subject to revision.

Short-term investments in marketable securities currently yield 2.25% interest per quarter.

The interest payments on bank loans and the interest received from investments in marketable securities are reported as Non-Operating Income on the firm's DIVISIONAL OPERATING STATEMENT each quarter. Bank loan interest charges would represent negative "Non-Operating Income."

On the DIVISIONAL OPERATING STATEMENT, "Non-Operating Income" is based on the marketable security or loan position at the end of the previous quarter. Thus, the presence of loans at the end of quarter "n" results in "Non-Operating Income" in quarter "n+1" being negative, which corresponds to interest paid on the quarter "n" loan.

Refinancing Arrangements and Dividends

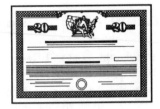

Periodically, refinancing of the capital structure of vaporware firms may be required. For example, dividends normally have to be paid to stockholders on a more or less regular basis, especially to your corporate parent (who owns about 50% of your outstanding stock). Also, increases in financing may be possible for firms with such needs. For example, larger firms may require greater financing to support a large capital budget for plant expansion. A larger equity base will, of course, permit greater borrowing possibilities. In addition, the equity base of each firm influences its ROI (return on investment).

There may be some room for creative negotiation with regard to positive and negative adjustments in your capital base. Your course instructor will advise you of the possibilities associated with such refinancing.

Cash Flow in BRANDMAPS™

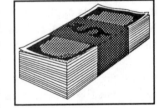

Just as in all businesses, management of cash flow is important in BRANDMAPS™. BRANDMAPS™ firms can never run out of cash, due to the provision for automatic loans. However, high levels of loans compared to a firm's capital base (common stock and retained earnings) result in substantial interest rate penalties on loans.

The marketable securities and loans positions can vary from quarter to quarter due to balance sheet activities (inventory and plant capacity) as well as due to operations activities (profit and loss). Sources of cash in BRANDMAPS™ include: profits derived from operations, reduction in finished goods inventory levels, and reductions in plant capacity levels through depreciation. Uses of cash in BRANDMAPS™ include: losses from operations (especially related to new product launches), investments in finished goods inventories, new investment in plant capacity, and payment of dividends.

The BRANDMAPS™ Stock Market

BRANDMAPS™ has its own stock market in which all vaporware industry firms' stock prices are reported. Stock prices are thought to reflect future earnings potential as well as recent past performance. Current stock prices (at the end of each quarter) are reported along with firms' other financial and operating results. Stock prices for all firms are $100 at the end of the initial BRANDMAPS™ quarter, quarter 1.

What determines stock prices in BRANDMAPS™? Presumably, the same things that influence stock prices on all stock exchanges. In the most general terms, financial theory and empirical results suggest that investors' future earnings expectations are the key drivers of current stock prices. What influences investors' future earnings expectations? Factors such as the current levels and trends in sales volume, market share, revenues, margins, profits, and operating efficiency are likely key influencers of investors' future earnings expectations. Absolute and relative (compared to other vaporware firms) considerations presumably both matter. New product launch activity normally receives special scrutiny in financial markets. Current earnings, of course, are presumably the primary factor influencing current stock prices.

If your BRANDMAPS™ exercise was run for a very large number of quarters (say, 50 or 100), then the firm with the largest stock price (presumably also the firm with the largest earnings, given that all firms start quarter 1 with an identical capital structure) would be the unambiguous winner. However, in any finite time horizon (say, 8 or 12 or 16 quarters), it is problematic to conclude that any single number fully describes the overall performance of a firm. These considerations resulted in the development of the multi-factor quantitative performance evaluation mechanism described in Chapter 9, which your course instructor may choose to use to evaluate firm performance in your BRANDMAPS™ exercise.

Dividend Payments

Firms may pay quarterly dividends of any amount (including $0) in each quarter. Dividends reduce cash, on the asset side of the balance sheet, and liabilities and equities (capitalization), on the liabilities and equities side of the balance sheet.

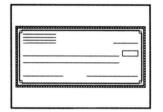

Since dividends reduce a firm's cash, they correspondingly reduce a firm's capitalization. It follows that a dividend reduces the "I" (Investment) in "ROI" (Return-on-Investment). Since ROI is an important factor in performance evaluation in BRANDMAPS™ as in all for-profit businesses, dividends permit firms to manage their capital structure to some extent. By having large dividend payments, ROI tends to increase. However, note that low capitalization can lead to high loans, with attendant interest charges. Such interest charges reduce the "R" in ROI. So, there is an obvious trade-off situation that must be dealt with explicitly in the dividend payment decision.

Dividends are expressed only in dollars, not in dollars per share and not in percentage terms.

Once you made a dividend payment, that amount of dividend payment is made in every subsequent quarter until you change the dividend payment value. For example, if you specify a dividend payment of $1,000,000, that dividend payment is ordered every quarter until the dividend payment value is explicitly changed to some other value. Thus, if you wish to make a one-time dividend payment of $1,000,000 (for one quarter only) and then have no additional dividend in subsequent quarters, be sure to reset your dividend payment variable to 0 after the next quarter.

Information Systems Costs

Firms are charged for information systems usage. For billing purposes, this charge is recorded as Marketing Research Study #55. The current charge is $1,000 per page of BRANDMAPS™ output (financial and operating statement results plus marketing research results). These costs are recorded in the quarter after they are incurred, like other marketing research charges.

Naming Your Firm

Firms are referenced within BRANDMAPS™ by their firm number. However, you may select a firm name and it is displayed at the top of each page of your financial reports and marketing research results. BRANDMAPS™ firm names may be a maximum of 50 standard typewriter-keyboard characters in length. You may change your firm name at any time.

## Chapter 5

BRANDMAPS™ Marketing Research Studies

Introduction

The marketing research studies currently available for purchase in BRANDMAPS™ are described in this chapter of the BRANDMAPS™ participant's manual.

Marketing research studies are primarily provided by your marketing research supplier, although some marketing research information is provided by the Vaporware Industry Trade Association. The vaporware industry marketing research supplier is well thought of in the marketing research supplier community, so you should have reasonable confidence in the general accuracy of the marketing research supplied. Of course, specific marketing research study types have strengths and weaknesses just as they do in the real world.

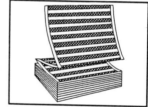

To execute a BRANDMAPS™ marketing research study, you complete the MARKETING RESEARCH STUDY PRE-ORDER REQUEST FORM. This form may be found in Chapter 7. This form must be submitted along with any other forms (required to effect changes in marketing and non-marketing decisions, described in Chapters 3 and 4) by the specified time deadlines for each game run. A catalog of available BRANDMAPS™ marketing research studies may be found in Tables 8-11.

Although marketing research is requested prior to a quarter, marketing research studies are executed after a quarter has concluded. Thus, marketing research reports always reflect the just-completed quarter's experience.

Marketing Research Strategy in BRANDMAPS™

BRANDMAPS™ is a competitive marketing strategy game. As such, participants focus continuously on issues associated with marketing analysis, strategy, and planning. However, the details associated with

Table 8

BRANDMAPS™ MARKETING RESEARCH STUDIES —
PRODUCT DEVELOPMENT AND TESTING RESEARCH

#	Marketing Research Study
2	Brand Composition Analysis
10	Conjoint Analysis
12	Concept Testing
13	Preference Testing, Two Existing Brands
14	Preference Testing, One Existing and One Hypothetical Brand
15	Preference Testing, Two Hypothetical Brands
18	Patent Search
30	Patent Zone Search
34	Another Conjoint Analysis
47	Self-Reported Attribute Preferences

Table 9

BRANDMAPS™ MARKETING RESEARCH STUDIES —
MARKETING PROGRAM ANALYSIS AND EVALUATION

#	Marketing Research Study
20	Test Marketing Experiment
35	Advertising Program Experiment
38	Promotion Experiment
43	Marketing Support Spending Productivity

Table 10

BRANDMAPS™ MARKETING RESEARCH STUDIES —
SALES FORECASTING

#	Marketing Research Study
31	Industry Sales Volume Forecasts
32	Brand Sales Volume Forecasts

Table 11

BRANDMAPS™ MARKETING RESEARCH STUDIES —
COMPETITIVE AND MARKET MONITORING RESEARCH

#	Marketing Research Study
1	Competitive Information — Dividends and Earnings
3	Industry Sales Force Size
4	Industry Advertising
5	Industry Sales Force Compensation
6	Industry Promotion
7	Industry R&D
8	Media Content Analysis
9	Promotional Type Analysis
11	Customer Brand Awareness
16	Operating Statistics Report
17	Brand Quality Ratings
19	Competitive Information — Balance Sheets
21	Brand Perceptual Ratings
22	Aggregate Market Statistics
23	Reformulation Activity
24	Market Shares
25	Dealer Prices
26	Dealer Rebates
27	Dealer Promotion Awareness
28	Dealer Availability
29	Competitive Position Audit
33	Reformulation Activity — Detailed
36	Competitive Information — Brand Marketing Profile
37	Competitive Information — Sales Force Compensation Statistics
39	Competitive Information — Unfilled Sales Volume Statistics
40	Competitive Information — Brand Margin Analysis
41	Regional Summary Analysis
42	Marketing Research Ordering Statistics
44	Population Forecasts
45	Per Capita Income Forecasts
46	Consumer Price Index Forecasts
48	Dealer Inventory Analysis — Own Brands
49	Dealer Inventory Analysis — All Brands
50	Price Sensitivity Analysis

implementing and executing marketing strategies and plans are not a part of BRANDMAPS™. It follows that BRANDMAPS™ participants do not design/place specific advertising copy in media outlets, recruit/train/supervise sales representatives, order raw materials and schedule production runs, or conduct marketing research. These things are all implicitly taken care of by your firm's advertising agency, sales managers, plant management staff, and marketing research suppliers, respectively. In essence, BRANDMAPS™ participants receive information from various sources (internal company information systems and marketing research suppliers, in particular) and, on the basis of that information, make decisions and communicate these decisions via decision forms or by direct data entry with BRANDMAPS™ program BRANDMAP.EXE (and sub-programs B_DV.EXE and B_PREMRS.EXE). Others actually implement and execute your decisions.

The military metaphor immediately comes to mind to describe your situation in BRANDMAPS™. Your team members are the officers (managers) commanding your forces (products, plant capacity, financial resources, and marketing program elements). You are located at headquarters, which is some distance from the actual battle field (the marketplace). Based on regular reports from the field (financial and operating reports) and special reconnaissance that you request (marketing research), you analyze the situation, choose strategies (select marketing program elements), make decisions, and communicate those decisions to your field officers. The field officers actually implement your decisions. Just as you do not have to be on the actual battle field to direct a successful military campaign, you do not have to be in the actual marketplace to design a successful marketing program. However, you cannot be successful in either the military battle field or the commercial marketplace without information.

Given that you cannot actually talk to other employees, your sales force, dealers, or customers, the role and importance of marketing research becomes readily apparent. Furthermore, since vaporware is an unspecified generic product, you cannot necessarily use standard rules-of-thumb (for example, "price high since vaporware customers are price insensitive") to assist you in BRANDMAPS™. You will have to use the routinely-provided financial and operating reports plus marketing research studies that you specifically request to provide the information necessary to manage your BRANDMAPS™ firm's affairs.

A wide range of marketing research studies are available in BRANDMAPS™. The existence of these marketing research studies is based on several premises.

- Marketing research is a routine fact of life in marketing. Since BRANDMAPS™ attempts to simulate marketing management to the fullest possible extent, it is only natural that marketing research opportunities would both exist and be a normal component of the marketing management activities within BRANDMAPS™.

- Marketing research is not free. Quite the contrary is true. Marketing research can be extraordinarily expensive, if not well-managed. BRANDMAPS™ marketing research studies have prices that are meant to be approximately representative of what such studies cost in the real world. The marketing research studies in BRANDMAPS™ range in price from a few hundred dollars to a few hundred thousand dollars. Be thoughtful! It is possible to spend several million dollars on marketing research in a single quarter. Such spending has important consequences for current profitability. Of course, some might argue that such spending on marketing research now is the only way to ensure future profitability.

- The existence of a particular marketing research study in BRANDMAPS™ is not an implicit endorsement that such a marketing research study is important, relevant, or even useful in the context of managing vaporware brands. Rather, these marketing research studies are included in BRANDMAPS™ because they exist in the real world and real-world managers sometimes or frequently use such studies. You will have to form your own opinions about whether these studies are valuable and worth their costs in the context of BRANDMAPS™ and the vaporware industry.

- There is normally a lag between ordering marketing research and receiving the associated study results. In BRANDMAPS™, this is simulated by the need to pre-order marketing research studies along with all other BRANDMAPS™ decisions.

- The sophisticated nature of the BRANDMAPS™ exercise implies the need for sophisticated marketing research capabilities. Indeed, BRANDMAPS™ has, by a considerable measure, the most extensive and sophisticated battery of marketing research studies of any commercially-available marketing simulation game.

All marketing research studies in BRANDMAPS™ are quantitative in nature. Qualitative research capabilities (such as focus groups and other exploratory research procedures) are not available. Furthermore, all marketing research results are in raw form. Only the direct results of the marketing research effort are reported in BRANDMAPS™. No managerial interpretation is provided. You must interpret the results of these marketing research studies yourself. Your interpretation efforts may require additional analysis, comparisons with previous results (from marketing research studies received in earlier quarters), and the like.

In thinking about marketing research strategy and tactics in BRANDMAPS™, some broad generalizations seem possible:

- Excellent marketing strategy can only be developed based on excellent marketing analysis and thinking. Since marketing research provides the raw data to perform excellent marketing analysis, marketing research should be an important component of your BRANDMAPS™ decision making process. Do not relegate your marketing research pre-ordering decisions to the last five minutes of team meetings. Rather, treat marketing research ordering decisions as a fundamental part of your whole BRANDMAPS™ decision making process.

- Plan ahead. To identify market patterns and trends, you will probably need to order some marketing research studies on a more-or-less regular basis. A formal marketing research plan should be a part of your marketing plans.

- Systematize the post-analysis of marketing research studies. This might involve, for example, the continual updating of specially-designed databases, charts, or graphs to reformat the raw BRANDMAPS™ marketing research results into more meaningful and useful forms.

- Share marketing insights derived from particular marketing research studies with all of your BRANDMAPS™ team members. These may require marketing research "experts" to assume coaching roles with marketing research "novices." This is a natural state of affairs. Given the complexity of BRANDMAPS™, it is not possible to be an "expert" on everything.

- If you do not understand the workings or technical details of a specific marketing research study, review the marketing research study description in the BRANDMAPS™ manual. If things are still unclear, consult with your course instructor. However, don't expect to receive particularly informative answers from your course instructor to broad questions of the form "Should we be ordering this marketing research study?" This sort of question is something with which you will have to struggle and ultimately resolve yourself within the context of your BRANDMAPS™ team.

A BRANDMAPS™ veteran offered the following summary advice about the BRANDMAPS™ marketing research milieu: *Think before ordering marketing research. The large number of marketing research studies available in BRANDMAPS™ provide reams and reams of data. However, data are not very useful if they cannot be turned quickly into information ("information" = "interpreted data"). Read the descriptions of the marketing research studies many, many times until you are familiar with what is available. Continue to re-read the descriptions throughout the BRANDMAPS™ exercise to refresh your memory. The usefulness of certain marketing research studies may not become apparent until several quarters have elapsed and you become completely familiar with the BRANDMAPS™ environment.*

BRANDMAPS™ Marketing Research Studies

In the rest of this chapter, each of the currently-available marketing research studies in BRANDMAPS™ is described. Several features about these descriptions should be noted. The current cost of executing each marketing research study is indicated in these marketing research study descriptions. Unless specifically mentioned, all marketing research studies report information based on the previous quarter (that is, the just-completed quarter).

Most of the competitive and market-monitoring marketing research studies may be performed on a custom or syndicated basis, with associated cost implications. Twice a year in the even-numbered quarters (Spring and Fall), your marketing research supplier conducts various studies and sells the results to any and all buyers. Since these syndicated studies may have many buyers, their cost is relatively low. However, in the odd-numbered quarters (Winter and Summer), these same marketing research studies are much more expensive since they must be conducted on a custom basis (that is, for a single client). The cost savings for syndicated studies are noted in this chapter.

The billing rate for custom or syndicated studies is based on the quarter that was just completed prior to the execution of the marketing research study requests. The full sequence of BRANDMAPS™ operations are described in the following example. Suppose that the next quarter is 10. Quarter 10 corresponds to Spring of year 3. Marketing research requests and decision variable changes for quarter 10 would be submitted at the designated time. Then, the BRANDMAPS™ game administrator would: (1) enter all decision variable changes; (2) run the game for quarter 10; and, (3) execute all marketing research study requests. Although these marketing research requests were actually made between the runs for quarters 9 and 10, they are executed after quarter 10, so quarter 10 marketing research billing rates would be in effect. Since quarter 10 corresponds to the Spring quarter, syndicated rates would be in effect for all marketing research studies with this feature.

Internal accounting records are maintained by the BRANDMAPS™ marketing research program regarding the number of times each study has been executed by each firm. Firms are billed for the cost of these studies in the following quarter's financial and operating reports. As the example above indicates, marketing research is executed after a quarter has concluded. Therefore, the billing for this research may only be made after the following quarter's run has occurred.

Some of the marketing research studies have maximum limits associated with them. These limits represent the absolute maximum number of times each study can be executed in any quarter. These maximums reflect the finite resources of your marketing research supplier. You cannot reasonably expect that your marketing research supplier is able to supply an unlimited number of marketing research studies during any single quarter.

Sample marketing research reports are displayed in this chapter. These sample reports are only meant to illustrate formatting and content; none of the numbers displayed in these sample reports are meant to be suggestive of actual operating policies or market situations.

An overview of all available BRANDMAPS™ marketing research studies is provided in Table 12. The following pages in the rest of this chapter provide all of the details of these marketing research studies.

Table 12

OVERVIEW OF BRANDMAPS™ MARKETING RESEARCH STUDIES

#	Marketing Research Study	Cost, Limitations on Availability, and Special Notes
1	Competitive Information — Dividends and Earnings	Cost: $1,000.
2	Brand Composition Analysis	Cost: $25,000. A maximum of four brand composition analyses may be requested in any quarter.
3	Industry Sales Force Size	Cost: syndicated, $2,500; custom, $7,500.
4	Industry Advertising	Cost: syndicated, $2,000; custom, $6,000.
5	Industry Sales Force Compensation	Cost: syndicated, $2,500; custom, $7,500.
6	Industry Promotion	Cost: syndicated, $3,000; custom, $9,000.
7	Industry R&D	Cost: syndicated, $4,000; custom, $12,000.
8	Media Content Analysis	Cost: $2,500.
9	Promotional Type Analysis	Cost: $5,000.
10	Conjoint Analysis	Cost (Per Market Region): $40,000 fixed cost plus $1 per product profile in the full factorial design implied by the total number of levels included. Only one conjoint analysis of this type (i.e., marketing research study #10) in a single market region or in all market regions simultaneously may be conducted in any quarter.
11	Customer Brand Awareness	Cost: syndicated, $7,000; custom, $21,000.
12	Concept Testing	Cost (Per Market Region): $3,000. A maximum of 20 concept tests may be requested in any quarter.
13	Preference Testing, Two Existing Brands	Cost (Per Market Region): $7,000. A maximum of 20 preference tests of this type may be requested in any quarter.
14	Preference Testing, One Existing and One Hypothetical Brand	Cost (Per Market Region): $14,000. A maximum of 20 preference tests of this type may be requested in any quarter.

15	Preference Testing, Two Hypothetical Brands	Cost (Per Market Region): $21,000. A maximum of 20 preference tests of this type may be requested in any quarter.
16	Operating Statistics Report	Cost: $25,000.
17	Brand Quality Ratings	Cost: syndicated, $5,000; custom, $15,000.
18	Patent Search	Cost: $1,000.
19	Competitive Information — Balance Sheets	Cost: $20,000.
20	Test Marketing Experiment	Cost: $100,000, $200,000, and $300,000 for one-, two-, and three-quarter test markets. Only a single test market (of one to three quarters duration) may be requested in any quarter.
21	Brand Perceptual Ratings	Cost: syndicated, $25,000; custom, $50,000.
22	Aggregate Market Statistics	Cost: $1,000.
23	Reformulation Activity	Cost: $1,000.
24	Market Shares	Cost: $2,500.
25	Dealer Prices	Cost: $2,500.
26	Dealer Rebates	Cost: $3,000.
27	Dealer Promotion Awareness	Cost: syndicated, $4,000; custom, $12,000.
28	Dealer Availability	Cost: syndicated, $8,000; custom, $24,000.
29	Competitive Position Audit	Cost: syndicated, $50,000 per brand for brands active in only one market region, $100,000 per brand for brands active in two or more market regions; custom, $100,000 per brand for brands active in only one market region, $200,000 per brand for brands active in two or more market regions. A maximum of four competitive position audits (for any of your brands) may be requested in any quarter.
30	Patent Zone Search	Cost: $20,000. A maximum of four patent zone searches may be requested in any quarter.
31	Industry Sales Volume Forecasts	Cost: $2,500.

32	Brand Sales Volume Forecasts	Cost: $5,000.
33	Reformulation Activity — Detailed	Cost: $5,000 plus $35,000 per reformulated brand (reformulated in the current quarter) that is currently actively distributed.
34	Another Conjoint Analysis	Cost (Per Market Region): $80,000 fixed cost plus $2 per product profile in the full factorial design implied by the total number of levels included. Only one conjoint analysis of this type (i.e., marketing research study #34) in a single market region or in all market regions simultaneously may be conducted in any quarter.
35	Advertising Program Experiment	Cost: $15,000. A maximum of 10 advertising program experiments may be conducted in any quarter.
36	Competitive Information — Brand Marketing Profiles	Cost: $10,000 per market region and $10,000 per product actively distributed in a market region.
37	Competitive Information — Sales Force Compensation Statistics	Cost: $40,000.
38	Promotion Experiment	Cost: $15,000. A maximum of 10 promotion experiments may be conducted in any quarter.
39	Competitive Information — Unfilled Sales Volume Statistics	Cost: $10,000.
40	Competitive Information — Brand Margin Analysis	Cost: $60,000.
41	Regional Summary Analysis	Cost: Depends on whether other marketing research studies upon which this marketing research study draws have already been ordered for the current quarter.
42	Marketing Research Ordering Statistics	Cost: $1,000.
43	Marketing Support Spending Productivity Analysis	Cost (Per Market Region): $5,000.
44	Population Forecasts	Cost: $2,000.

45	Per Capita Income Forecasts	Cost: $2,000.
46	Consumer Price Index Forecasts	Cost: $2,000.
47	Self-Reported Attribute Preferences	Cost (Per Market Region): $5,000.
48	Dealer Inventory Analysis — Own Brands	Cost: $5,000.
49	Dealer Inventory Analysis — All Brands	Cost: $15,000.
50	Price Sensitivity Analysis	Cost (Per Market Region): $25,000.

Marketing Research Study #1: Competitive Information — Dividends and Earnings

Purpose: To obtain estimates of current quarter dividends, current quarter after-tax earnings, and cumulative after-tax year-to-date earnings of a firm.

Description of the Research Process: These estimates are based on publicly available information.

Cost: $1,000.

Sample
Study
Output

```
==============================================================================
MARKETING RESEARCH STUDY # 1 (COMP INFO - DIVIDENDS AND EARNINGS          )
==============================================================================

                               CURRENT QUARTER           CUMULATIVE
                           --------------------------     YEAR-TO-DATE
                           DIVIDENDS      EARNINGS          EARNINGS
                           ---------     ----------       ------------

              FIRM 1       1,000,000      -155,440         -2,355,433
              FIRM 2               0     2,640,000          2,641,010
              FIRM 3       6,343,242     9,029,727         19,029,727
              ...
```

Marketing Research Study #2: Brand Composition Analysis

Purpose: To obtain the current composition and patent protection zone of a specific vaporware brand.

Description of the Research Process: Your firm's research and development group reverse engineers the specified brand. Past patent filings are reviewed to determine patent protection zones.

Cost: $25,000.

Availability: A maximum of four brand composition analyses may be requested in any quarter.

Other Comments: A composition analysis may be conducted only for a brand that is actively distributed in at least one BRANDMAPS™ market region. The composition analysis is based on the brand's formulation during the last quarter, since reverse engineering can be conducted only on an existing brand. For example, if quarter "n" has just finished, and this study is executed on product 2-1, then an estimate of the brand composition of 2-1 in quarter "n" is reported. The composition of a reformulated brand is protected until the next quarter after the reformulation has taken place (that is, until the reformulated brand is actually sold on the market).

```
=====================================================================
MARKETING RESEARCH STUDY # 2 (BRAND COMPOSITION ANALYSIS           )
=====================================================================

PRODUCT 7-2 COMPOSITION:  65/23/25/45/ 5/5/8  [Patent Protection Zone 19]
```

Marketing Research Study #3: Industry Sales Force Size

Purpose: To obtain estimates of sales force sizes of all firms in the industry within all market regions for the current and previous four quarters.

Description of the Research Process: These figures are compiled by the Vaporware Industry Trade Association.

Cost: $2,500 on a syndicated basis, in the Spring and Fall quarters; $7,500 on a custom basis, in the Winter and Summer quarters.

```
=====================================================================
MARKETING RESEARCH STUDY # 3 (INDUSTRY SALES FORCE SIZE           )
=====================================================================

                      QUARTER 25  QUARTER 26  QUARTER 27  QUARTER 28  QUARTER 29
                      ----------  ----------  ----------  ----------  ----------

REG. 1 (U.S.    )        310         390         450         480         575
REG. 2 (U.K.    )        295         195         100         150         125
REG. 3 (C.EUROPE)        320         375         375         190         210
REG. 4 (CANADA  )        300         200         255         270         225
REG. 5 (PACIFIC )        100          80          90          85          92
TOTAL                  1,325       1,240       1,270       1,175       1,227
```

Marketing Research Study #4: Industry Advertising

Purpose: To obtain an estimate of total advertising expenditures for all brands of all firms in the industry within all market regions for the current and previous four quarters. These estimates are for all firms in total, and not for each individual firm.

Description of the Research Process: These figures are compiled by the Vaporware Industry Trade Association.

Cost: $2,000 on a syndicated basis, in the Spring and Fall quarters; $6,000 on a custom basis, in the Winter and Summer quarters.

```
===============================================================
MARKETING RESEARCH STUDY # 4 (INDUSTRY ADVERTISING                )
===============================================================

                     QUARTER 12   QUARTER 13   QUARTER 14   QUARTER 15   QUARTER 16
                     ----------   ----------   ----------   ----------   ----------

REG. 1 (EASTERN )    7,500,000    1,600,000    1,000,000    3,000,000    5,500,000
REG. 2 (SOUTHERN)    6,400,000    2,650,000    2,750,000    7,000,000    6,500,000
REG. 3 (CENTRAL )    9,050,000    7,900,000    8,600,000    8,000,000    5,500,000
...
TOTAL               28,950,000   25,200,000   43,050,000   45,200,000   42,000,000
```

Marketing Research Study #5: Industry Sales Force Compensation

Purpose: To obtain estimate of average sales force compensation (salary and commissions) of all firms.

Description of the Research Process: These figures are compiled by the Vaporware Industry Trade Association. Your marketing research supplier then adjusts these raw figures based on other publicly available information and their own expert judgement.

Cost: $2,500 on a syndicated basis, in the Spring and Fall quarters; $7,500 on a custom basis, in the Winter and Summer quarters.

Sample
Study
Output

```
===============================================================
MARKETING RESEARCH STUDY # 5 (INDUSTRY SALES FORCE COMPENSATION        )
===============================================================

                        ALL       REGION 1     REGION 2     REGION 3     REGION 4
                      REGIONS     (EASTERN )   (SOUTHERN)   (CENTRAL )   (PACIFIC )
                     ----------   ----------   ----------   ----------   ----------

Salaries               2,580        2,602        2,533        2,611        2,568
Commissions              650          699          979          484          464
Compensation           3,230        3,301        3,512        3,095        3,032
Compensation (SD)        278          281          321          219          234
Commission Rate          1.8          1.7          2.0          1.5          2.0
```

Notes Regarding This Study Output: In this study output, compensation equals salaries plus commissions and "Compensation (SD)" is the standard deviation (across firms) of compensation.

Marketing Research Study #6: Industry Promotion

Purpose: To obtain estimates of the total promotion expenditures of all firms in the industry in all market regions in the current and previous four quarters. These estimates are for all firms in total, and not for each individual firm.

Description of the Research Process: These figures are compiled by the Vaporware Industry Trade Association.

Cost: $3,000 on a syndicated basis, in the Spring and Fall quarters; $9,000 on a custom basis, in the Winter and Summer quarters.

Sample
Study
Output

```
==============================================================================
MARKETING RESEARCH STUDY # 6 (INDUSTRY PROMOTION                           )
==============================================================================

                    QUARTER  5   QUARTER  6   QUARTER  7   QUARTER  8   QUARTER  9
                    ----------   ----------   ----------   ----------   ----------

REG. 1 (EASTERN )    5,960,000    7,192,000    5,725,186    9,200,000    5,200,000
REG. 2 (SOUTHERN)    4,760,000    2,408,000    1,500,000    4,500,000    3,000,000
REG. 3 (CENTRAL )    6,250,000    4,500,000    9,225,186    5,500,000    4,750,000
REG. 4 (WESTERN )    7,000,000    4,650,000    6,306,483    1,300,000    6,700,000
TOTAL               23,970,000   18,750,000   22,756,856   20,500,000   24,650,000
```

Marketing Research Study #7: Industry R&D

Purpose: To obtain an estimate of the average research and development expenditures of all firms in the industry. This estimate is for average research and development spending for vaporware brands.

Description of the Research Process: These figures are compiled by the Vaporware Industry Trade Association.

Cost: $4,000 on a syndicated basis, in the Spring and Fall quarters; $12,000 on a custom basis, in the Winter and Summer quarters.

Sample
Study
Output

```
==============================================================================
MARKETING RESEARCH STUDY # 7 (INDUSTRY R&D                                 )
==============================================================================

                    QUARTER 15   QUARTER 16   QUARTER 17   QUARTER 18   QUARTER 19
                    ----------   ----------   ----------   ----------   ----------

AVERAGE R&D            571,250      497,500      412,500      302,666      244,375
```

Marketing Research Study #8: Media Content Analysis

Purpose: To obtain an analysis of the media content currently being employed by firms in their advertising efforts associated with each brand in all market regions for the current and previous four quarters.

Description of the Research Process: Your marketing research supplier observes and analyzes the advertising of all firms' brands.

Cost: $2,500.

Other Comments: Entries of "0" refer to actively distributed brands without any advertising activity in this quarter.

Sample Study Output

MARKETING RESEARCH STUDY # 8 (MEDIA CONTENT ANALYSIS)

	QUARTER 55	QUARTER 56	QUARTER 57	QUARTER 58	QUARTER 59
REGION 1 (U.S.)					
Product 1-1	12	12	12		15
Product 2-1	1	0	21	7	14
Product 4-2	19	19	13	14	11
Product 6-1	8	15	15	15	15
REGION 2 (EUROPE)					
Product 1-3			7	7	7
Product 3-2				9	10
Product 4-3	16	7	7	7	15
...					

Marketing Research Study #9: Promotional Type Analysis

Purpose: To obtain an analysis of the promotional type currently being employed by firms in their promotion efforts associated with each brand in all market regions in the current and previous four quarters.

Description of the Research Process: Your marketing research supplier observes and analyzes the promotional types of all firms' brands. Promotional types are determined by dealer surveys and other means.

Cost: $5,000.

Other Comments: Entries of "0" refer to actively distributed brands without any promotional activity in this quarter.

Sample Study Output

MARKETING RESEARCH STUDY # 9 (PROMOTIONAL TYPE ANALYSIS)

	QUARTER 8	QUARTER 9	QUARTER 10	QUARTER 11	QUARTER 12
REGION 1 (EASTERN)					
Product 1-1	10	0	0		32
Product 2-1	48	0	23	26	92
Product 5-1	9	9	0	6	10
Product 6-1	0	10	10	10	10
REGION 2 (SOUTHERN)					
Product 3-2				43	94
Product 4-3	96	10	10	10	10
...					

A data analysis technique in which respondents ranking of the importance of various product attributes is seen in the preferences they show for different combinations of these attributes.

① Which attributes to include
② the levels of the attributes
③ the combination of the attributes.

Marketing Research Study #10: Conjoint Analysis

Purpose: To perform a conjoint analysis in a specified market region or in all market regions simultaneously.

Description of the Research Process: It is assumed that the potential user of this BRANDMAPS™ marketing research study is familiar with conjoint analysis. Your course instructor should have provided the necessary background information about this product/service design tool.

A representative sample of potential vaporware users in the specified market region is used to evaluate the product profiles in the conjoint judgement task. Each customer in the sample evaluates a number of profiles describing possible vaporware. These profiles are descriptions of hypothetical vaporware brands. These descriptions include all seven attributes which comprise vaporware (Syntech, Plumbo, Glomp, Trimicro, Fralange, Compatibility, and Warranty) plus dealer price.

The output from this study consists of the estimated conjoint weights for each level of each attribute (the seven product composition attributes and dealer price). In addition, the relative importance of each attribute is provided. Note that these relative importances are derived from the conjoint weights themselves.

In specifying the design of this study, you choose the levels of each of eight product components, the seven product composition attributes and dealer prices (per unit). Each of these attributes may have at most four levels (and they must, of course, have at least one level).

Within the conjoint analysis study itself, there is no attempt to see if the product profiles are technologically feasible according to the current BRANDMAPS™ technology.

As an illustrative example, consider the following conjoint analysis design:

Attribute	Levels
Attribute 1 [Syntech]	10, 20, 30
Attribute 2 [Plumbo]	20, 25, 30
Attribute 3 [Glomp]	12, 15
Attribute 4 [Trimicro]	20, 40, 60, 80
Attribute 5 [Fralange]	5
Attribute 6 [Compatibility]	2, 4, 6, 8
Attribute 7 [Warranty]	3, 5, 7
Attribute 8 [Dealer Price]	800, 1100, 1400, 1700

Note that a full factorial design for this illustrative conjoint analysis study would include (3)(3)(2)(4)(1)(4)(3)(4) = 3,456 different possible product profiles. In conducting this marketing research study, your marketing research supplier uses an orthogonal array to only require that the respondents evaluate a small subset of the full factorial possibilities.

Cost (Per Market Region): This study has a fixed set-up cost of $40,000 associated with it. This fixed cost covers the design of the study and the respondent recruitment efforts. In addition, a further variable cost of $1 per product profile in the equivalent full factorial design implied by the number of attribute levels included in the conjoint study design is incurred. Therefore, the illustrative experimental design described above would cost $40,000 + ($1)(3,456) = $43,456. This variable cost reflects the extra burdens imposed on conjoint analysis efforts when there are a large number of attribute levels.

A conjoint analysis may be conducted either for a single market region or for all market regions simultaneously. This permits the same conjoint design (a single set of specified attribute-levels) to be used in all market regions simultaneously. To execute two different conjoint designs in the same quarter (in the same market region or in different market regions), studies #10 and #34 would have to be executed.

Availability: Only one Marketing Research Study #10 ("Conjoint Analysis") may be conducted in any quarter. A second conjoint analysis study is available in BRANDMAPS™, at a 100% cost premium above this study's cost. See Marketing Research Study #34 ("Another Conjoint Analysis").

Sample
Study
Output

Importance = 65.3 - 7.2 difference between highest utilities and lowest utilities.

```
================================================================
MARKETING RESEARCH STUDY #10 (CONJOINT ANALYSIS              )
================================================================

                                           REGION 6
                                          (PACIFIC )
                                          ----------

   RELATIVE            SYNTECH               13.7%
   IMPORTANCES         PLUMBO                23.2%
   (given the          GLOMP                 23.6%
   attribute           TRIMICRO              17.6%
   levels in the       FRALANGE                .0%
   design of           COMPATIBILITY          4.6%
   this conjoint       WARRANTY               3.1%
   study)              DEALER PRICE          14.1%

   WEIGHTS FOR         Level #1 (10)          65.3
   ATTRIBUTE #1,       Level #2 (40)          64.4
   SYNTECH             Level #3 (60)          37.8
                       Level #4 (70)           7.2

   WEIGHTS FOR         Level #1 (20)           1.6
   ATTRIBUTE #2,       Level #2 (40)          25.4
   PLUMBO              Level #3 (60)         100.0

   WEIGHTS FOR         Level #1 (20)          99.9
   ATTRIBUTE #3,       Level #2 (40)          84.4
   GLOMP               Level #3 (60)          17.6
                       Level #4 (80)            .0

   WEIGHTS FOR         Level #1 (10)          10.6
   ATTRIBUTE #4,       Level #2 (20)          39.1
   TRIMICRO            Level #3 (30)          67.8
                       Level #4 (40)          85.2

   WEIGHTS FOR         Level #1 ( 5)          13.5
   ATTRIBUTE #5,
   FRALANGE

   WEIGHTS FOR         Level #1 ( 2)          43.8
   ATTRIBUTE #6,       Level #2 ( 4)          51.3
   COMPATIBILITY       Level #3 ( 6)          56.9
                       Level #4 ( 8)          63.4

   WEIGHTS FOR         Level #1 ( 2)          47.1
   ATTRIBUTE #7,       Level #2 ( 4)          52.9
   WARRANTY            Level #3 ( 6)          56.5
                       Level #4 ( 8)          60.3

   WEIGHTS FOR         Level #1 (   500)      90.3
   ATTRIBUTE #8,       Level #2 (   750)      67.2
   DEALER PRICE        Level #3 ( 1,000)      44.4
                       Level #4 ( 1,250)      30.4
```

standard β ? = utilities .

Other Comments: The prospective user of the conjoint analysis study is reminded that this study is based on customers' judgements (assessments) of "hypothetical" vaporware brand profiles. As such, conjoint analysis is really just a more complex form of multiple concept testing. This study is not based on actual product usage. Therefore, this study should not be expected to yield information that is as accurate as the product preference tests (Marketing Research Studies #13, #14, and #15). Marketing Research Study #47,

"Self-Reported Attribute Preferences," also provides information on customer preferences for vaporware formulations.

Marketing Research Study #11: Customer Brand Awareness

Purpose: To obtain an estimate of the percentage of customers who are aware of each actively distributed vaporware brand of all firms in all market regions in the current and previous four quarters.

Description of the Research Process: This marketing research study is based on data obtained from a customer panel operated by your marketing research supplier. The awareness of vaporware brands is evaluated with reference to the percentage of customers in the panel who identify a brand in response to the question: "Could you tell me about the brands of vaporware that you know about?" The percentage of customers who mention each brand of vaporware are defined as being aware.

Cost: $7,000 on a syndicated basis, in the Spring and Fall quarters; $21,000 on a custom basis, in the Winter and Summer quarters.

Sample
Study
Output

```
===================================================================
MARKETING RESEARCH STUDY #11 (CUSTOMER BRAND AWARENESS            )
===================================================================

                      QUARTER 6   QUARTER 7   QUARTER 8   QUARTER 9   QUARTER 10
                      ---------   ---------   ---------   ---------   ---------

REGION 1 (NORTHERN)
   Product 1-1          37.92       28.82       24.92                   42.42
   Product 3-1          43.00       62.67       63.17       50.16       53.64
   Product 4-2          32.60       36.32       43.51       40.50       66.13
   Product 6-1          30.60       59.16       76.32       79.95       78.74

REGION 2 (EASTERN )
   Product 1-3                                  19.15       42.37       47.02
   Product 3-2                                              17.62       47.28
   Product 4-3          17.92       28.76       46.27       48.79       73.25

...
```

Marketing Research Study #12: Concept Testing

Purpose: To conduct a concept test in a specified market region or in all market regions simultaneously.

Description of the Research Process: This marketing research study is conducted with a representative sample of actual and potential vaporware users in the specified BRANDMAPS™ market region. In a BRANDMAPS™ concept test, respondents are presented with a verbal description of one possible vaporware brand, and their potential degree of interest in purchasing such a product is elicited. The respondents are asked to evaluate the proposed vaporware brand on a ten-point probability-of-purchase scale (from "absolutely no chance of purchasing" to "certain to purchase"). The percentage of respondents reporting "likely to purchase" or higher is reported. Note that this is not a usage test, since the proposed vaporware product does not have to exist.

Cost (Per Market Region): $3,000.

Availability: A maximum of 20 concept tests may be requested in any quarter. In a six-region industry, ordering this study for all market regions simultaneously results in a total of six concept tests being conducted.

Other Comments: See the product preference testing studies (Marketing Research Studies #13, #14, and #15) for usage-type tests. Also, see the conjoint analysis study (Marketing Research Study #10). Conjoint analysis may be thought of as being a much more sophisticated form of product concept testing. In conjoint analysis studies, a range of product concepts are tested simultaneously.

Sample
Study
Output

```
================================================================================
MARKETING RESEARCH STUDY #12 (CONCEPT TESTING                                  )
================================================================================

CONCEPT TESTING RESULTS FOR REGION 3 (S.EUROPE):   QUARTER 33
        CONCEPT 34/76/12/91/ 5/2/6 :     13.9% DEGREE-OF-INTEREST
```

Marketing Research Study #13: Preference Testing, Two Existing Brands

Purpose: To conduct a blind product preference test (including dealer prices) between two existing vaporware brands in a specified market region or in all market regions simultaneously. By definition, an existing product is one that is currently actively distributed in at least one BRANDMAPS™ market region.

Description of the Research Process: This marketing research study is conducted with a representative sample of actual and potential vaporware users in the specified market region. By executing this marketing research study, a firm receives a report of the percentage of users tested who preferred each of the two products in the test. This study involves an actual usage test of the two products.

This test is conducted on a blind basis since only the product's formulation and dealer price are at work here. The two products are repackaged in unmarked (unbranded) containers, so the users do not know which real brands the test products really are. Thus, none of the other marketing mix variables (advertising, promotion, sales force activities, and so forth) are at work in this test situation; only formulation and dealer price differ between the two tested brands. The actual execution of this study involves leaving the two products (in unlabeled packages) with the customers for a period of time and then later, after the customers have used the two products, asking them which product is most preferred. After using both products, the customers in the test are asked which they would prefer if the dealer prices of the two products were as specified. Thus, this blind product preference test isolates two of the marketing mix decision variables: product formulation and dealer price.

Cost (Per Market Region): $7,000.

Availability: A maximum of 20 preference tests of this type may be requested in any quarter. In a six-region industry, ordering this study for all market regions simultaneously results in a total of six preference tests being conducted.

Other Comments: A product preference test on an existing product can only be conducted for a brand that is currently being actively distributed in at least one BRANDMAPS™ market region. This restriction exists because your marketing research supplier must purchase a quantity of these brands for use in this study.

Sample
Study
Output

```
========================================================================
MARKETING RESEARCH STUDY #13 (PREFERENCE TESTING, 2 EXISTING BRANDS   )
========================================================================

TEST RESULTS FOR REGION 1 (NORTHERN):  QUARTER  6 (SPRING )
        PRODUCT 1-2,              DEALER PRICE =    880 :  12.9% PREFERENCE
        PRODUCT 9-3,              DEALER PRICE =  1,222 :  81.1% PREFERENCE
```

Marketing Research Study #14: Preference Testing, One Existing and One Hypothetical Brand

Purpose: To conduct a blind product preference test (including dealer prices) between one existing product and one hypothetical product in a specified market region or in all market regions simultaneously. By definition, an existing product is one which is currently actively distributed in at least one BRANDMAPS™ region and a hypothetical product is any technologically valid formulation, whether available on the market now or not.

Description of the Research Process: See Marketing Research Study #13. A suitable quantity of the specified hypothetical product is created by your firm's research and development group.

Cost (Per Market Region): $14,000. This cost is composed of $7,000 to create the hypothetical product in sufficient quantity to conduct the test and $7,000 to actually conduct the study.

Availability: A maximum of 20 preference tests of this type may be requested in any quarter. In a six-region industry, ordering this study for all market regions simultaneously results in a total of six preference tests being conducted.

Other Comments: A product preference test on an existing product can only be conducted for a brand that is currently being actively distributed in at least one market region. This restriction exists because your marketing research supplier must purchase a quantity of these brands for use in this study.

In conducting this product preference test with a hypothetical product formulation, no reference is made to the possibility that the proposed composition of the hypothetical product might violate one or more patents if an attempt were made to actually reformulate an existing brand to have this composition. Existing patent laws do not prohibit the creation of a small quantity of a hypothetical product of the kind employed in a marketing research study of this type.

Sample
Study
Output

```
========================================================================
MARKETING RESEARCH STUDY #14 (PREFERENCE TESTING, 1 EX AND 1 HYP     )
========================================================================

TEST RESULTS FOR REGION 2 (WESTERN ):  QUARTER 22 (SPRING )
        PRODUCT 8-3,                 DEALER PRICE = 1,841 :  12.9% PREFERENCE
        PRODUCT 33/35/67/12/ 5/7/8, DEALER PRICE = 1,922 :  87.1% PREFERENCE
```

Marketing Research Study #15: Preference Testing, Two Hypothetical Brands

Purpose: To conduct a blind product preference test (including dealer prices) between two hypothetical products in a specified market region or in all market regions simultaneously. By definition, a hypothetical product is any technologically valid formulation, whether available on the market now or not.

Description of the Research Process: See Marketing Research Study #13. A suitable quantity of the user-specified hypothetical products is created by your firm's research and development group.

Cost (Per Market Region): $21,000. This cost is composed of $7,000 to create each of the hypothetical products in sufficient quantity to conduct the test and $7,000 to actually conduct the study.

Availability: A maximum of 20 preference tests of this type may be requested in any quarter. In a six-region industry, ordering this study for all market regions simultaneously results in a total of six preference tests being conducted.

Other Comments: In conducting this product preference test with a hypothetical product formulation, no reference is made to the possibility that the proposed composition of the hypothetical product might violate one or more patents if an attempt were made to actually reformulate an existing brand to have this composition. Existing patent laws do not prohibit the creation of a small quantity of a hypothetical product of the kind employed in a marketing research study of this type.

Sample
Study
Output

```
================================================================
MARKETING RESEARCH STUDY #15 (PREFERENCE TESTING, 2 HYP BRANDS    )
================================================================

TEST RESULTS FOR REGION 3 (EUROPE  ):   QUARTER 36 (FALL    )
    PRODUCT 22/12/27/43/ 5/3/2, DEALER PRICE = 1,520 :  41.2% PREFERENCE
    PRODUCT 94/44/ 4/11/ 5/9/3, DEALER PRICE = 1,110 :  58.8% PREFERENCE
```

Marketing Research Study #16: Operating Statistics Report

Purpose: To obtain an Operating Statistics Report. This report contains statistics on operating ratios (usually of spending in various categories as a percentage of sales revenues). These ratios are calculated across all of the firms in the vaporware industry. The summary measures reported include the firm's data plus the industry minimum, mean, and maximum for each ratio. The operating ratios reported include the following:
- Advertising/Revenues
- Emergency Premiums/Revenues
- Inventory Charges/Revenues
- (Emergency Premiums + Inventory Charges)/Revenues
- Marketing Research/Revenues
- Promotion/Revenues

- Research & Development/Revenues
- Sales Force Spending/Revenues
- Depreciation/Production Volume (where Depreciation includes both fixed and variable depreciation)
- Support Spending/Revenues (where Support Spending includes Advertising, Promotion, Research & Development, and Sales Force Spending)
- Profits/Revenues (where Profits is net after-tax income)
- Lost Margin Due To Stockouts/Revenues
- Sales Forecasting Score
- Operating Efficiency Score.

These operating ratios are based on cumulative year-to-date financial and operating data for all firms in a industry.

Some traditional balance sheet financial ratios are also reported in this marketing research study's results:

- Debt Leverage (%): Liabilities (loans) divided by net worth (total assets minus loans), expressed in percentage terms. Lower is better. This is a measure of financial and credit risk.
- Inventory Turns: Sales volume divided by finished goods inventory volume. Higher is generally better. This is a measure of finished goods inventory management efficiency (a low number may indicate too much inventory on hand; a high number may indicate that sales are being lost due to too little inventory on hand). Here, "inventory" = (beginning inventory + regular production + emergency production + ending inventory)/13 & "sales volume" = (sales in units)/13.
- Revenue To Working Capital: Sales revenues divided by working capital (cash plus marketable securities). Higher is better. This is a measure of working capital management efficiency.
- Return on Assets (%): Net income after taxes divided by total assets, expressed in percentage terms. Higher is better. This is a measure of total asset management efficiency.
- Return on Equity (%): Net income after taxes divided by net worth (total assets minus loans), expressed in percentage terms. Higher is better. This is a measure of management's ability to obtain a good return for the firm's net worth.

Description of the Research Process: These data are derived from reports of the Vaporware Industry Trade Association.

Cost: $25,000.

```
================================================================
MARKETING RESEARCH STUDY #16 (OPERATING STATISTICS REPORT          )
================================================================
```

		INDUSTRY NORMS		
	FIRM 6	MINIMUM	AVERAGE	MAXIMUM
OPERATING STATISTICS (YTD)				
ADVERTISING/REVENUES	7.0%	2.5%	5.7%	9.4%
EMERGENCY PRODUCTION PREMIUMS/REVENUES	.0%	.0%	.0%	.0%
INVENTORY CHARGES/REVENUES	1.4%	.2%	1.5%	2.7%
[EMERG PREMIUMS + INV CHARGES]/REVENUES	1.4%	.2%	1.5%	2.7%
MARKETING RESEARCH/REVENUES	.1%	.1%	.4%	.9%
PROMOTION/REVENUES	4.4%	1.3%	4.3%	6.8%
RESEARCH AND DEVELOPMENT/REVENUES	.5%	.3%	.9%	1.8%
SALES FORCE SPENDING/REVENUES	8.3%	2.7%	4.8%	8.3%
DEPRECIATION/PRODUCTION VOLUME	112.2	108.2	119.6	129.0
LOST MARGIN DUE TO STOCKOUTS/REVENUES	.0%	.0%	.6%	2.6%
MARKETING SUPPORT SPENDING/REVENUES	20.2%	6.9%	15.8%	22.3%
PROFITS/REVENUES	6.5%	3.9%	8.2%	14.4%
SALES FORECASTING ACCURACY SCORE	22.8%	22.8%	55.4%	95.5%
OPERATING EFFICIENCY SCORE	29.0	25.0	35.0	55.5
FINANCIAL RATIOS				
DEBT LEVERAGE	4.3%	.0%	17.6%	56.1%
INVENTORY TURNS	3.9	3.9	6.8	12.2
REVENUE TO WORKING CAPITAL	20.0	2.2	14.2	20.0
RETURN ON ASSETS	4.4%	2.1%	6.0%	11.9%
RETURN ON EQUITY	4.6%	2.1%	7.2%	15.3%

Marketing Research Study #17: Brand Quality Ratings

Purpose: To obtain quality perception ratings of each vaporware brand.

Description of the Research Process: This study is based on a survey of vaporware users. Results are reported on a rating scale. The actual summary quality measure for each brand is the percentage of potential and actual vaporware customers who evaluated each brand to be of "good" or "excellent" quality. The actual scale used in this marketing research study is a four-point scale, where the points are described by the adjectives "poor," "fair," "good," and "excellent."

Cost: $5,000 on a syndicated basis, in the Spring and Fall quarters; $15,000 on a custom basis, in the Winter and Summer quarters.

```
================================================================
MARKETING RESEARCH STUDY #17 (BRAND QUALITY RATINGS              )
================================================================

                 QUARTER 25  QUARTER 26  QUARTER 27  QUARTER 28  QUARTER 29
                 ----------  ----------  ----------  ----------  ----------

   Product 1-1     45.57       35.29       28.11                   24.77
   Product 1-2      2.28        4.63        6.11       24.78       46.77
   Product 1-3                              2.17       22.54       47.18
   Product 2-1     31.67       23.71       27.49       42.20       49.84
   Product 2-2     36.49       43.91       48.65       52.93       59.65
   Product 2-3     20.50       32.05       42.03       48.93       52.66
   Product 3-1     58.54       50.28       58.11       62.11       63.41
   Product 3-2     37.10       49.08       55.92       51.82       58.26
   ...
```

Marketing Research Study #18: Patent Search

Purpose: To request a patent search to be conducted for a specified vaporware formulation.

Description of the Research Process: By requesting this study, a firm receives a report from the legal staff of the marketing research supplier as to whether a specified product composition would violate any existing patents held by any firm in the vaporware industry.

Cost: $1,000.

Other Comments: The specified product composition must be technologically feasible.

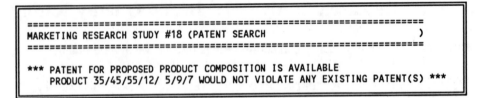

```
================================================================
MARKETING RESEARCH STUDY #18 (PATENT SEARCH                      )
================================================================

*** PATENT FOR PROPOSED PRODUCT COMPOSITION IS AVAILABLE
    PRODUCT 35/45/55/12/ 5/9/7 WOULD NOT VIOLATE ANY EXISTING PATENT(S) ***
```

Marketing Research Study #19: Competitive Information — Balance Sheets

Purpose: To obtain estimates of the balance sheet of a firm. A balance sheet estimate consists of a standard vaporware industry balance sheet with numerical estimates for all line items provided.

Description of the Research Process: These estimates are based on publicly available information, investment analysts' assessments, general market intelligence, and the expert judgement of your marketing research supplier.

Cost: $20,000.

```
===================================================================
MARKETING RESEARCH STUDY #19 (COMPETITIVE INFORMATION - BALANCE SHEETS)
===================================================================


****************************************************
DIVISIONAL BALANCE SHEET FOR FIRM 1, QUARTER 55
****************************************************

ASSETS
------

  CASH                                                       5,431,851
  MARKETABLE SECURITIES                                     19,045,029
  FINISHED GOODS INVENTORY:
    PRODUCT 1        (   10,467 Units)  [$  601.25 Per Unit]  6,293,331
    PRODUCT 2        (        0 Units)  [$     .00 Per Unit]          0
    PRODUCT 3        (   44,795 Units)  [$  468.01 Per Unit] 20,964,326
  PLANT:
    CURRENT PLANT                       [CAPACITY =  99,716] 71,741,712
    PLANT ON ORDER FOR 1 QUARTER HENCE  [CAPACITY =      0]          0
  TOTAL ASSETS                                             123,476,249

LIABILITIES AND EQUITY
----------------------

  LOANS                                                             0
  INITIAL (QUARTER 0) CORPORATE CAPITALIZATION            120,000,000
  - DIVIDENDS PAID, PRIOR TO THIS YEAR                     -3,608,825
  - DIVIDENDS PAID, END OF QUARTER 1 OF THIS YEAR            -880,000
  - DIVIDENDS PAID, END OF QUARTER 2 OF THIS YEAR                   0
  - DIVIDENDS PAID, END OF QUARTER 3 OF THIS YEAR                   0
  - DIVIDENDS PAID, END OF QUARTER 4 OF THIS YEAR                   0
  + RETAINED EARNINGS (AFTER-TAX INCOME PRIOR TO THIS YEAR)  5,325,074
  + YEAR-TO-DATE EARNINGS (AFTER-TAX INCOME THIS YEAR)       2,640,000
  TOTAL LIABILITIES AND EQUITY                            123,476,249
```

Marketing Research Study #20: Test Marketing Experiment

Purpose: To conduct a test marketing experiment in a specified market region or in all market regions simultaneously. This test marketing experiment may be one to three quarters in duration.

In BRANDMAPS™, test marketing experiments may be used to test all aspects of a brand's marketing program. Test marketing may be used to test non-design marketing program elements such as price, advertising, promotion, research and development, and sales force — either singly or in combination with each other. Test marketing may also be used to test product design variations, as well as launching currently non-active brands.

Test marketing results are received along with all other marketing research results. Test marketing results for multi-quarter tests are reported immediately. There is no time lag between ordering a multi-quarter test marketing experiment and receiving the results associated with the test marketing experiment.

Description of the Research Process: The execution of this study results in a test marketing experiment being conducted in a specified market region or regions.

Cost (Per Market Region): $100,000, $200,000, and $300,000 for one-, two-, and three-quarter test markets.

Sample Study Output

```
===================================================================
MARKETING RESEARCH STUDY #20 (TEST MARKETING EXPERIMENT            )
===================================================================
EXPERIMENTAL (TEST CASE) SCENARIO
TEST MARKETING RESULTS FOR PRODUCT 1-1 FOR REGION 2 (EUROPE  )
===================================================================
```

	QUARTER 11 [Actual]	QUARTER 12 [Forecast]	QUARTER 13 [Forecast]	QUARTER 14 [Forecast]
MARKET SHARE	8.51%	5.65%	5.12%	4.90%
INDUSTRY SALES (Units)	85,497	92,499	96,290	89,470
**PRICE	570	700	700	700
BRAND SALES (Units)	7,278	5,224	4,930	4,381
REVENUE	4,148,460	3,656,800	3,451,000	3,066,700
PRODUCT COSTS	1,519,578	1,090,722	1,029,338	914,712
REBATES	0	0	0	0
SALES COMMISSIONS	41,484	109,704	103,530	92,001
TRANSPORTATION	189,228	135,824	128,180	113,906
GROSS MARGIN	2,398,170	2,320,550	2,189,952	1,946,081
TOTAL FIXED COSTS	4,841,484	6,209,704	6,203,530	6,192,001
OPERATING INCOME	-2,443,314	-3,889,154	-4,013,578	-4,245,920
**Product Composition	11/12/13/ 24/ 5/5/6	11/12/13/ 24/ 5/7/7	11/12/13/ 24/ 5/7/7	11/12/13/ 24/ 5/7/7
Advertising Spending	2,000,000	2,000,000	2,000,000	2,000,000
Media Content & Mix	1 & 55555	1 & 55555	1 & 55555	1 & 55555
**Promotion Spending	1,000,000	2,000,000	2,000,000	2,000,000
Promotional Type	10	10	10	10
Res & Dev Spending	250,000	250,000	250,000	250,000
**Sales Force Salary + Commis	2,500 + 1	3,000 + 3	3,000 + 3	3,000 + 3
Sales Force Size	200	200	200	200
Sales Force Time Allocation	50%	50%	50%	50%
Sales Force Spending	1,541,484	1,909,704	1,903,530	1,892,001
Customer Brand Awareness	76.96%	75.96%	75.72%	72.75%
Dealer Promotion Awareness	93.83%	98.32%	96.05%	96.10%
Dealer Availability	74.98%	74.31%	68.75%	65.01%
Product Quality Rating	55.93%	54.94%	56.03%	55.06%
Perceived Performance	.01%	.01%	.01%	.01%
Perceived Convenience	39.42%	26.98%	25.49%	23.43%

```
*** NOTES ***
In this test marketing experiment, OPERATING INCOME is calculated assuming
that administrative overhead for this brand is at its base level and that
research and development spending associated with this brand is completely
allocated to this market region.  Double asterisks ("**") to the left denote
decision variables that have been changed in this test marketing experiment.
```

Notes Regarding This Sample Study Output: This is an example of a three-quarter test market conducted for firm #1. The just-completed quarter's actual results are shown for reference purposes, along with the forecast values for the three-quarter test marketing period. Test marketing results include both "Base Case" and "Experimental (Test) Case" scenarios, facilitating direct comparisons of the differences between the control and the experimental cases.

Other Comments: This test marketing experiment is executed in a small but representative part of the specified market region. The length of the test marketing experiment may be from one to three quarters. The reported results for each quarter in the test marketing experiment include market shares for all brands and the corresponding sales volumes. This test marketing experiment is executed using your current decision variables (and the past decision variables of all of your competitors). Your competitors will not be aware of the existence of this test marketing experiment, and they have no opportunity to intervene to attempt to influence the results of this test marketing experiment. Your competitors' marketing decision variables are held constant during the experiment. Your competitors' marketing decision variables are held constant at their values in the previous quarter.

Within the test marketing experiment, it is assumed that there is sufficient finished goods inventory (due to inventory on hand at the beginning of each quarter and to production orders during the quarter) to meet all sales orders. Therefore, there is no unfilled demand within a test marketing experiment.

Be sure to provide complete instructions for test marketing experiment changes on the Marketing Research Pre-Order Request Form. In particular, specify all brands using the normal BRANDMAPS™ terminology. For example, brand #1 of firm #4 is described as brand 4-1. See the sample instructions included below:

What marketing decision variables, if any, are to be changed prior to this test marketing experiment being conducted? Be sure to specify specific firm and brand numbers for decision variable changes.

Change advertising spending of brand 4-1 in region 2 to $2,000,000.

Change sales force time allocations in region 2 for brands 4-1, 4-2, and 4-3 to 100, 0, 0, and 0, respectively.

Change sales force size in region 2 to 175.

Change price of brand 4-1 in region 2 to $1,005.

Alternatively, if no decision variable changes are required in a test marketing experiment, the following directions would be appropriate:

What marketing decision variables, if any, are to be changed prior to this test marketing experiment being conducted? Be sure to specify specific firm and brand numbers for decision variable changes.

No changes are required.

Marketing Research Study #21: Brand Perceptual Ratings

Purpose: To obtain product perceptual ratings of each vaporware brand along the overall perceptual dimensions of product "performance" and "convenience."

Raw and dollar-scaled perceptual maps of all vaporware brands in each BRANDMAPS™ market region are reported. Dollar-scaled perceptual ratings are equal to the raw perceptual rating divided by dealer price (in $000s). Additionally, two types of relative importance weight information are reported: correlations of raw and dollar-scaled "performance" and "convenience" (and dealer price) with volume market shares for the last two quarters and self-reported relative importance weights.

Description of the Research Process: This study is based on a survey of potential and actual vaporware users. The "performance" and "convenience" results are reported on a six-point "terrible" to "excellent" rating scale. The actual summary perceptual measures for each brand are the percentage of survey respondents who evaluated each brand "very good" or "excellent" on each of the "performance" and "convenience" perceptual ratings scales. The self-reported importance weights are based on dividing 100 "degree-of-importance points" across the buying factors of "performance," "convenience," and dealer price.

Cost: $25,000 on a syndicated basis, in the Spring and Fall quarters; $50,000 on a custom basis, in the Winter and Summer quarters.

Other Comments: Past research in the vaporware industry has indicated that product "performance" consists of product preference and product quality perceptions and that "convenience" refers to the convenience of both buying and using vaporware brands.

Sample
Study
Output

```
==============================================================
MARKETING RESEARCH STUDY #21 (BRAND PERCEPTUAL RATINGS          )
==============================================================
```

		CORRELATION BETWEEN VOLUME MARKET SHARE AND ..					
	Data Points	PERFOR	CONVEN	DEALER PRICE	PREVIOUS VOLUME MK SHARE	PERFOR PER $000	CONVEN PER $000
REGION 1 (EASTERN)	11	-.01	.35	-.01	.65	.08	.49
REGION 2 (SOUTHERN)	9	.58	.61	.01	.87	.64	.64
REGION 3 (CENTRAL)	6	.78	.83	.00	.80	.75	.82
REGION 4 (WESTERN)	10	.59	.84	.39	.85	.63	.86
REGION 5 (PACIFIC)	14	.34	.23	.48	.65	.23	.34
REGION 6 (EUROPE)	15	.56	.38	.32	.70	.44	.46
REGION 7 (CANADA)	8	.44	.33	.22	.36	.41	.51

	MEAN SELF-REPORTED IMPORTANCE WEIGHTS		
	PERFORMANCE PERCEPTION	CONVENIENCE PERCEPTION	DEALER PRICE	SUM
REGION 1 (EASTERN)	19.42	30.86	49.72	100.00
REGION 2 (SOUTHERN)	24.62	33.04	42.34	100.00
REGION 3 (CENTRAL)	32.82	29.18	37.99	100.00
REGION 4 (WESTERN)	29.96	27.01	43.03	100.00
REGION 5 (PACIFIC)	33.21	32.12	34.67	100.00
REGION 6 (EUROPE)	41.22	21.22	37.56	100.00
REGION 7 (CANADA)	28.98	51.01	20.01	100.00

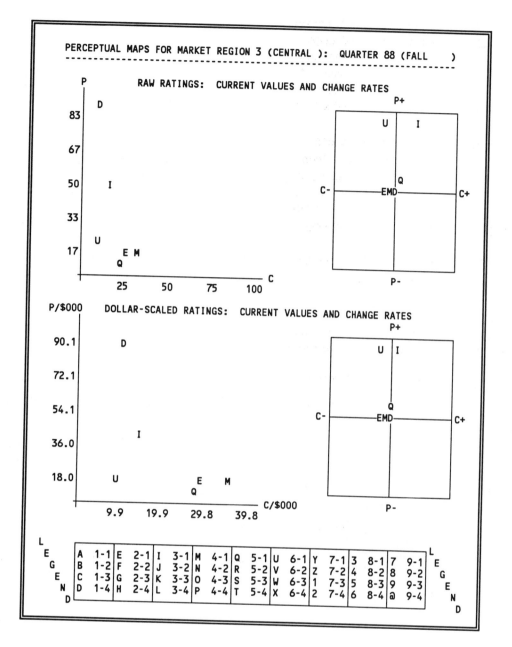

PERCEPTUAL MAPS FOR MARKET REGION 3 (CENTRAL):   QUARTER 88 (FALL   )

RAW RATINGS: CURRENT VALUES AND CHANGE RATES

DOLLAR-SCALED RATINGS: CURRENT VALUES AND CHANGE RATES

A	1-1	E	2-1	I	3-1	M	4-1	Q	5-1	U	6-1	Y	7-1	3	8-1	7	9-1
B	1-2	F	2-2	J	3-2	N	4-2	R	5-2	V	6-2	Z	7-2	4	8-2	8	9-2
C	1-3	G	2-3	K	3-3	O	4-3	S	5-3	W	6-3	1	7-3	5	8-3	9	9-3
D	1-4	H	2-4	L	3-4	P	4-4	T	5-4	X	6-4	2	7-4	6	8-4	@	9-4

Notes Regarding This Sample Study Output:

For each of the regions, performance-convenience charts for raw and dollar-scaled perceptual ratings are provided. The raw performance-convenience charts display current positions of vaporware brands on performance and convenience. Of course, a third key buying factor — dealer price — is not accounted for in this raw performance-convenience chart. Dollar-scaled performance-convenience charts attempt to account simultaneously for performance, convenience, and dealer price in a single chart. In addition to these current-quarter charts, change rates of raw and dollar-scaled perceptual ratings are displayed in another chart.

   With regard to the scaling of the raw and dollar-scaled charts:

● Natural 0%-100% scales are used in the raw performance-convenience charts, since performance and convenience perceptions are defined to be in the 0%-100% range by the nature of this marketing research study.

- Dollar-scaled performance-convenience charts plot brands according to the dimensions "performance perception per $000 (of dealer price)" and "convenience perception per $000 (of dealer price)." The ranges of the vertical and horizontal dimensions of the dollar-scaled performance-convenience chart are automatically adjusted for the corresponding ranges of the vaporware brands in a BRANDMAPS™ market region. This implies that the vertical and horizontal dimensions typically have somewhat different scalings, reflecting the current relative ranges in dollar-scaled performance and convenience.

These performance-convenience charts are derived directly from the tabulations of current-quarter performance and convenience data provided at the beginning of this study's output (plus current-quarter and previous-quarter dealer prices and previous-quarter performance and convenience values). While containing no new information not provided elsewhere in this and other BRANDMAPS™ marketing research studies, the visual impact of the performance-convenience charts is notable. A glance at the charts quickly reveals the leading vaporware brands and the current relative competitive standing of a specific vaporware brand.

The change rate charts show the direction and rates of change of the raw and dollar-scaled perceptual positions of all vaporware brands. Brands with increasing performance [convenience] appear in the upper-half [right-side] of a change rate chart; brands with decreasing performance [convenience] appear in the lower-half [left-side] of a change rate chart. Vaporware brands with little or no change from the previous quarter appear at or near the center of a change rate chart. Change rates are expressed as percentage changes from the corresponding values in the previous quarter. The change rate chart has outer boundaries of +100% and -100% for the vertical and horizontal axes. Change rates exceeding these amounts are displayed at the outer boundary limits.

A traditional problem of percentage change rates with small bases should be noted: small absolute changes on a very small base can result in very large percentage change rates. For example, a change in performance from 1.2 to 2.4 is a small absolute change (only 1.2 on a 0-100 scale), but a large percentage change (100%).

Some sample interpreted change rate charts are shown below:

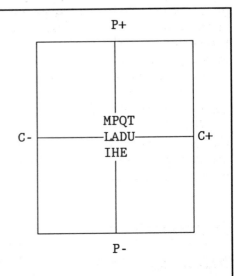

This change rate chart shows a large number of vaporware brands clustered at or near the chart's center. These brands have little or no change in either performance or convenience from the previous quarter. Apparently, this is a fairly stable market. No vaporware brands are presently sharply changing either their performance or their convenience.

All brand codes are displayed in this change range chart. If the positions of two brands are identical (and would be plotted at the same point in the chart), the second brand would be plotted as close as possible to the first. This implies that the cluster of points shown in the change rate chart on the right could actually correspond to brands which all have performance and convenience change rates of approximately zero.

Most of the brands in this change rate chart are clustered near the center, denoting little change in performance or convenience since the previous quarter.

However, brand Y is located at the extreme upper right-hand corner. This might correspond to a just-introduced brand. Inactive brands have performance and conveniences of zero, by definition, when not actively distributed. After introduction, a brand's performance and convenience perceptions become positive numbers. It follows that any newly-introduced brand automatically has the maximum change rate for both performance and convenience in the initial quarter of introduction.

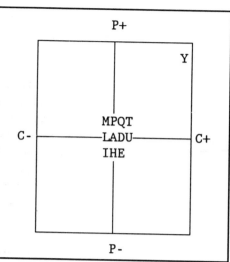

In this change rate chart, brand Y is rapidly increasing its convenience perception while performance has remained approximately constant since the previous quarter. This might correspond to the second quarter after an introduction in this BRANDMAPS™ market region. Convenience is still increasing, perhaps due to the impact of on-going marketing support spending and dealer/customer acceptance. Performance, presumably already at a high absolute level for brand Y (after all, a brand would not be introduced into a region unless it has high potential performance), is not changing much.

For the other brands in this market region (A, D, E, H, I, L, and U) clustered at or near the center of the change rate chart, there is apparently little or no change in performance or convenience at the present time.

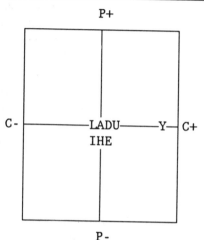

In this change rate chart, brand Y is apparently in serious difficulties. Its location, in the bottom left-hand quadrant, corresponds to rapidly decreasing performance and rapidly decreasing convenience. This might represent a situation where brand Y has just been reformulated and targeted for another BRANDMAPS™ market region. It's new formulation apparently is not at all of interest to customers in this market region, so performance is decreasing. The rapidly decreasing convenience perception could be due to associated reduced marketing support spending (with corresponding reductions in customer awareness, etc.), which is preparatory to withdrawing the brand from this BRANDMAPS™ market region.

For the other brands in this market region (A, D, E, H, I, L, and U) clustered at or near the center of the change rate chart, there is apparently little or no change in performance or convenience at the present time.

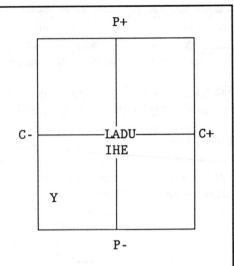

Marketing Research Study #22: Aggregate Market Statistics

Purpose: To generate a market statistics report. The marketing statistics report includes some frequently referenced market statistics such as major economic indicators (Population, Per Capita Income, and Consumer Price Index) and current aggregate industry sales volume.

Description of the Research Process: These market statistics are compiled from government statistical sources and by the Vaporware Industry Trade Association. These market statistics are provided to vaporware firms under an information-sharing arrangement administered by the Vaporware Industry Trade Association.

Cost: $1,000.

Sample
Study
Output

```
=====================================================================
MARKETING RESEARCH STUDY #22 (AGGREGATE MARKET STATISTICS         )
=====================================================================

                                   CONSUMER    PER    INDUSTRY SALES VOLUME
                                    PRICE     CAPITA   ---------------------
                       POPULATION   INDEX     INCOME   PREVIOUS    CURRENT
                      ------------  --------  ------   ----------  --------
REGION 1 (EASTERN )   91,715,304    1,130     13,562   255,093     278,035
REGION 2 (SOUTHERN)   40,534,496      975     11,383    99,532     103,557
REGION 3 (CENTRAL )   72,766,512    1,096     13,022   237,398     233,082
REGION 4 (WESTERN )   51,312,308    1,073     12,474   192,002     205,160
...
```

Marketing Research Study #23: Reformulation Activity

Purpose: To provide summary reformulation activity information for the current quarter.

Description of the Research Process: Summary statistics about the current quarter's reformulation activity and bidding statistics are compiled and reported.

Cost: $1,000.

Other Comments: See Marketing Research Study #33 ("Reformulation Activity — Detailed") for another version of this study.

Sample
Study
Output

```
=================================================================
MARKETING RESEARCH STUDY #23 (REFORMULATION ACTIVITY          )
=================================================================

NUMBER OF REFORMULATION BIDS SUBMITTED  =             4
LOWEST REFORMULATION BID SUBMITTED      = $         555
AVERAGE REFORMULATION BID SUBMITTED     = $     404,438
HIGHEST REFORMULATION BID SUBMITTED     = $     673,198
NUMBER OF SUCCESSFUL REFORMULATION BIDS =             4
LOWEST SUCCESSFUL REFORMULATION BID     = $         555

Product 1-3 Has Been Reformulated Since Last Quarter
Product 2-3 Has Been Reformulated Since Last Quarter
Product 7-4 Has Been Reformulated Since Last Quarter
Product 9-1 Has Been Reformulated Since Last Quarter
```

Marketing Research Study #24: Market Shares

Purpose: To obtain volume and dollar market share estimates of all vaporware brands of all firms in all market regions for the current and previous four quarters.

Description of the Research Process: These data are provided to vaporware firms under an information-sharing arrangement administered by the Vaporware Industry Trade Association.

Cost: $2,500.

```
=============================================================================
MARKETING RESEARCH STUDY #24 (MARKET SHARES                               )
=============================================================================

OVERALL VOLUME MARKET SHARES [CURRENT]
--------------------------------------
FIRM 1 OVERALL MARKET SHARE =   11.44      [Previous Market Share =    9.99]
FIRM 2 OVERALL MARKET SHARE =   26.58      [Previous Market Share =   27.07]
FIRM 3 OVERALL MARKET SHARE =    8.79      [Previous Market Share =    6.68]
FIRM 4 OVERALL MARKET SHARE =   23.34      [Previous Market Share =   22.89]
FIRM 5 OVERALL MARKET SHARE =   25.03      [Previous Market Share =   24.16]
FIRM 6 OVERALL MARKET SHARE =    4.82      [Previous Market Share =    9.21]

VOLUME MARKET SHARES
--------------------
```

	QUARTER 41	QUARTER 42	QUARTER 43	QUARTER 44	QUARTER 45
REGION 1 (EASTERN)					
Product 1-1	12.72	6.84	.08		5.59
Product 2-1	11.66	4.62	10.74	17.20	12.70
Product 3-1	9.39	12.90	16.51	15.44	15.84
Product 4-2	37.11	43.28	26.89	29.23	32.30
Product 5-1	15.28	13.59	17.15	9.84	19.37
Product 6-1	6.62	17.54	28.62	28.29	14.20
REGION 2 (SOUTHERN)					
Product 1-3			6.29	13.50	13.01
Product 2-2				1.25	.98
Product 3-2				5.28	13.59
Product 4-3	19.08	54.42	74.43	68.98	72.42

```
...

OVERALL DOLLAR MARKET SHARES [CURRENT]
--------------------------------------
FIRM 1 OVERALL MARKET SHARE =    9.69      [Previous Market Share =    8.75]
FIRM 2 OVERALL MARKET SHARE =   24.94      [Previous Market Share =   23.47]
FIRM 3 OVERALL MARKET SHARE =   10.24      [Previous Market Share =    8.88]
FIRM 4 OVERALL MARKET SHARE =   21.70      [Previous Market Share =   18.37]
FIRM 5 OVERALL MARKET SHARE =   22.66      [Previous Market Share =   25.98]
FIRM 6 OVERALL MARKET SHARE =   10.77      [Previous Market Share =   14.55]

DOLLAR MARKET SHARES
--------------------
```

	QUARTER 41	QUARTER 42	QUARTER 43	QUARTER 44	QUARTER 45
REGION 1 (EASTERN)					
Product 1-1	9.42	3.16	.05		4.02
Product 2-1	8.53	2.10	8.58	12.96	10.97
Product 3-1	8.66	19.59	20.50	18.12	16.91
Product 4-2	48.14	38.22	19.52	22.56	29.01
Product 5-1	12.20	10.84	17.58	9.81	13.84
Product 6-1	5.70	25.09	33.76	36.55	25.26
REGION 2 (SOUTHERN)					
Product 1-3			8.25	15.32	14.63
Product 2-2				1.11	.85
Product 3-2				6.42	14.20
Product 4-3	22.15	55.38	75.06	68.78	70.33

```
...
```

Marketing Research Study #25: Dealer Prices

Purpose: To obtain estimates of dealer prices (the prices at which dealers sell vaporware brands to customers) associated with each brand of vaporware in all market regions in the current and previous four quarters.

Description of the Research Process: These data are based on a survey of a sample of dealers in each region. This study is conducted by the field audit staff of your marketing research supplier.

Cost: $2,500.

Sample Study Output

```
=================================================================
MARKETING RESEARCH STUDY #25 (DEALER PRICES                     )
=================================================================

                    QUARTER 5   QUARTER 6   QUARTER 7   QUARTER 8   QUARTER 9
                    ---------   ---------   ---------   ---------   ---------

REGION 1 (EASTERN )
  Product 1-1           735         733       1,288                   1,288
  Product 2-1           727         722       1,550       1,399       1,546
  Product 3-1           916       2,415       2,409       2,179       1,912
  Product 4-2         1,288       1,403       1,408       1,433       1,608
  Product 5-1           793       1,268       1,988       1,851       1,280
  Product 6-1           855       2,274       2,289       2,398       3,185

  ...
```

Marketing Research Study #26: Dealer Rebates

Purpose: To obtain estimates of dealer rebates associated with each brand of vaporware in all regions in the current and previous four quarters.

Description of the Research Process: These data are based on a survey of a sample of dealers in each region. This study is conducted by the field audit staff of your marketing research supplier.

Cost: $3,000.

```
================================================================
MARKETING RESEARCH STUDY #26 (DEALER REBATES                    )
================================================================

                   QUARTER 5   QUARTER 6   QUARTER 7   QUARTER 8   QUARTER 9
                   ---------   ---------   ---------   ---------   ---------

REGION 1 (U.S.    )
  Product 1-1          0           0           0                       0
  Product 2-1          0           0          20           0           0
  Product 3-1          0           0           5          10           0
  Product 4-2          0           0           0          50           0
  Product 5-1          0         100           0           0         100
  Product 6-1          0           0           0           0           0

REGION 2 (CANADA  )
  Product 1-3                                  0           0           0
  Product 2-2                                             40           0
  Product 3-2                                              0           0

...
```

Marketing Research Study #27: Dealer Promotion Awareness

Purpose: To obtain estimates of the percentage of dealers who are aware of the promotion activities associated with each brand of vaporware in all market regions in the current and previous four quarters.

Description of the Research Process: These data are based on a survey of a sample of dealers in each market region. This study is conducted by the field audit staff of your marketing research supplier. Deal awareness is defined with reference to the following question posed to the sample of dealers: "Have any vaporware brands that you stock had any special promotional activity within the last quarter?" The proportion of dealers who mention each vaporware brand are defined to be aware of brand dealing (promotion) activity.

Cost: $4,000 on a syndicated basis, in the Spring and Fall quarters; $12,000 on a custom basis, in the Winter and Summer quarters.

Sample
Study
Output

```
================================================================
MARKETING RESEARCH STUDY #27 (DEALER PROMOTION AWARENESS        )
================================================================

                   QUARTER 5   QUARTER 6   QUARTER 7   QUARTER 8   QUARTER 9
                   ---------   ---------   ---------   ---------   ---------

REGION 1 (CANADA  )
  Product 1-1        80.81        1.94         .01                   90.57
  Product 2-1        23.85         .13       82.31       87.71       89.74
  Product 3-1        75.09       77.27       77.51       49.43       88.59
  Product 4-2        82.35       87.46       88.00       86.68       77.47
  Product 5-1        42.20       14.52         .07       49.84       72.34
  Product 6-1          .01       89.01       89.15       91.53       96.85

...
```

Marketing Research Study #28: Dealer Availability

Purpose: To obtain estimates of the percentage of dealers who sell each vaporware brand in all regions in the current and previous four quarters.

Description of the Research Process: These data are based on a survey of a sample of dealers in each market region. This study is conducted by the field audit staff of your marketing research supplier. Dealer availability refers to whether dealers currently stock a particular vaporware brand.

Cost: $8,000 on a syndicated basis, in the Spring and Fall quarters; $24,000 on a custom basis, in the Winter and Summer quarters.

Sample Study Output

```
=================================================================
MARKETING RESEARCH STUDY #28 (DEALER AVAILABILITY            )
=================================================================

                     QUARTER 5  QUARTER 6  QUARTER 7  QUARTER 8  QUARTER 9
                     ---------  ---------  ---------  ---------  ---------

REGION 1 (EASTERN )
  Product 1-1          53.45      45.47      33.83                 11.62
  Product 2-1          46.14      40.42      29.18      27.17      39.38
  Product 3-1          59.87      57.69      57.30      56.83      61.84
  Product 4-2          31.85      78.21      81.01      74.25      75.38
  Product 5-1          65.37      60.61      56.10      55.99      45.75
  Product 6-1          51.48      49.59      68.65      86.33      89.87

REGION 2 (SOUTHERN)
  Product 1-3                                 4.33      19.57      49.90
  Product 2-2                                            1.01       1.01
  Product 3-2                                            3.77      10.26
  Product 4-3           5.46      32.81      64.32      81.99      85.83

...
```

Marketing Research Study #29: Competitive Position Audit

Purpose: The competitive position audit for a brand summarizes the current standing of the brand in each of the BRANDMAPS™ market regions. Here, "current standing" is interpreted as being relative to all brands actively distributed in a market region.

Each brand's competitive position audit summarizes results for each of the BRANDMAPS™ market regions, whether the brand is actively distributed in each region or not. Inactive brands in particular regions have blank columns of results in the audit. The elements in the competitive position audit are things that BRANDMAPS™ participants might review to size up the current competitive market position and marketing program of a brand. The audit is really of the "checklist" variety. A wide range of marketing position statistics is examined, and the relative position of a brand (compared to all other brands currently actively distributed in the market region) is reported.

Description of the Research Process: To develop the data necessary for a competitive position audit, various other marketing research studies must be executed by your marketing research supplier.

Cost: Syndicated (Spring and Fall): $50,000 per brand for brands active in only one market region; $100,000 per brand for brands active in two or more market regions. Custom (Winter and Summer): $100,000 per brand for brands active in only one market region; $200,000 per brand for brands active in two or more market regions.

Availability: A maximum of four competitive position audits (for any of your brands or for competitors' brands) may be requested in any quarter.

Other Comments: The competitive position audit report attempts to summarize most (but not all) relevant marketing and financial position statistics. For each reported statistic (except things involving "Yes" or "No" answers), the brand's value is compared to the average of all brands currently actively distributed in a market region. The difference between a brand's value and the average market value is expressed in standard deviate form (in increments of 0.5 standard deviations). The relative standing of a brand on a market position statistic is then reported in standard deviate form, with the following labels being used (these label definitions appear at the bottom of the page of each brand's competitive position audit):

++++	More Than 2.0 Standard Deviations Above Mean
+++	Between 1.5 and 2.0 Standard Deviations Above Mean
++	Between 1.0 and 1.5 Standard Deviations Above Mean
+	Between 0.5 and 1.0 Standard Deviations Above Mean
Average	Between -0.5 and +0.5 Standard Deviations From Mean
-	Between 0.5 and 1.0 Standard Deviations Below Mean
--	Between 1.0 and 1.5 Standard Deviations Below Mean
---	Between 1.5 and 2.0 Standard Deviations Below Mean
----	More Than 2.0 Standard Deviations Below Mean
Zero	Variable Has Value of Zero (0)
Zero&Ave	Variable Has Value of Zero (0) Which Also Equals Average

Values near the market region average (within 0.5 standard deviations of the average) are reported as being "Average." Since the value zero (0) is especially notable, a special label ("Zero") is used for any marketing position statistic that has this value. The value "Zero" overrides the usual standard deviate form of summarization. Also, if the value of a statistic is zero and the market region average is also zero, then the label "Zero&Ave" is used.

Most things reported in the competitive position audit are straight forward and self explanatory. The things that are novel are defined below:

- "Current" refers to the current quarter.
- "Previous" refers to the previous quarter (i.e., one quarter ago).
- "Change in Manufacturer Price?" refers to a change in manufacturer price since the previous quarter.
- "Relative Performance," "Relative Convenience," and "Relative Product Quality" all refer to perceptual measures.
- "Dealer Margin" refers to VOLUME*((PRICE*MARKUP)+REBATE), where VOLUME is the unit sales volume, PRICE is the manufacturer price, MARKUP is the customary markup rate, and REBATE is the dealer (per unit) rebate. Rebates through promotions are not included in this "Dealer Margin" calculation.
- "Sales Force Size" refers to the effective number of sales representatives associated with this brand in this market region (which equals sales force size times time allocation).

Reminder: Even though all regions are shown on the same page (or successive pages, if more than four market regions exist in your BRANDMAPS™ industry), the competitive position audit refers to comparisons involving all actively distributed brands ("own" and competitors' brands) in each market region separately. Do not compare across regions on each page of a competitive position audit, since the "relative" calculations are based on within-region brands only.

Sample
Study
Output

```
====================================================================
MARKETING RESEARCH STUDY #29 (COMPETITIVE POSITION AUDIT          )
====================================================================

********************************************************************
COMPETITIVE POSITION AUDIT FOR PRODUCT 6-2        QUARTER 81 (WINTER )
********************************************************************

                              REGION 1   REGION 2   REGION 3   REGION 4
                              (U.S.   )  (CANADA )  (EUROPE )  (JAPAN  )
                              ---------- ---------- ---------- ----------
Product Actively Distributed?       Yes        Yes         No        Yes
Current Volume Market Share       15.36       4.74        .00      15.98
Previous Volume Market Share      24.13      14.61        .00      22.11
Relative Sales Revenues               -          -                Average
Relative Gross Margin           Average          -                Average
Relative Operating Income       Average    Average                    ++

Relative Distributor Price      Average    Average            Average
Change in Manufacturer Price?        No         No                    No
Relative Performance                  -    Average            Average
Relative Convenience            Average    Average            Average

Relative Product Desirability         -    Average            Average
Relative Product Quality        Average    Average            Average
Relative R&D Spending                 -    Average            Average
Product Just Reformulated?           No         No                    No

Relative Customer Awareness     Average         --            Average
Relative Advertising Spending         -       Zero                     -
Change in Media Content?             No         No                    No
Relative Deal Awareness             ---         --                     -
Relative Promotion Spending          --       Zero                     -
Relative Dealer Availability          +          +            Average
Relative Dealer Margin               --          -            Average
Relative Dealer Rebate             Zero    Zero&Ave              Zero
Relative Sales Force Effort           +    Average            Average
Relative Sales Force Size             +          -                     -
Relative Sales Force Compens         ---          +                    --


Legend:    ++++   More Than 2.0 Standard Deviations Above Mean
            +++   Between  1.5 and  2.0 Standard Deviations Above Mean
             ++   Between  1.0 and  1.5 Standard Deviations Above Mean
              +   Between  0.5 and  1.0 Standard Deviations Above Mean
        Average   Between -0.5 and +0.5 Standard Deviations From Mean
              -   Between  0.5 and  1.0 Standard Deviations Below Mean
             --   Between  1.0 and  1.5 Standard Deviations Below Mean
            ---   Between  1.5 and  2.0 Standard Deviations Below Mean
           ----   More Than 2.0 Standard Deviations Below Mean
           Zero   Variable Has Value of Zero (0)
       Zero&Ave   Variable Has Value of Zero (0) Which Also Equals Average
```

Marketing Research Study #30: Patent Zone Search

Purpose: To search for all valid patents available within the "vicinity" of a specified brand formulation.

Description of the Research Process: "Vicinity" means within one unit of the specified formulation on each of the first five vaporware attributes. The sixth and seventh vaporware attributes (Compatibility and Warranty) are held constant at their user-specified values in this patent zone search. A patent zone search involves 3^5 (243) patent searches. The results of each patent search are reported, with "OK" indicating that a formulation is patentable (i.e., this formulation currently does not violate any product's existing patent) and "XX" indicating that a formulation would violate one or more existing vaporware brand patents.

Cost: $20,000.

Availability: A maximum of four patent zone searches may be requested in any quarter.

Sample
Study
Output

```
=================================================================
MARKETING RESEARCH STUDY #30 (PATENT ZONE SEARCH                 )
=================================================================

PATENT ZONE SEARCH AROUND 12/23/34/45/ 5/6/6:
   11/22/33/44/ 5/6/6 OK    11/22/33/45/ 5/6/6 XX    11/22/33/46/ 5/6/6 OK
   ...
```

Marketing Research Study #31: Industry Sales Volume Forecasts

Purpose: To provide next-quarter industry sales volume forecasts for all market regions.

Description of the Research Process: These industry sales volume forecasts are based on an extrapolation of current market trends, seasonality, and competitive activity. These are unconditional sales volume forecasts. They assume that current marketing activities of all firms in the industry continue on their present course during the forecast period.

Cost: $2,500.

Sample
Study
Output

```
=================================================================
MARKETING RESEARCH STUDY #31 (INDUSTRY SALES VOLUME FORECASTS         )
=================================================================

                    QUARTER 7   QUARTER 8   QUARTER 9      QUARTER 10
                    [History]   [History]   [History]   [Forecast +/- Error]
                    ---------   ---------   ---------   --------------------

REGION 1 (U.S.    )   252,347     255,093     278,035     299,996 +/-  7,083
REGION 2 (U.K.    )    52,407      99,532     103,557     107,544 +/-  2,922
REGION 3 (C.EUROPE)   211,294     237,398     233,082     228,580 +/-  4,845
REGION 4 (JAPAN   )   235,875     192,002     205,160     220,616 +/-  5,035
REGION 5 (HK/T/K/S)    35,875      92,002     105,160     120,616 +/-  6,036


*** NOTE ***
"Error" corresponds to the 90% confidence interval for the forecast value.
For example, a forecast of "110,120 +/- 4,451" corresponds to a 90% degree-
of-confidence that the true value lies between 105,669 (110,120-4,451) and
114,571 (110,120+4,451). Of course, this also implies that there is a 10%
chance that the true value will be less than 105,669 or more than 114,571.
```

Marketing Research Study #32: Brand Sales Volume Forecasts

Purpose: To provide next-quarter brand sales volume forecasts for all actively distributed products of a firm for all market regions.

Description of the Research Process: These brand sales volume forecasts are based on an extrapolation of current market trends, seasonality, and competitive activity. These are unconditional sales volume forecasts. They assume that current marketing activities of all firms in the industry continue on their present course during the forecast period.

Cost: $5,000.

Sample Study Output

```
=====================================================================
MARKETING RESEARCH STUDY #32 (BRAND SALES VOLUME FORECASTS          )
=====================================================================

                     QUARTER  7   QUARTER  8   QUARTER  9    QUARTER 10
                     [History]    [History]    [History]   [Forecast +/- Error]
                     ----------   ----------   ----------   --------------------

REGION 1 (EASTERN )
  Product 6-1          72,231       72,177       39,494      14,028 +/-     918

REGION 2 (SOUTHERN)

REGION 3 (CENTRAL )
  Product 6-1                                    12,981      21,232 +/-     879
  Product 6-3          12,321       15,634       21,321      34,543 +/-   1,243

REGION 4 (WESTERN )
  Product 6-2         101,981      123,123       56,712      21,321 +/-   2,123


*** NOTE ***
"Error" corresponds to the 90% confidence interval for the forecast value.
For example, a forecast of "110,120 +/- 4,451" corresponds to a 90% degree-
of-confidence that the true value lies between 105,669 (110,120-4,451) and
114,571 (110,120+4,451).  Of course, this also implies that there is a 10%
chance that the true value will be less than 105,669 or more than 114,571.
```

Marketing Research Study #33: Reformulation Activity — Detailed

Purpose: To provide detailed reformulation activity information for the current quarter.

Description of the Research Process: This study is similar to Marketing Research Study #23, except that this marketing research study also reports the new formulation of brands that have been reformulated in the current quarter.

Cost: The costs associated with this study are $5,000 plus an additional $40,000 for reverse engineering each newly reformulated brand (in the current quarter) that is currently actively distributed in at least one market region.

Other Comments: Reverse engineering is only possible on actively distributed brands. A reformulated brand not currently actively distributed in any market region will, of course, have no formulation reported in this study. Such a brand could only be reverse engineered with Marketing Research Study #2 at such time as it was actively distributed in at least one market region.

Sample
Study
Output

```
=======================================================================
MARKETING RESEARCH STUDY #33 (REFORMULATION ACTIVITY - DETAILED        )
=======================================================================

NUMBER OF REFORMULATION BIDS SUBMITTED  =           4
LOWEST REFORMULATION BID SUBMITTED      = $       555
AVERAGE REFORMULATION BID SUBMITTED     = $   404,438
HIGHEST REFORMULATION BID SUBMITTED     = $   673,198
NUMBER OF SUCCESSFUL REFORMULATION BIDS =           4
LOWEST SUCCESSFUL REFORMULATION BID     = $       555

Product 3-4 Has Been Reformulated Since Last Quarter To 80/30/40/20/50/7/5
Product 6-3 Has Been Reformulated Since Last Quarter
...
```

Marketing Research Study #34: Another Conjoint Analysis

Purpose: To provide a second conjoint analysis marketing research study.

Description of the Research Process: See Marketing Research Study #10 ("Conjoint Analysis").

Cost (Per Market Region): $80,000 fixed cost plus $2 per product profile in the equivalent full factorial design implied by the number of attribute levels included in the conjoint study design. This conjoint analysis is 100% more expensive than Marketing Research Study #10 ("Conjoint Analysis").
     A conjoint analysis may be conducted either for a single market region or for all market regions simultaneously. This permits the same conjoint design (a single set of specified attribute-levels) to be used in all market regions simultaneously. To execute two different conjoint designs in the same quarter (in the same market region or in different market regions), studies #10 and #34 would have to be executed.

Availability: Only one Marketing Research Study #34 may be conducted in any quarter. Conjoint analyses may be conducted for a single market region or all market regions simultaneously.

Other Comments: Given the more costly nature of this study, firms interested in only a single conjoint analysis study in a quarter obviously should use Marketing Research Study #10 ("Conjoint Analysis").

Sample Study Output: See Marketing Research Study #10 ("Conjoint Analysis").

Marketing Research Study #35: Advertising Program Experiment

Purpose: To conduct an advertising program experiment. The estimated customer brand awareness associated with a specified advertising program (a combination of advertising spending level, media content, and media mix for a specific product in a specific market region) is reported.

Description of the Research Process: This advertising program experiment is executed in a small but representative part of the specified market region. This advertising program experiment is executed using your advertising program and all other current marketing mix variables of your brand and all competitors' brands. Your competitors will not be aware of the existence of this advertising program experiment, and they have no opportunity to intervene to attempt to influence the results of this experiment. Competitors' marketing decision variables are held constant at their values in the previous quarter.

Cost: $15,000.

Availability: A maximum of ten advertising program experiments may be requested in any quarter.

Sample
Study
Output

```
================================================================
MARKETING RESEARCH STUDY #35 (ADVERTISING PROGRAM EXPERIMENT       )
================================================================

RESULTS OF ADVERTISING EXPERIMENT FOR PRODUCT 5-2 IN REGION 2 (CANADA  ):
        Advertising Spending = $ 1,250,000
        Media Content (#)    =         21
        Media Mix (#s)       =      22559
        Estimated Customer Awareness For Product 5-2 = 50.5%
```

Marketing Research Study #36: Competitive Information — Brand Marketing Profiles

Purpose: To provide estimates of a number of specific brand marketing mix variables for all actively-distributed brands in a specified market region.

Description of the Research Process: Your marketing research supplier uses a variety of publicly available information and proprietary sources to provide these data.

Cost: $10,000 per market region and $10,000 per product actively distributed in a market region. Therefore, if this marketing research study is requested for a market region with six actively distributed vaporware brands, the associated study cost would be $(1+6)($10,000)=$70,000$.

```
=============================================================
MARKETING RESEARCH STUDY #36 (COMPETITIVE INFORMATION - BRAND PROFILES)
=============================================================

                    DEALER        ADVERTISING        PROMOTION      SALES
                 ------------    ---------------    --------------   FORCE
                 Price Rebate    $ Amount MC Media  $ Amount  Type   SIZE
                 ------ ------   ---------- -- ----- ----------  ----  -----

REGION 1 (U.S.   )
   Product 1-3      901     0   1,750,000 15 55555  1,250,000   26     44
   Product 4-4      905     0   2,000,000  6 33456    500,000   96    200
   Product 5-2    1,223   100   2,000,000 14 23433    500,000   74    100
   Product 7-3      905     0   5,000,000  6 33456    500,000   96     20

REGION 2 (EUROPE )
   Product 1-2      867    50     500,000 15 55555          0    0     40
   Product 3-1    1,180     0   2,000,000 14 12789  3,000,000   69    100
   ...
```

Marketing Research Study #37: Competitive Information — Sales Force Compensation Statistics

Purpose: To provide firm-specific sales force compensation statistics for all vaporware industry firms.

Description of the Research Process: Your marketing research supplier uses a variety of publicly available information and proprietary sources to provide these data.

Cost: $40,000.

```
=============================================================
MARKETING RESEARCH STUDY #37 (COMPETITIVE INFORMATION - SFC STATISTICS)
=============================================================

                    ALL       REGION 1    REGION 2    REGION 3     REGION 4
                  REGIONS     (U.S.   )   (U.K.   )  (C.EUROPE)   (CANADA  )
                  ---------   ---------   ---------  -----------  -----------

FIRM 1
Salaries            2,665      2,790       2,500       2,700        2,650
Commissions           469        687         439         228          562
Compensation        3,134      3,477       2,939       2,928        3,212
Commission Rate       1.3        1.0         2.0         1.0          2.0
Sales Force Size      870        220         200         250          200

...

INDUSTRY
Salaries            2,580      2,602       2,533       2,611        2,568
Commissions           650        699         979         484          464
Compensation        3,230      3,301       3,512       3,095        3,032
Compensation (SD)     387        312         479         299          374
Commission Rate       1.8        1.7         2.0         1.5          2.0
Sales Force Size    3,270        870         750         850          800
```

Notes Regarding This Study Output: In this study output, compensation equals salaries plus commissions and "Compensation (SD)" is the standard deviation (across firms) of compensation.

Marketing Research Study #38: Promotion Experiment

Purpose: To conduct a promotion experiment. The estimated dealer promotion awareness associated with a specific in-market promotion test (a combination of promotion spending level and promotional type for a specific product in a specific market region) is reported.

Description of the Research Process: One direct outcome of a product's promotion program, dealer promotion awareness, is reported. (This marketing research study would be of no value for promotional types directed at consumers.)

This promotion program experiment is executed in a small but representative part of the specified market region. This promotion program experiment is executed using your promotion program and all other current marketing mix variables of your brand and all competitors' brands. Your competitors will not be aware of the existence of this promotion program experiment, and they have no opportunity to intervene to attempt to influence the results of this experiment. Competitors' marketing decision variables are held constant at their values in the previous quarter.

Cost: $15,000.

Availability: A maximum of ten promotion experiments may be requested in any quarter.

Sample Study Output

```
=================================================================
MARKETING RESEARCH STUDY #38 (PROMOTION EXPERIMENT            )
=================================================================

RESULTS OF PROMOTION EXPERIMENT FOR PRODUCT 9-3 IN REGION 8 (AUST&NZ ):
    Promotion Spending    = $ 1,500,000
    Promotional Type (#) =        18
    Estimated Dealer Promotion Awareness For Product 9-3 = 69.0%
```

Marketing Research Study #39: Competitive Information — Unfilled Sales Volume Statistics

Purpose: To obtain estimates of the current quarter's unfilled sales volumes for all vaporware brands.

Description of the Research Process: These estimates are based on various on-going market analyses conducted by your marketing research supplier.

Cost: $10,000.

Sample
Study
Output

```
==================================================================
MARKETING RESEARCH STUDY #39 (COMPETITIVE INFORMATION - UNFILLED SALES)
==================================================================

                     ALL      REGION 1    REGION 2    REGION 3    REGION 4
                   REGIONS    (U.S.   )   (U.K.   )   (FRANCE  )  (GERMANY )
                 ----------- ----------- ----------- ----------- -----------

FIRM 1
  Product 1-1          0                       0           0
  Product 1-2     15,000      14,000
  Product 1-3          0           0           0                       0
  Firm 1 Total    15,000      14,000           0           0           0

FIRM 2
  Product 2-1          0                       0           0
  Product 2-2      1,016       1,000
  Product 2-3          0           0         245                       0
  Firm 2 Total     1,016       1,000           0           0           0

...

INDUSTRY          20,056      15,000       5,056           0           0
```

Marketing Research Study #40:   Competitive Information — Brand Margin Analysis

Purpose: To obtain estimates of the current margins (price less variable costs) associated with all actively distributed vaporware brands in all market regions.

Description of the Research Process: These estimates are based on various on-going market analyses conducted by your marketing research supplier.

Other Comments: To estimate margins, formulations of brands are required. BRANDMAPS™ tracks each firm's formulations. All firm's formulations are known as of quarter 1. Subsequently, formulation information is only updated in each firm's reformulation record data base in the following circumstances: (a) when a firm reformulates any brand; (b) when a firm requests a composition analysis of any product via Marketing Research Study #2 ("Brand Composition Analysis"); and, (c) when a firm requests detailed reformulation activity via Marketing Research Study #33 ("Reformulation Activity — Detailed"). See the detailed notes at the end of this sample marketing research study output.

Cost: $60,000.

Note: This marketing research study concerns brand margins. It is not a marketing research study to obtain current formulations of competitors' brands. Review the notes associated with this marketing research study output.

```
=====================================================================
MARKETING RESEARCH STUDY #40 (COMPETITIVE INFORMATION - BRAND MARGINS )
=====================================================================

                                            ESTIMATED [PER UNIT] PRICES,
                                                COSTS, AND MARGINS
                                            ---------------------------
                          BRAND FORMULATION [AND    Dealer Manuf  Unit
                          REFORMULATION QUARTER]    Price  Price  Cost   Margin
                          ----------------------    ------ -----  ------ ------

REGION 1 (EASTERN )
   Product 1-4            40/40/40/40/ 5/5/5 [**]    920   575    320    255
   Product 2-4            40/40/40/40/ 5/5/5 [**]    924   578    320    258
   Product 9-4            44/44/44/44/ 5/4/4 [ 3]    897   560    293    267

REGION 2 (SOUTHERN)
   Product 1-1            41/23/81/22/ 5/1/1 [ 2]    899   580    153    427
   ...


*** NOTES ***
(1) "Brand Formulation" refers to the last "recorded" formulation of a brand.
    Formulations are only "recorded" when a firm executes Marketing Research
    Study #2 ("Brand Composition Analysis") or Marketing Research Study #33
    ("Reformulation Activity - Detailed").
(2) "Reformulation Quarter" refers to the quarter in which the last recorded
    brand formulation occurred.  Quarter "**" refers to brands that have not
    been reformulated since quarter 0.
(3) "Dealer Price" is the price at which dealers sell brands to customers.
(4) "Manuf Price" is the price at which manufacturers sell brands to dealers.
(5) "Unit Cost" is the raw materials, production, labor, plant depreciation
    (assuming full capacity usage), and transportation and shipping costs.
    Experience curve cost reductions and smoothing adjustment costs, if any,
    in production and labor are not included within these "Unit Cost"
    figures.  Other components of variable costs (dealer rebates and sales
    commissions) are also not included in these "Unit Cost" figures.
(6) "Margin" equals "Manuf Price" minus "Unit Cost."
```

Marketing Research Study #41: Regional Summary Analysis

Purpose: To obtain a regional summary analysis of a variety of aggregate industry statistics and to obtain a brand performance statistics chart (volume market shares, dealer prices, and brand perception ratings) summarizing the current status of all actively distributed brands in a specified market region.

Description of the Research Process: These estimates are based on various on-going market analyses conducted by your marketing research supplier.

Cost: This marketing research study is based on data generated by other marketing research studies. Thus, the costs associated with this marketing research study depend on whether other marketing research studies have already been executed in the current quarter. The base cost of this marketing research study is $5,000 per market region. In addition, 1/NAREAS (where NAREAS is number of market areas in your BRANDMAPS™ industry) of the cost of each of the following marketing research studies are incurred, if these marketing research studies have not already been executed this quarter:

Marketing Research Study #3 (Industry Sales Force Size)
Marketing Research Study #4 (Industry Advertising)
Marketing Research Study #6 (Industry Promotion)

Marketing Research Study #7 (Industry R&D)
Marketing Research Study #21 (Brand Perceptual Ratings)
Marketing Research Study #22 (Aggregate Market Statistics)
Marketing Research Study #23 (Reformulation Activity)
Marketing Research Study #24 (Market Shares)
Marketing Research Study #25 (Dealer Prices)
Marketing Research Study #39 (Competitive Information - Unfilled Orders).

At current BRANDMAPS™ costs, executing this marketing research study in a single market would result in $18,375 and $30,375 in costs being incurred in syndicated (Spring and Fall) and custom (Winter and Summer) quarters, respectively. These costs assume that none of the marketing research studies on which this marketing research study is based (marketing research studies #3, #4, #6, #7, #21, #22, #23, #24, #25, and #39) have already been executed in the current quarter.

Sample
Study
Output

```
=====================================================================
MARKETING RESEARCH STUDY #41 (REGIONAL SUMMARY ANALYSIS            )
=====================================================================


REGION STATISTICS, REGION 2 (MEXICO  ), QUARTER 44 (FALL  )
```

	Quarter		Change (%)
	Previous	Current	
Population	40,979,028	41,357,708	.9
Consumer Price Index	930	949	2.0
Per Capita Income	11,146	11,496	3.1
Industry Sales Volume	71,125	66,361	-6.7
Industry Advertising	8,000,000	4,000,000	-50.0
Industry Average D_Price	878	887	-1.0
Industry Promotion	3,000,000	4,000,000	33.3
Industry Average R&D	250,000	350,000	20.0
Industry Sales Force	400	350	-12.5

```
BRAND PERFORMANCE STATISTICS, REGION 2 (MEXICO  ), QUARTER 44 (FALL  )
```

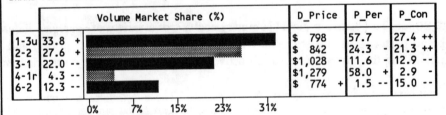

	Volume Market Share (%)	D_Price	P_Per	P_Con
1-3u	33.8 +	$ 798	57.7	27.4 ++
2-2	27.6 +	$ 842	24.3 -	21.3 ++
3-1	22.0 --	$1,028 -	11.6 -	12.9 --
4-1r	4.3 --	$1,279	58.0 +	2.9 -
6-2	12.3 --	$ 774 +	1.5 --	15.0 --

0%   7%   15%   23%   31%

```
*** NOTES ***
(1) An "r" after a product number denotes a reformulation in this quarter.
    A "u" denotes unfilled orders in this quarter.  A "*" denotes a product
    that has been reformulated and that has unfilled orders in this quarter.
(2) Changes of more than 25%, from the previous-quarter value, are flagged
    by "++" and "--" to the right of the current-quarter entry for increases
    and decreases, respectively.  Changes of more than 5% but less than 25%,
    from the previous-quarter value, are flagged by "+" and "-" to the right
    of the current-quarter entry for increases and decreases, respectively.
    Changes of less than 5% from the previous quarter are not flagged.
(3) "D_Price" is dealer price, "P_Per" is perceived performance, and "P_Con"
    is perceived convenience.
```

Marketing Research Study #42: Marketing Research Ordering Statistics

Purpose: To obtain a summary of the frequency with which various BRANDMAPS™ marketing research studies are ordered by vaporware industry firms.

Description of the Research Process: Frequency estimates are provided by your marketing research supplier. Frequencies are reported in categories, as follows: Ordered by 100% of Vaporware Firms, "Always"; Ordered by 80%-99.9% of Vaporware Firms, "Very High"; Ordered by 60%-79.9% of Vaporware Firms, "High"; Ordered by 40%-59.9% of Vaporware Firms, "Moderate"; Ordered by 20%-39.9% of Vaporware Firms, "Low"; Ordered by 5%-19.9% of Vaporware Firms, "Very Low"; and, Ordered by 0%-4.9% of Vaporware Firms, "Rarely/Never." Frequency estimates are based on marketing research ordering frequency for all vaporware industry firms over the previous four quarters.

Cost: $1,000.

Sample
Study
Output

```
================================================================
MARKETING RESEARCH STUDY #42 (MARKETING RESEARCH ORDERING STATISTICS  )
================================================================

MR #            Marketing Research Study           Ordering Frequency
----    -------------------------------------      ------------------
  1     COMPETITIVE INFORMATION - YTD EARNINGS      High
  2     BRAND COMPOSITION ANALYSIS                  Moderate
  3     INDUSTRY SALES FORCE SIZE                   Very Low
  4     INDUSTRY ADVERTISING                        Very Low
  5     INDUSTRY SALES FORCE COMPENSATION           Low
  6     INDUSTRY PROMOTION                          Very Low
  7     INDUSTRY R&D                                Low
  8     MEDIA CONTENT ANALYSIS                      Moderate
  9     PROMOTIONAL TYPE ANALYSIS                   Low
 10     CONJOINT ANALYSIS                           Very High
 ...
```

Marketing Research Study #43: Marketing Support Spending Productivity Analysis

Purpose: To obtain a marketing support spending productivity analysis (ratios of marketing support spending to sales volume and sales revenues) in a specified market region.

Description of the Research Process: The data reported include ratios of advertising, promotion, research and development, and sales force compensation (salaries, commissions, and overhead) spending to sales revenue and to sales volume for all of your firm's actively distributed brands in a specified market region. The marketing support spending, sales volume, and sales revenue data are derived directly from your firm's financial and operating reports.

For comparative purposes, an industry norm for the specified market region is also provided. The industry norms estimates are based on various on-going market analyses conducted by your marketing research supplier.

Cost (Per Market Region): $5,000.

Other Comments: Only brands with a current-quarter volume market share of at least 5.0% are included in the industry norm calculations. In addition, only ratios with non-zero marketing support spending are included and reported in this marketing research study.

Sample
Study
Output

```
=========================================================================
MARKETING RESEARCH STUDY #43 (MARKETING SUPPORT SPENDING PRODUCTIVITY )
=========================================================================


    MARKETING SUPPORT SPENDING PRODUCTIVITY ANALYSIS, REGION 6 (JAPAN   )
    -----------------------------------------------------------------------
                                                          COMPARATIVE NORMS
                                                          -----------------
                                                          FIRM 2   INDUSTRY
                                    Product Product Product (In All (In This
                                      2-1     2-2    2-3   Regions)  Region)
                                    ------- ------- -------  -------- --------
    SALES VOLUME PER $000 OF:
      Advertising                     4.0           13.7     17.0      8.5
      Promotion                      10.9           37.1     45.8     23.0
      Research & Development         32.3          109.8    135.6     68.0
      Sales Force Compensation        5.1           15.3     13.0      9.8
    SALES REVENUE PER $ OF:
      Advertising                     2.3            7.5      9.7      4.8
      Promotion                       6.3           20.3     26.1     13.1
      Research & Development         18.7           60.0     77.3     38.7
      Sales Force Compensation        2.9            8.3      7.4      5.6
    -----------------------------------------------------------------------
```

Marketing Research Study #44: Population Forecasts

Purpose: To provide population forecasts for the next four quarters for all market regions.

Description of the Research Process: These population forecasts are based on an extrapolation of current trends.

Cost: $2,000.

Sample
Study
Output

```
=========================================================================
MARKETING RESEARCH STUDY #44 (POPULATION FORECASTS                      )
=========================================================================

                 QUARTER 31   QUARTER 32   QUARTER 33   QUARTER 34   QUARTER 35
                 [History]    [Forecast]   [Forecast]   [Forecast]   [Forecast]
                 ----------   ----------   ----------   ----------   ----------

REG. 1 (U.S.     ) 110,281,568 111,381,656 112,619,728 113,866,448 115,062,488
                   [100.00]    [101.00]     [102.12]     [103.25]     [104.34]

REG. 2 (U.K.     )  50,397,428  50,919,024  51,528,744  52,120,060  52,777,044
                   [100.00]    [101.03]     [102.24]     [103.42]     [104.72]

REG. 3 (GERMANY )   84,437,184  85,300,120  86,142,776  87,087,536  87,972,984
                   [100.00]    [101.02]     [102.02]     [103.14]     [104.19]

REG. 4 (FRANCE   )  62,765,016  63,546,976  64,411,756  65,203,948  65,973,252
                   [100.00]    [101.25]     [102.62]     [103.89]     [105.11]
```

Marketing Research Study #45: Per Capita Income Forecasts

Purpose: To provide per capita income forecasts for the next four quarters for all market regions.

Description of the Research Process: These per capita income forecasts are based on an extrapolation of current trends.

Cost: $2,000.

Sample
Study
Output

```
===========================================================================
MARKETING RESEARCH STUDY #45 (PER CAPITA INCOME FORECASTS               )
===========================================================================

                     QUARTER 80   QUARTER 81   QUARTER 82   QUARTER 83   QUARTER 84
                     [History]    [Forecast]   [Forecast]   [Forecast]   [Forecast]
                     ----------   ----------   ----------   ----------   ----------

REG.  1 (EASTERN )      15,905       16,051       16,250       16,419       16,594
                       [100.00]     [100.92]     [102.17]     [103.23]     [104.34]

REG.  2 (SOUTHERN)      13,400       13,530       13,669       13,807       13,944
                       [100.00]     [100.96]     [102.01]     [103.03]     [104.06]

REG.  3 (CENTRAL )      14,930       15,082       15,261       15,383       15,545
                       [100.00]     [101.02]     [102.22]     [103.03]     [104.12]

REG.  4 (WESTERN )      14,318       14,478       14,627       14,799       14,964
                       [100.00]     [101.12]     [102.16]     [103.36]     [104.52]
```

Marketing Research Study #46: Consumer Price Index Forecasts

Purpose: To provide consumer price index forecasts for the next four quarters for all market regions.

Description of the Research Process: These consumer price index forecasts are based on an extrapolation of current trends.

Cost: $2,000.

```
===================================================================
MARKETING RESEARCH STUDY #46 (CONSUMER PRICE INDEX FORECASTS        )
===================================================================

                    QUARTER 43  QUARTER 44  QUARTER 45  QUARTER 46  QUARTER 47
                    [History]   [Forecast]  [Forecast]  [Forecast]  [Forecast]
                    ----------  ----------  ----------  ----------  ----------

REG. 1 (CANADA  )       1,407       1,427       1,452       1,472       1,491
                     [100.00]    [101.40]    [103.17]    [104.64]    [106.01]

REG. 2 (U.K.    )       1,121       1,132       1,143       1,154       1,166
                     [100.00]    [100.98]    [101.90]    [102.89]    [104.00]

REG. 3 (U.S.    )       1,373       1,392       1,414       1,432       1,454
                     [100.00]    [101.43]    [102.98]    [104.29]    [105.91]

REG. 4 (C.EUROPE)       1,319       1,339       1,355       1,378       1,399
                     [100.00]    [101.55]    [102.77]    [104.50]    [106.11]
```

Marketing Research Study #47: Self-Reported Attribute Preferences

Purpose: To provide distributions of customers' direct self-reported preferences for each vaporware raw material ingredient in a specified market region or regions.

Description of the Research Process: A representative sample of vaporware customers is asked, for each vaporware raw material ingredient, "What is your most preferred level of ... ?" The results are tabulated and reported as frequency distributions in eight categories, centered on the attribute-levels 8, 20, 32, 44, 56, 68, 80, and 92.

Cost (Per Market Region): $5,000.

Other Comments: In this marketing research study output, the percentages reported for the frequencies refer to a range of attribute-levels. For example, if 13.3% of survey respondents report favoring a level of 20 for a particular raw material, this is interpreted as corresponding to 13.3% of customers preferring a raw material value in the range 14.0% to 25.9%.

Since Compatibility and Warranty are strictly of the "more-is-better" variety, there is no doubt about the most preferred level of these product attributes — the maximum possible level is preferred by all customers. Thus, customers' direct self-reported preferences for Compatibility and Warranty are obvious and there is no need to actually query customers about Compatibility and Warranty.

Sample
Study
Output

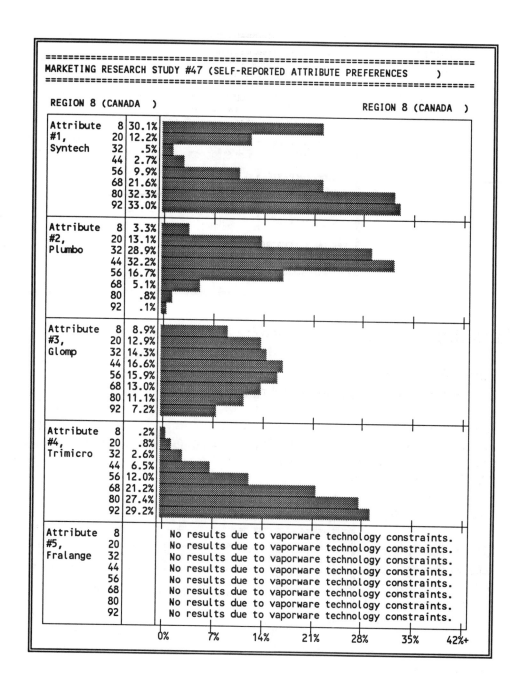

```
===================================================================
MARKETING RESEARCH STUDY #47 (SELF-REPORTED ATTRIBUTE PREFERENCES    )
===================================================================

REGION 8 (CANADA  )                              REGION 8 (CANADA  )
```

Attribute #1, Syntech	8	30.1%
	20	12.2%
	32	.5%
	44	2.7%
	56	9.9%
	68	21.6%
	80	32.3%
	92	33.0%
Attribute #2, Plumbo	8	3.3%
	20	13.1%
	32	28.9%
	44	32.2%
	56	16.7%
	68	5.1%
	80	.8%
	92	.1%
Attribute #3, Glomp	8	8.9%
	20	12.9%
	32	14.3%
	44	16.6%
	56	15.9%
	68	13.0%
	80	11.1%
	92	7.2%
Attribute #4, Trimicro	8	.2%
	20	.8%
	32	2.6%
	44	6.5%
	56	12.0%
	68	21.2%
	80	27.4%
	92	29.2%
Attribute #5, Fralange	8	No results due to vaporware technology constraints.
	20	No results due to vaporware technology constraints.
	32	No results due to vaporware technology constraints.
	44	No results due to vaporware technology constraints.
	56	No results due to vaporware technology constraints.
	68	No results due to vaporware technology constraints.
	80	No results due to vaporware technology constraints.
	92	No results due to vaporware technology constraints.

```
0%   7%   14%   21%   28%   35%   42%+
```

Marketing Research Study #48:   Dealer Inventory Analysis - Own Brands

Purpose: To provide estimates of current dealer inventory levels of your actively distributed brands in all market regions.

Description of the Research Process: These dealer inventory level estimates are based on a survey of vaporware dealers.

Cost: $5,000.

```
================================================================================
MARKETING RESEARCH STUDY #48 (DEALER INVENTORY ANALYSIS - OWN BRANDS  )
================================================================================

                      QUARTER 22  QUARTER 23  QUARTER 24  QUARTER 25  QUARTER 26
                      ----------  ----------  ----------  ----------  ----------


REGION 1 (EASTERN  )

REGION 2 (SOUTHERN)
   Product 9-1          5,775       5,083       6,794      10,492       7,672
   Product 9-2                                     60         291      20,922

REGION 3 (CENTRAL  )

REGION 4 (WESTERN  )
   Product 9-3          2,982       3,090       1,998       2,242       6,590
```

Marketing Research Study #49: Dealer Inventory Analysis - All Brands

Purpose: To provide estimates of current dealer inventory levels of all actively distributed brands (your brands and your competitors' brands) in all market regions.

Description of the Research Process: These dealer inventory level estimates are based on a survey of vaporware dealers.

Cost: $15,000.

```
================================================================================
MARKETING RESEARCH STUDY #49 (DEALER INVENTORY ANALYSIS - ALL BRANDS  )
================================================================================

                      QUARTER 12  QUARTER 13  QUARTER 14  QUARTER 15  QUARTER 16
                      ----------  ----------  ----------  ----------  ----------


REGION 1 (U.S.   )
   Product 1-2                                              11,552      12,771
   Product 2-2                                      0           0           0
   Product 3-1         12,556       6,930           0           0      28,482
   Product 4-2                                     60         291      20,922
   Product 6-3          9,048       6,189       3,179       2,310         986

REGION 2 (U.K.   )
   Product 1-1          7,840       6,120           0       6,314      10,716

...
```

Marketing Research Study #50: Price Sensitivity Analysis

Purpose: To perform a price sensitivity analysis on products which are currently actively distributed (at current formulations and current dealer prices) in a specified market region or regions.

Description of the Research Process: Price sensitivity analysis involves the execution of a series of preference tests on existing products. See Marketing Research Study #13 for details of preference testing with two existing products.

Preference shares are estimated for all current actively distributed products at their existing formulations and their existing dealer prices. Preference shares refer to market shares if only two aspects of the whole marketing program, formulation and dealer price, matter to customers. These preference shares should be viewed as long-run "full information" estimates to which market shares might stabilize assuming that customers have equal access (i.e., equal awareness, equal distribution, equal "convenience," etc.) to all products actively distributed in this market.

A 20% range around current dealer price is used in this price sensitivity analysis. Extrapolations beyond the vicinity of current dealer price are likely to be unreliable. Substantial dealer price changes are likely to lead to competitive counter-responses thus making preference share predictions problematic.

Cost (Per Market Region): $25,000.

Special Ordering Instructions: To order this study, write in and circle the marketing research study number, 50, at the bottom of the Marketing Research Pre-Order Request Form. Be sure to indicate the market regions for which this marketing research study is to be executed.

Sample
Study
Output

```
=========================================================================
MARKETING RESEARCH STUDY #50 (PRICE SENSITIVITY ANALYSIS          )
=========================================================================

REGION 7 (HK/T/K/S)                                REGION 7 (HK/T/K/S)

 ┌─────────────────────────────────┐    Product 1-1 a $  919:  25.5%
 │ Estimated Preference Shares Given│    Product 2-2 a $  803:  24.4%
 │ Product Formulations and Dealer  │    Product 5-2 a $  913:  27.9%
 │ Prices of All Actively           │    Product 8-3 a $1,033:  22.2%
 │ Distributed Products             │
 └─────────────────────────────────┘

 ┌─────────────────────────────────┐    Product 1-1 a $  700:  42.0%
 │ Product 1-1 Estimated Preference │    Product 1-1 a $  750:  37.5%
 │ Shares at Various Dealer Prices  │    Product 1-1 a $  800:  33.4%
 │ Given Current Product            │    Product 1-1 a $  850:  29.8%
 │ Formulations and Dealer Prices   │    Product 1-1 a $  900:  26.6%
 │ of All Other Actively            │    Product 1-1 a $  950:  23.8%
 │ Distributed Products             │    Product 1-1 a $1,000:  21.4%
 │                                  │    Product 1-1 a $1,050:  19.2%
 └─────────────────────────────────┘    Product 1-1 a $1,100:  17.3%

*** NOTES ***
(1) Preference shares refer to market shares if only two aspects of the whole
    marketing program, formulation and dealer price, matter to customers.
(2) A 20% range around current dealer price is used in this price sensitivity
    analysis. Extrapolations beyond the immediate vicinity of current dealer
    price are likely to be unreliable. Substantial dealer price changes are
    likely to lead to competitive counter-responses thus making preference
    share predictions problematic.
(3) These preference shares should be viewed as long-run "full information"
    estimates to which market shares might stabilize assuming that customers
    have equal access (i.e., equal awareness, equal distribution, equal
    "convenience," etc.) to all products actively distributed in this market.
```

## Chapter 6

Financial and Operating Results Reports

After a game run, BRANDMAPS™ teams receive a variety of reports. These financial and operating results reports are described and documented in this chapter. The sample financial and operating reports displayed in this chapter are only meant to illustrate formatting and content.

Note: None of the numbers displayed in these sample reports are meant to be suggestive of actual operating policies or market situations. The actual page numbers shown on these sample reports may differ from your reports, depending on the particular financial results reporting style (discussed at the end of this chapter) that you select.

Current Product Operating Statement and Status of Decision Variables

This part of the financial and operating reports consists of a CURRENT PRODUCT OPERATING STATEMENT for each vaporware brand and, at the bottom of the page, information on the current status of the brand's other decision variables as well as some firm-wide decision variables, followed by a year-to-date CUMULATIVE PRODUCT OPERATING STATEMENT for each brand. See Exhibit 1 for a sample CURRENT PRODUCT OPERATING STATEMENT. The CURRENT PRODUCT OPERATING STATEMENT data for a vaporware brand includes two pages of information for each set of four market regions.

Financial results for each brand in all market regions are reported on the CURRENT PRODUCT OPERATING STATEMENT. Only those marketing support expenditures and other fixed costs which are unambiguously attributable to a specific brand in a specific market region are reported on the CURRENT PRODUCT OPERATING STATEMENT. Thus, for example, research and development expenditures for a brand are not included on the CURRENT PRODUCT OPERATING STATEMENT since they cannot be

Exhibit 1

SAMPLE CURRENT PRODUCT OPERATING STATEMENT

```
**********************************************************************
FIRM 4:  INTERGALACTIC VAPORWARE                           INDUSTRY T
CURRENT PRODUCT OPERATING STATEMENT, PRODUCT 4-1, QUARTER  5     PAGE  1
**********************************************************************
```

	ALL REGIONS	REGION 1 (EASTERN)	REGION 2 (SOUTHERN)	REGION 3 (CENTRAL)	REGION 4 (WESTERN)
ACTIVE PRODUCT?	YES	NO	YES	YES	NO
SALES (Units)	49,622	0	7,779	41,843	0
UNFILLED ORDERS	0	0	0	0	0
PRICE	566	570	550	570	550
DEALER REBATES	0	0	0	0	0
REVENUE	28,128,960	0	4,278,450	23,850,510	0
PRODUCT COSTS	10,176,756	0	1,595,360	8,581,396	0
REBATES OFFERED	0	0	0	0	0
SALES COMMISSIONS	562,578	0	85,568	477,010	0
TRANSPORTATION	1,080,957	0	202,254	878,703	0
GROSS MARGIN	16,308,669	0	2,395,268	13,913,401	0
FIXED COSTS:					
ADMINISTRAT O/H	110,425	0	57,848	52,577	0
ADVERTISING	3,000,000	0	500,000	2,500,000	0
PROMOTION	502,500	0	500,000	2,500	0
SALES SALARIES	1,650,000	0	150,000	1,500,000	0
SALES O/H	2,212,578	0	235,568	1,977,010	0
TOTAL FIXED COSTS	7,475,503	0	1,443,416	6,032,087	0
OPERATING INCOME	8,833,166	0	951,852	7,881,314	0

```
*****************************************************
OTHER DECISION VARIABLES FOR PRODUCT 4-1 AND FIRM 4
*****************************************************
```

MEDIA CONTENT & MIX	1 & 55555	9 & 55555	10 & 55555	9 & 91191
PROMOTIONAL TYPE	10	10	21	10
SALES FORCE:				
SIZE	200	200	200	200
TIME ALLOCATION (%s)	0	10	100	0
EFFORT	.00	20.00	200.00	.00
SALARY + COMMISSION	2,500 + 2	2,500 + 2	2,500 + 2	2,500 + 2

SALES FORECAST (Units)	0 9,000 44,000 0
PRODUCT COMPOSITION	10/10/10/15/ 5/5/5
PRODUCTION ORDER (Units)	47,000
EMERGENCY PRODUCTION LIMIT (%)	50
RESEARCH & DEVELOPMENT	500,000
PLANT CAPACITY ORDER (Units)	55,000

Exhibit 1 [continued]

```
*************************************************************************
FIRM 4:  INTERGALACTIC VAPORWARE                            INDUSTRY T
ADVERTISING MEDIA MIX ALLOCATIONS, PRODUCT 4-1, QUARTER  5    PAGE  2
*************************************************************************
```

	ALL REGIONS	REGION 1 (EASTERN)	REGION 2 (SOUTHERN)	REGION 3 (CENTRAL)	REGION 4 (WESTERN)
MEDIA MIX [#s]		55555	55555	55555	91191
ADVERTISING SPENDING					
Direct Marketing	600,000	0	100,000	500,000	0
Magazines	600,000	0	100,000	500,000	0
Newspapers	600,000	0	100,000	500,000	0
Radio	600,000	0	100,000	500,000	0
Television	600,000	0	100,000	500,000	0
Total	3,000,000	0	500,000	2,500,000	0

```
*************************************************************************
CUMULATIVE PRODUCT OPERATING STATEMENT, PRODUCT 4-1, QUARTER  5   PAGE  2
*************************************************************************
```

	ALL REGIONS	REGION 1 (EASTERN)	REGION 2 (SOUTHERN)	REGION 3 (CENTRAL)	REGION 4 (WESTERN)
SALES (Units)	49,622	0	7,779	41,843	0
UNFILLED ORDERS	0	0	0	0	0
PRICE	566	0	550	570	0
DEALER REBATES	0	0	0	0	0
REVENUE	28,128,960	0	4,278,450	23,850,510	0
PRODUCT COSTS	10,176,756	0	1,595,360	8,581,396	0
REBATES OFFERED	0	0	0	0	0
SALES COMMISSIONS	562,578	0	85,568	477,010	0
TRANSPORTATION	1,080,957	0	202,254	878,703	0
GROSS MARGIN	16,308,669	0	2,395,268	13,913,401	0
FIXED COSTS:					
ADMINISTRAT O/H	110,425	0	57,848	52,577	0
ADVERTISING	3,000,000	0	500,000	2,500,000	0
PROMOTION	502,500	0	500,000	2,500	0
SALES SALARIES	1,650,000	0	150,000	1,500,000	0
SALES O/H	2,212,578	0	235,568	1,977,010	0
TOTAL FIXED COSTS	7,475,503	0	1,443,416	6,032,087	0
OPERATING INCOME	8,833,166	0	951,852	7,881,314	0

unambiguously allocated across the regions in which a brand is actively distributed.

On the CURRENT PRODUCT OPERATING STATEMENT:

- "Active Product?" refers to whether a brand is actively distributed in a market region.
- "Unfilled Orders" refers to the number of units of sales volume that were stock-outs, for which sales orders were received but available inventory was insufficient to meet this demand (even after accounting for emergency production orders).

Note: "Unfilled Orders" are not back orders. Only some part of "Unfilled Orders" will involve customers who will wait (patiently) for the next quarter in which to have their purchase requests fulfilled. Other customers will shift to competing brands or not make any purchase.

- "Dealer Rebates" refers to the per-unit value of dealer rebates, if any.
- "Product Costs" refers to per-unit cost-of-goods sold.
- "Sales Commissions" refers to the dollar value of sales commission.
- "Rebates Offered" refers to the total dollar value of dealer rebates offered, if any. This equals sales volume times per-unit rebate ("Dealer Rebates").
- "Administrat O/H" refers to the administrative overhead attributable to each active brand in a market region. This reflects adjustments in the base administrative overhead amount for sales volume forecasting performance.
- "Sales O/H" refers to the sales overhead charges, which is equal to "Sales Salaries" plus "Sales Commissions."

The current status of other decision variables associated with the brand are reported on the bottom of the page containing the CURRENT PRODUCT OPERATING STATEMENT. The implicit dollar allocations of overall advertising to media types implied by the five-digit media mix allocation code are shown on the top of the second page. This compact form of reporting is designed to permit quick review of the current status of a brand's marketing program. Plant capacity orders and production orders are also reported here. There is some built-in redundancy here, since these operations variables are reported on each brand's CURRENT PRODUCT OPERATING STATEMENT page.

In the decision variable status area under the "Sales Force" subheading, "Effort" is just the product of "Size" times "Time Allocation" (expressed as a proportion). "Effort" is automatically calculated by the BRANDMAPS™ software. BRANDMAPS™ firms control only "Size" and "Time Allocation." "Effort" is the equivalent number of full-time sales representatives devoting their time to supporting a particular vaporware brand in a specific BRANDMAPS™ market region.

Divisional Operating Statement

After the CURRENT PRODUCT OPERATING STATEMENTS, the next two pages of the financial and operations report contain the CURRENT DIVISIONAL OPERATING STATEMENT and year-to-date CUMULATIVE DIVISIONAL OPERATING STATEMENT. These summarize the CURRENT PRODUCT OPERATING STATEMENTS for the individual brands as well as accounting for the various fixed costs that were not attributable to individual brands. They also include some other costs which could not be unambiguously allocated to a particular brand in a specific BRANDMAPS™ market region. The CURRENT DIVISIONAL OPERATING STATEMENT is the P&L (profit and loss) statement for the vaporware division of your firm. Exhibit 2 contains a sample CURRENT DIVISIONAL OPERATING STATEMENT.

In the CURRENT DIVISIONAL OPERATING STATEMENT:

- "Corporate O/H" refers to corporate overhead.
- "Consulting Fees" include several possible components. As mentioned earlier, dealer inventory adjustment payments for reformulated brands are included here. Also, special financial adjustments (for incorrect marketing research billings, for special plant capacity transfers, etc.) made by the course

Exhibit 2

SAMPLE DIVISIONAL OPERATING STATEMENT

```
*************************************************************************
FIRM 2:  VAPORWARE, INC.                                    INDUSTRY Q
CURRENT DIVISIONAL OPERATING STATEMENT, FIRM 2, QUARTER  9     PAGE  7
*************************************************************************
```

	ALL PRODUCTS	PRODUCT 2-1	PRODUCT 2-2	PRODUCT 2-3
SALES (Units)	217,901	35,323	127,782	54,796
UNFILLED ORDERS	0	0	0	0
PRICE	812	975	773	800
DEALER REBATES	0	0	0	0
REVENUE	177,105,175	34,439,925	98,828,450	43,836,800
PRODUCT COSTS	85,699,065	16,511,764	38,150,491	31,036,810
REBATES OFFERED	0	0	0	0
SALES COMMISSIONS	3,530,452	688,798	1,964,918	876,736
TRANSPORTATION	5,215,442	883,075	2,688,487	1,643,880
GROSS MARGIN	82,660,216	16,356,288	56,024,554	10,279,374
FIXED COSTS:				
ADMINISTRAT O/H	583,527	155,705	318,325	109,497
ADVERTISING	10,000,000	3,000,000	4,000,000	3,000,000
CONSULTING FEES	0			
CORPORATE O/H	750,000			
DEPRECIATION	5,680,403			
DISPOSAL SALES	0	0	0	0
EMERG PREMIUMS	0	0	0	0
INTRODUCTIONS	0	0	0	0
INVENTORY CHARG	1,672,995	574,786	397,247	700,962
MARKET RESEARCH	149,500			
PROD ORDER COST	300,000	100,000	100,000	100,000
PROMOTION	12,000,000	6,000,000	3,000,000	3,000,000
REFORMULATIONS	0	0	0	0
RESEARCH & DEV	1,160,000	330,000	500,000	330,000
SALES EXPENSES	75,000			
SALES SALARIES	1,837,500	562,500	750,000	525,000
SALES O/H	5,367,952	1,251,298	2,714,918	1,401,736
TOTAL FIXED COSTS	39,576,877	11,974,289	11,780,490	9,167,195
OPERATING INCOME	43,083,339	4,381,999	44,244,064	1,112,179
NON-OPERAT INCOME	-5,023,886			
LESS: TAXES	19,029,726			
NET INCOME	19,029,727			

instructor are recorded as "Consulting Fees." These adjustments may be either positive or negative "Consulting Fees."

- "Depreciation" refers to the fixed depreciation component.
- "Disposal Sales" accounts for the 25% loss in value (from the DIVISIONAL BALANCE SHEET inventory cost) associated with disposal sales due to reformulations. Reimbursements to dealers for losses on reformulated brands' inventory are also recorded here.
- "Emerg Premiums" accounts for the emergency production premiums for a brand.
- "Introductions" accounts for the fixed costs of introducing a brand into a market region.
- "Inventory Charg" refers to the finished goods inventory charges.
- "Market Research" refers to marketing research charges.
- "Prod Order Cost" refers to the fixed cost of production orders.
- "Reformulations" accounts for the fixed costs associated with reformulating a brand. Also, the bid prices for position in the reformulation queue are recorded in this line of the CURRENT DIVISIONAL OPERATING STATEMENT.
- "Sales Expenses" refers to the hiring and firing costs associated with changes in the size of a sales force in a market region.
- "Non-Operat Income" accounts for non-operating income from marketable securities (a positive contribution to income) and from loans (a negative contribution to income).

The figures in the CURRENT DIVISIONAL OPERATING STATEMENT add down and across separately to the appropriate totals. However, they do not add down and across simultaneously, since some items included in the "All Products" column are not included in the individual brand columns.

Balance Sheet, Finished Goods Inventory Transactions, Cash Flow Analysis Report, and Operating Performance Report

After the CURRENT DIVISIONAL OPERATING STATEMENT and the year-to-date CUMULATIVE DIVISIONAL OPERATING STATEMENT, the next page of the financial and operating report contains a DIVISIONAL BALANCE SHEET and a statement of FINISHED GOODS INVENTORY TRANSACTIONS. Then, the following page includes a CASH FLOW ANALYSIS REPORT and an OPERATING PERFORMANCE REPORT. See Exhibit 3 and 4 for samples.

The DIVISIONAL BALANCE SHEET documents the current asset and liability position. Included in the DIVISIONAL BALANCE SHEET report are the current finished goods inventory position and the current plant capacity situation.

The FINISHED GOODS INVENTORY TRANSACTIONS report documents the adjustments to finished goods inventory due to sales, production, and emergency production.

Variable Cost Calculations and Production Cost Analysis Estimates

The next page of the financial and operating results reports contains a detailed calculation of the various variable costs associated with each current vaporware brand. This detailed calculation is provided because the various components that combine to yield total variable costs of a vaporware brand are very complex.

The bottom part of this page contains a Production Cost Analysis Report, which provides estimates of variable costs for the next quarter. Experience curve cost savings are reported here. Also, this report provides margin analysis calculations.

See Exhibit 4 for a sample variable cost calculation and production cost analysis reports.

Exhibit 3

SAMPLE BALANCE SHEET AND FINISHED GOODS INVENTORY TRANSACTIONS

```
*********************************************************************
FIRM 3:  NORTHERN VAPORWARE                              INDUSTRY G
DIVISIONAL BALANCE SHEET, FIRM 3, QUARTER  9               PAGE   9
*********************************************************************


ASSETS
------
  CASH                                                   8,855,258
  MARKETABLE SECURITIES                                          0
  FINISHED GOODS INVENTORY:
    PRODUCT 3-1   (   23,698 Units) [$  467.45 Per Unit]  11,077,651
    PRODUCT 3-2   (   33,683 Units) [$  298.56 Per Unit]  10,056,372
    PRODUCT 3-3   (    6,395 Units) [$  566.41 Per Unit]   3,622,170
  PLANT:
    CURRENT PLANT                  [CAPACITY =   195,106] 163,548,349
    PLANT ON ORDER FOR 1 QUARTER HENCE [CAPACITY =     0]          0
  TOTAL ASSETS                                           197,159,800

LIABILITIES AND EQUITY
----------------------
  LOANS                                                   28,208,131
  INITIAL (QUARTER 0) CORPORATE CAPITALIZATION           120,000,000
  - DIVIDENDS PAID, PRIOR TO THIS YEAR                   -19,032,274
  - DIVIDENDS PAID, END OF QUARTER 1 OF THIS YEAR         -6,343,242
  - DIVIDENDS PAID, END OF QUARTER 2 OF THIS YEAR                  0
  - DIVIDENDS PAID, END OF QUARTER 3 OF THIS YEAR                  0
  - DIVIDENDS PAID, END OF QUARTER 4 OF THIS YEAR                  0
  + RETAINED EARNINGS (AFTER-TAX INCOME PRIOR TO THIS YEAR) 55,297,458
  + YEAR-TO-DATE EARNINGS (AFTER-TAX INCOME THIS YEAR)    19,029,727
  TOTAL LIABILITIES AND EQUITY                           197,159,800




*********************************************************************
                                                           PAGE   9
FINISHED GOODS INVENTORY TRANSACTIONS, FIRM 3, QUARTER  9
*********************************************************************

                              PRODUCT    PRODUCT    PRODUCT
                                3-1        3-2        3-3
                             ---------  ---------  ---------


  BEGINNING INVENTORY          24,021     16,465     41,191
+ PRODUCTION                   35,000    145,000     20,000
+ EMERGENCY PRODUCTION              0          0          0
= AVAILABLE FOR SALE           59,021    161,465     61,191
- SALES
      REGION 1 (U.S.     )    -35,323          0          0
      REGION 2 (U.K.     )          0     -1,013          0
      REGION 3 (C.EUROPE)           0   -126,769          0
      REGION 4 (JAPAN    )           0          0    -54,796
      REGION 5 (CANADA   )           0          0          0
= ENDING INVENTORY            23,698     33,683      6,395
```

Exhibit 4

SAMPLE CASH FLOW ANALYSIS REPORT AND
OPERATING PERFORMANCE REPORT

```
*****************************************************************************
FIRM 6:  INTERGALACTIC VAPORWARE                             INDUSTRY D
CASH FLOW ANALYSIS REPORT, FIRM 6, QUARTER 19                  PAGE 10
*****************************************************************************


    STARTING "CASH" BALANCE (FINAL "CASH" BALANCE, QUARTER 18)      8,486,138
 + "MARKETABLE SECURITIES" (CONVERTED TO "CASH" IN QUARTER 19)              0
 - "LOANS" (LIQUIDATED DURING QUARTER 19)                         -83,731,436
 + "FINISHED GOODS INVENTORY" INVESTMENT CHANGES
       PRODUCT 6-1 (From 11,913,821 To 11,077,651)                   836,170
       PRODUCT 6-2 (From  5,833,543 To 10,056,372)                -4,222,829
       PRODUCT 6-3 (From 24,416,327 To  3,622,170)                20,794,157
 + "PLANT" INVESTMENT CHANGE (From 189,346,791 To 163,548,349)     25,798,442
 + "NET INCOME"                                                    19,029,727
 = INITIAL END-OF-QUARTER "CASH" BALANCE                          -13,009,631
 - "DIVIDENDS" (PAID AT END OF QUARTER 19)                         -6,343,242
 = ACTUAL "CASH" BALANCE (END OF QUARTER 19)                      -19,352,873
 - OPERATING "CASH" EXCESS (TO "MARKETABLE SECURITIES")                     0
 + OPERATING "CASH" DEFICIT (FROM "LOANS")                         28,208,131
 = FINAL "CASH" BALANCE (END OF QUARTER 19)                         8,855,258


*** NOTES ***
(1) "MARKETABLE SECURITIES" and "LOANS" in the second and third lines above
    refer to the values on last quarter's balance sheet.
(2) INVESTMENT CHANGEs can be positive, negative, or zero.  A positive
    (negative) {zero} INVESTMENT CHANGE corresponds to an increase (a
    decrease) {no change} in the dollar-value of the investment from last
    quarter to this quarter which leads to a decrease (an increase) {no
    change} in current-quarter "CASH" balance.
(3) In every quarter, plant capacity depreciates.  The depreciation process
    results in additions to cash, by converting investment in plant capacity
    to cash which may be used for other operating and investment purposes.
    The net "PLANT" INVESTMENT CHANGE includes this cash-increasing effect
    as well as the cash-decreasing impact of ordering new plant capacity.
(4) At most, one of OPERATING "CASH" EXCESS and OPERATING "CASH" DEFICIT will
    be non-zero; it is possible for both to be zero.  Recall that "CASH" must
    be between  5.0% and  8.0% of current-quarter sales revenues.  Excess
    "CASH" (above  8.0% of revenues) is invested in marketable securities;
    shortfalls in "CASH" (below  5.0% of revenues) result in loans.




*****************************************************************************
OPERATING PERFORMANCE REPORT, FIRM 6, QUARTER 19                PAGE 10
*****************************************************************************
```

	REVENUES ($)	EARNINGS ($)	ROI (%)	MARKET SHARES (%)	
				VOLUME	DOLLAR
CURRENT QUARTER	177,105,175	19,029,727	50.2	26.58	24.94
PREVIOUS QUARTER	169,722,775	9,596,858	33.2	27.07	23.47
CHANGE RATE	4.3%	98.3%	51.4%	-1.8%	6.3%

Other Financial and Operating Reports

Subsequent pages of the financial and operating results reports include a SALES FORECASTING ACCURACY REPORT, a STOCK MARKET REPORT, a detailed listing of MARKETING RESEARCH BILLINGS, FINANCIAL AND OPERATING STATEMENT MESSAGES, and SPECIAL BRANDMAPS NOTICES. See Exhibits 5-9 for samples.

Financial Results Reporting Options

BRANDMAPS™ has four options for reporting the brand-specific profit-and-loss statements. These four presentation styles are described in the table below:

Style #	Content and Focus	Details Reported	Pages
1	Product Operating Statement	Total and all regions for each product.	Two pages for each product — current and cumulative year-to-date.
2	Regional Operating Statement	Total and all products for each region.	Two pages for each region — current and cumulative year-to-date.
3	Operating Statement	Previous quarter, current quarter, percentage change rates from previous quarter, and cumulative year-to-date.	One page for each brand actively distributed in each market region.
4	Historical Operating Statement	Current quarter and previous three quarters.	One page for each brand actively distributed in each market region.

Only one of these presentation styles may be used at any one time. You may change your financial results presentation style at any time. Samples of each of these financial results presentations styles are shown in Exhibits 10-13 on pages 120-123.

Exhibit 5

SAMPLE DETAILED VARIABLE COST CALCULATIONS AND
PRODUCT COST ANALYSIS ESTIMATES

```
*********************************************************************
FIRM 7:  WORLDWIDE VAPORWARE, INC.                      INDUSTRY B
DETAILED VARIABLE COST CALCULATIONS, FIRM 7, QUARTER  5    PAGE  8
*********************************************************************
```

COST COMPONENTS	PRODUCT 7-1	PRODUCT 7-2	PRODUCT 7-3
RAW MATERIAL #1 [SYNTECH]	13.50	11.25	60.00
RAW MATERIAL #2 [PLUMBO]	96.60	46.20	46.20
RAW MATERIAL #3 [GLOMP]	6.75	4.50	14.40
RAW MATERIAL #4 [TRIMICRO]	11.70	10.50	27.60
RAW MATERIAL #5 [FRALANGE]	.75	.75	.75
RAW MATERIAL (Experience Curve Adjust.)	-6.68	-28.27	-20.05
LABOR (Base)	30.00	30.00	30.00
LABOR (Smoothing Adjustment)	3.33	.54	.00
LABOR (Experience Curve Adjustment)	-2.06	-13.53	-4.78
PRODUCTION (Base)	60.00	60.00	60.00
PRODUCTION (Smoothing Adjustment)	3.33	.54	.00
PRODUCTION (Experience Curve Adjustment)	-3.91	-26.83	-9.56
PACKAGING	10.00	10.00	10.00
VARIABLE DEPRECIATION	100.59	100.59	100.59
SUB-TOTAL VARIABLE COSTS	323.91	206.23	315.16
COMPATIBILITY (Cost Premium Impact)	51.83	18.56	78.79
WARRANTY (Cost Premium Impact)	72.14	67.44	118.18
TOTAL VARIABLE COSTS	447.87	292.23	512.13

```
*********************************************************************
PRODUCT COST ANALYSIS ESTIMATES, FIRM 7, QUARTER 10       PAGE  8
*********************************************************************
```

	ESTIMATES OF NEXT QUARTER EXPERIENCE CURVE ADJUSTED VARIABLE (Per Unit) COSTS				MARGIN ANALYSIS		
	RAW MATERI	PDCOST +PKCST	PROD +LABOR	TOTAL	PRICE	COST	MARGIN
PRODUCT 7-1	111.90	110.59	75.67	412.26	975.00	412.26	562.74
PRODUCT 7-2	41.23	110.59	45.19	279.16	773.00	279.16	493.84
PRODUCT 7-3	123.63	110.59	71.97	497.56	800.00	497.56	302.44

*** NOTES ***

(1) The variable depreciation cost (PDCOST) figure in this table has been estimated under the assumption that production next quarter is equal to plant capacity.

(2) In this table, PKCST refers to packaging cost.

(3) MARGIN ANALYSIS figures do not include transportation and shipping costs; also, dealer rebates have been assumed to be $0.

(4) TOTAL includes cost-premium impacts of Compatibility and Warranty.

Exhibit 6

SAMPLE SALES FORECASTING ACCURACY REPORT
AND STOCK MARKET REPORT

```
****************************************************************************
FIRM 4:  UNIVERSAL VAPORWARE                                   INDUSTRY A
SALES FORECASTING ACCURACY REPORT, FIRM 4, QUARTER 15           PAGE 12
****************************************************************************

             MARKET       SALES       ACTUAL      ACCURACY
PRODUCT      REGION      FORECAST      SALES        SCORE
-------      ------      --------      -------     --------

  4-1          2           9,000        7,779       84.30
  4-1          3          44,000       41,843       94.85
  4-2          2          50,000       41,142       78.47
  4-3          4          20,000        3,742         .00
  4-3          5          50,000       29,985       33.25
  4-3          6          11,000        7,770       58.43
  4-3          7          27,000       15,470       25.47
AVERAGE (Current Quarter)                           53.54

ON  7 SALES VOLUME FORECASTS IN THE CURRENT YEAR:
   CUMULATIVE (Total) FORECASTING SCORE POINTS =    374.77
   AVERAGE FORECASTING SCORE (Per Forecast)    =     53.54


*** NOTE ***
Only forecasts associated with actual market shares of at least  2.5% in a
market region are counted in the calculation of forecasting accuracy scores.



****************************************************************************
STOCK MARKET REPORT, FIRM 4, QUARTER 15                        PAGE 12
****************************************************************************

CURRENT STOCK PRICE (Per Share), FIRM 1    $    80 1/2
CURRENT STOCK PRICE (Per Share), FIRM 2    $    66 1/2
CURRENT STOCK PRICE (Per Share), FIRM 3    $    96 1/8
CURRENT STOCK PRICE (Per Share), FIRM 4    $   137 5/8
...
```

Exhibit 7

SAMPLE MARKETING RESEARCH BILLINGS

```
**************************************************************************
FIRM 4:  INTERGALACTIC VAPORWARE                             INDUSTRY T
MARKETING RESEARCH BILLINGS, FIRM 4, QUARTER 25                PAGE 13
**************************************************************************


STUDY                                       UNIT
  #      MARKETING RESEARCH STUDY DESCRIPTION   COST    TIMES    COST
-----    ------------------------------------ -------  -------  ---------

  1      COMP INFO - DIVIDENDS AND EARNINGS     1,000      4      4,000
  3      INDUSTRY SALES FORCE SIZE              5,000      1      5,000
  4      INDUSTRY ADVERTISING                   4,000      1      4,000
  5      INDUSTRY SALES FORCE COMPENSATION      5,000      1      5,000
  8      MEDIA CONTENT ANALYSIS                 2,500      1      2,500
  9      PROMOTIONAL TYPE ANALYSIS              2,500      1      2,500
 10      CONJOINT ANALYSIS                          1  105,536  105,536
 11      CUSTOMER BRAND AWARENESS               7,000      1      7,000
 16      OPERATING STATISTICS REPORT           25,000      1     25,000
 17      BRAND QUALITY RATINGS                  7,000      1      7,000
 22      AGGREGATE MARKET STATISTICS            1,000      1      1,000
 23      REFORMULATION ACTIVITY                 1,000      1      1,000
 24      MARKET SHARES                          2,500      1      2,500
 25      DEALER PRICES                          2,500      1      2,500
 26      DEALER REBATES                         3,000      1      3,000
 27      DEALER PROMOTION AWARENESS             4,000      1      4,000
 28      DEALER AVAILABILITY                    8,000      1      8,000
 31      INDUSTRY SALES VOLUME FORECASTS        2,000      1      2,000
 32      BRAND SALES VOLUME FORECASTS           4,000      1      4,000
 35      ADVERTISING PROGRAM EXPERIMENT        15,000      5     75,000
 36      COMPETITIVE INFORMATION - BRAND PROFILES 10,000   14    140,000
 37      COMPETITIVE INFORMATION - SFC STATISTICS 40,000    1     40,000

TOTAL                                                           450,536


*** NOTE ***
This marketing research billing report is based on marketing research pre-
ordered for quarter 24 and billed in connection with quarter 25.  Marketing
research study premium rates, in connection with syndicated and custom
marketing research, are based on quarter 24.
```

Exhibit 8

SAMPLE FINANCIAL AND OPERATING STATEMENT MESSAGES

```
********************************************************************************
FIRM 4:  ASIAN VAPORWARE PTY.                                      INDUSTRY C
FINANCIAL AND OPERATING STATEMENT MESSAGES, FIRM 4, QUARTER  5         PAGE 14
********************************************************************************


CAPACITY USAGE SITUATION
     Current capacity is 175,150 units; pending capacity is  55,000 units.
     With no change in production, next quarter capacity usage will be 115.3%.
     Next quarter capacity is 118.6% of current quarter sales volume.
     Forecast capacity utilization is more than 100%.
     ### WARNING:  Major Overcapacity Utilization Problem May Be Imminent ###

EMERGENCY PRODUCTION ACTIVITY
     No products have emergency production this quarter.

INVENTORY LEVELS
     Product 4-2 inventory is  13,858 units, which represents    .3 quarters
        of sales, at the current sales volume levels for this product.
     Product 4-3 inventory is  16,258 units, which represents   4.3 quarters
        of sales, at the current sales volume levels for this product.

PRODUCT FORMULATION STATUS
     Product 4-1 has formulation 10/10/10/15/ 5/5/5 and patent zone of  7.
     Product 4-2 has formulation 30/40/30/80/ 5/6/5 and patent zone of 22.
     Product 4-3 has formulation 40/65/25/35/ 5/4/5 and patent zone of 25.

SALES FORECASTING ACCURACY SCORES
     Product 4-3, region 4, sales forecasting accuracy is very poor [   .00].
     Product 4-3, region 5, sales forecasting accuracy is very poor [ 33.25].
     Product 4-3, region 6, sales forecasting accuracy is very poor [ 25.47].

REGIONAL GROSS MARGINS
     All products in all regions have contribution margins greater than 25%.

QUARTERLY MARKETING SUPPORT SPENDING BUDGET REPORT
            Current quarter "adjusted sales revenue" is      90,927,844.
            Current quarter "marketing support spending" is  26,890,280.
     Maximum "marketing support spending" next quarter is    36,371,138.

SPECIAL NOTES, REMINDERS, AND WARNING MESSAGES
     Spending violation:  product 4-1, area 3 [promotion =   688,327].
     Spending violation:  product 4-2, area 1 [promotion =   917,770].
     Spending violation:  product 4-3, area 5 [promotion =   458,885].
     Spending violation:  product 4-3, area 7 [promotion =   458,885].
     Product 4-3 reformulated to 40/65/25/35/ 5/4/5; successful on try #1.
     Product 4-1, area 2, has unfilled sales orders of   3,178 units.
     Product 4-3, area 6, has unfilled sales orders of  12,190 units.
     Emergency plant capacity order executed for firm 1:
        Current quarter total production orders are   500,000 units.
        Without an emergency plant capacity order, next quarter available
        plant capacity would be only   200,000 units, which is less than 50%
        of current quarter total production orders.
     Emergency plant capacity order executed for    50,000 units.
     Next quarter available plant capacity (current plant capacity as
        recorded on these financial statements) is   250,000 units.
```

Exhibit 9

SAMPLE SPECIAL BRANDMAPS NOTICES

```
********************************************************************************
FIRM 1:  NORTH AMERICAN VAPORWARE                                    INDUSTRY T
SPECIAL BRANDMAPS NOTICES, FIRM 1, QUARTER  9                           PAGE 15
********************************************************************************


BRANDS:  ONLY SOME BRANDMAPS BRANDS ARE AVAILABLE FOR USE AT THIS TIME
    Brand 1 is available for use.
    Brand 2 is available for use.
    Brand 3 is available for use.
    Brand 4 is not available for use.

VAPORWARE TECHNOLOGY CONSTRAINTS
    Product attributes #1-#5 must sum to between  50 and 300.
    Attribute #5 [Fralange    ] must equal   5.

TRANSPORTATION AND SHIPPING COSTS
    Transportation and shipping costs for Region 1 (U.S.    ) = $ 25.00/unit.
    Transportation and shipping costs for Region 2 (U.K.    ) = $ 26.00/unit.
    Transportation and shipping costs for Region 3 (FRANCE  ) = $ 27.00/unit.
    Transportation and shipping costs for Region 4 (GERMANY ) = $ 30.00/unit.
    Transportation and shipping costs for Region 5 (JAPAN   ) = $ 35.00/unit.
    Transportation and shipping costs for Region 6 (HK/T/K/S) = $ 37.00/unit.
    Transportation and shipping costs for Region 7 (CANADA  ) = $ 26.00/unit.
    Transportation and shipping costs for Region 8 (MEXICO  ) = $ 29.00/unit.
```

Exhibit 10

SAMPLE PRODUCT OPERATING STATEMENT

```
**********************************************************************
FIRM 4:  INTERCONTINENTAL VAPORWARE, LTD.                   INDUSTRY A
CURRENT PRODUCT OPERATING STATEMENT, PRODUCT 4-1, QUARTER  5     PAGE  1
**********************************************************************
```

	ALL REGIONS	REGION 1 (U.S.)	REGION 2 (U.K.)	REGION 3 (C.EUROPE)	REGION 4 (PACIFIC)
ACTIVE PRODUCT?	YES	NO	YES	YES	NO
SALES (Units)	49,622	0	7,779	41,843	0
UNFILLED ORDERS	0	0	0	0	0
PRICE	566	570	550	570	550
DEALER REBATES	0	0	0	0	0
REVENUE	28,128,960	0	4,278,450	23,850,510	0
PRODUCT COSTS	10,176,756	0	1,595,360	8,581,396	0
REBATES OFFERED	0	0	0	0	0
SALES COMMISSIONS	562,578	0	85,568	477,010	0
TRANSPORTATION	1,080,957	0	202,254	878,703	0
GROSS MARGIN	16,308,669	0	2,395,268	13,913,401	0
FIXED COSTS:					
ADMINISTRAT O/H	110,425	0	57,848	52,577	0
ADVERTISING	3,000,000	0	500,000	2,500,000	0
PROMOTION	502,500	0	500,000	2,500	0
SALES SALARIES	1,650,000	0	150,000	1,500,000	0
SALES O/H	2,212,578	0	235,568	1,977,010	0
TOTAL FIXED COSTS	7,475,503	0	1,443,416	6,032,087	0
OPERATING INCOME	8,833,166	0	951,852	7,881,314	0

```
****************************************************
OTHER DECISION VARIABLES FOR PRODUCT 4-1 AND FIRM 4
****************************************************
```

		REGION 1	REGION 2	REGION 3	REGION 4
MEDIA CONTENT & MIX		1 & 55555	9 & 55555	10 & 55555	9 & 91191
PROMOTIONAL TYPE		10	10	21	10
SALES FORCE:					
SIZE		200	200	200	200
TIME ALLOCATION (%s)		0	10	100	0
EFFORT		.00	20.00	200.00	.00
SALARY + COMMISSION		2,500 + 2	2,500 + 2	2,500 + 2	2,500 + 2
SALES FORECAST (Units)		0	9,000	44,000	0

PRODUCT COMPOSITION   10/10/10/15/ 5/5/5

PRODUCTION ORDER (Units)   47,000
EMERGENCY PRODUCTION LIMIT (%)   50
RESEARCH & DEVELOPMENT   500,000

PLANT CAPACITY ORDER (Units)   55,000

Exhibit 11

SAMPLE REGIONAL OPERATING STATEMENT

```
*************************************************************************
FIRM 5:  FIFTH-WHEEL VAPORWARE
                                                             INDUSTRY B
CURRENT REGIONAL OPERATING STATEMENT, FIRM 5, REGION 2, QUARTER  9   PAGE  3
*************************************************************************
```

	ALL PRODUCTS	PRODUCT 5-1	PRODUCT 5-2	PRODUCT 5-3
ACTIVE PRODUCT?	YES	YES	NO	YES
SALES (Units)	41,097	1,038	0	40,059
UNFILLED ORDERS	0	0	0	0
PRICE	978	520	530	990
DEALER REBATES	0	0	0	0
REVENUE	40,198,170	539,760	0	39,658,410
PRODUCT COSTS	18,349,966	228,260	0	18,121,706
REBATES OFFERED	0	0	0	0
SALES COMMISSIONS	401,981	5,397	0	396,584
TRANSPORTATION	1,068,522	26,988	0	1,041,534
GROSS MARGIN	20,377,701	279,115	0	20,098,586
FIXED COSTS:				
ADMINISTRAT O/H	107,997	51,830	0	56,167
ADVERTISING	3,000,000	0	0	3,000,000
PROMOTION	1,000,000	0	0	1,000,000
SALES SALARIES	2,062,500	0	0	2,062,500
SALES O/H	2,464,481	5,397	0	2,459,084
TOTAL FIXED COSTS	8,634,978	57,227	0	8,577,751
OPERATING INCOME	11,742,723	221,888	0	11,520,835

```
**********************************************************
OTHER DECISION VARIABLES FOR REGION 2 AND FIRM 5
**********************************************************
```

		PRODUCT 5-1	PRODUCT 5-2	PRODUCT 5-3
MEDIA CONTENT & MIX		1 & 55555	15 & 11111	21 & 11111
PROMOTIONAL TYPE		9	10	10
SALES FORCE (Region 2):				
SIZE		250	250	250
TIME ALLOCATION (%s)		0	0	100
EFFORT		.00	.00	250.00
SALARY + COMMISSION		2,750 + 1	2,750 + 1	2,750 + 1
SALES FORECAST (Units)		1,000	0	45,000
PRODUCT COMPOSITION		7/15/18/ 19/ 5/1/5	65/23/36/ 5/ 5/3/3	40/60/20/ 95/ 5/6/6
PRODUCTION ORDER (Units)		0	48,000	85,000
EMERGENCY PRODUCTION LIMIT (%s)		50	50	50
RESEARCH & DEVELOPMENT		500,000	500,000	300,000
PLANT CAPACITY ORDER (Units)			46,242	

Exhibit 12

SAMPLE CURRENT OPERATING STATEMENT

```
*****************************************************************************
FIRM 3:  THREE'S COMPANY                                         INDUSTRY C
CURRENT OPERATING STATEMENT, PRODUCT 3-3, REGION 2, QUARTER 10    PAGE  5
*****************************************************************************
```

	PREVIOUS QUARTER	CURRENT QUARTER	Change Rate	CUMULATIVE YEAR-TO-DATE
ACTIVE PRODUCT?	YES	YES		YES
SALES (Units)	27,000	60,626	124.5%	87,626
UNFILLED ORDERS	34,893	25,645	-26.5%	60,538
PRICE	810	810	.0%	810
DEALER REBATES	0	0	.0%	0
REVENUE	21,870,000	49,107,060	124.5%	70,977,060
PRODUCT COSTS	10,761,174	26,119,426	142.7%	36,880,600
REBATES OFFERED	0	0	.0%	0
SALES COMMISSIONS	656,100	1,473,210	124.5%	2,129,310
TRANSPORTATION	783,000	1,758,154	124.5%	2,541,154
GROSS MARGIN	9,669,726	19,756,270	104.3%	29,425,996
FIXED COSTS:				
ADMINISTRAT O/H	142,222	137,073	-3.6%	279,295
ADVERTISING	2,000,000	1,500,000	-25.0%	3,500,000
PROMOTION	1,000,000	1,000,000	.0%	2,000,000
SALES SALARIES	826,800	831,885	.6%	1,658,685
SALES O/H	1,482,900	2,305,095	55.4%	3,787,995
TOTAL FIXED COSTS	5,451,922	5,774,053	5.9%	11,225,975
OPERATING INCOME	4,217,804	13,982,217	231.5%	18,200,021

```
*****************************************************************************
OTHER DECISION VARIABLES FOR PRODUCT 3-3, REGION 2, AND FIRM 3
*****************************************************************************
```

MEDIA CONTENT & MIX	15 & 55555	11 & 13732
PROMOTIONAL TYPE	46	16
SALES FORCE:		
SIZE	130	109
TIME ALLOCATION (%s)	80	96
EFFORT	104.00	104.64
SALARY + COMMISSION	2,650 + 3	2,650 + 3
SALES FORECAST (Units)	22,000	52,000
PRODUCT COMPOSITION	30/50/22/ 97/ 5/5/4	30/50/22/ 97/ 5/5/4
PRODUCTION ORDER (Units)	27,000	52,000
EMERGENCY PRODUCTION LIMIT (%)	0	10
RESEARCH & DEVELOPMENT	450,000	400,000
PLANT CAPACITY ORDER (Units)	0	0

Exhibit 13

SAMPLE HISTORICAL OPERATING STATEMENT

```
*****************************************************************************
FIRM 4:  ABSON, JORDAN, SMYTH, & WILLIAMS VAPORWARE INC.          INDUSTRY D
HISTORICAL OPERATING STATEMENT, PRODUCT 4-1, REGION 6, QUARTER 10    PAGE  1
*****************************************************************************
```

	QUARTER 7	QUARTER 8	QUARTER 9	QUARTER 10
ACTIVE PRODUCT?	YES	YES	YES	YES
SALES (Units)	66,690	47,852	47,307	54,650
UNFILLED ORDERS	0	0	0	0
PRICE	650	725	725	725
DEALER REBATES	0	0	0	0
REVENUE	43,348,500	34,692,700	34,297,575	39,621,250
PRODUCT COSTS	20,234,158	13,660,736	13,546,401	17,342,057
REBATES OFFERED	0	0	0	0
SALES COMMISSIONS	866,970	1,040,781	1,028,925	1,188,636
TRANSPORTATION	1,533,870	1,100,596	1,135,368	1,311,600
GROSS MARGIN	20,713,502	18,890,587	18,586,881	19,778,957
FIXED COSTS:				
ADMINISTRAT O/H	110,031	125,386	151,218	134,602
ADVERTISING	2,000,000	2,000,000	1,600,000	1,700,000
PROMOTION	1,000,000	1,000,000	750,000	800,000
SALES SALARIES	1,500,000	1,800,000	1,800,000	1,800,000
SALES O/H	2,366,970	2,840,781	2,828,925	2,988,636
TOTAL FIXED COSTS	6,977,001	7,766,167	7,130,143	7,423,238
OPERATING INCOME	13,736,501	11,124,420	11,456,738	12,355,719

```
*****************************************************************
OTHER DECISION VARIABLES FOR PRODUCT 4-1, REGION 6 AND FIRM 4
*****************************************************************
```

	QUARTER 7	QUARTER 8	QUARTER 9	QUARTER 10
MEDIA CONTENT & MIX	9 & 53588	12 & 95522	2 & 55555	2 & 55555
PROMOTIONAL TYPE	91	96	10	10
SALES FORCE:				
SIZE	200	200	200	200
TIME ALLOCATION (%s)	100	100	100	100
EFFORT	200.00	200.00	200.00	200.00
SALARY + COMMISSION	2,500 + 2	3,000 + 3	3,000 + 3	3,000 + 3
SALES FORECAST (Units)	60,000	60,000	35,000	48,000
PRODUCT COMPOSITION	15/ 5/25/ 7/ 5/5/5	15/ 5/25/ 7/ 5/5/5	15/ 5/25/ 7/ 5/5/5	15/ 5/25/ 7/ 5/5/5
PRODUCTION ORDER (Units)	110,000	65,000	10,000	28,000
EMERGENCY PRODUCTION LIMIT (%)	50	50	50	50
RESEARCH & DEVELOPMENT	275,000	275,000	300,000	300,000
PLANT CAPACITY ORDER (Units)	45,000	25,000	10,000	20,000

Chapter 7

Decision Making
Logistics and
Related Paperwork

To make changes in current marketing and non-marketing decisions in BRANDMAPS™, firms must complete appropriate decision change forms and submit these forms to the BRANDMAPS™ Game Administrator. The BRANDMAPS™ Game Administrator will ensure that the changes are made prior to the next game run. There are specific decision change forms in BRANDMAPS™. These forms are included in this chapter.

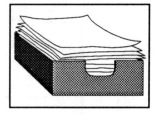

All decision variable changes are of the form "make this decision equal to ... ," *not* "change this decision by this much ... ."

All BRANDMAPS™ decisions are "permanent." That is, BRANDMAPS™ decisions stay the same from quarter to quarter until they are explicitly changed. Thus, only changes need to be entered on these decision variable change forms. Leave current decision variables blank if no change is necessary.

To request marketing research studies, it is necessary to complete marketing research study request forms. The multi-page marketing research study request form is included in this chapter. Marketing research is executed after the next game run, so marketing research results will reflect the most recent quarter's activities. Note that the various product development and testing marketing research requests that require a "price" to be associated with existing or proposed vaporware formulations refer to "dealer price," *not* "manufacturer price." The key here is that the relevant "price" is the price seen by the customer in the context of the marketing research study.

These forms, for decision changes and for marketing research, must be submitted no later than the announced time for each decision period. Decision change forms submitted after this deadline may not be entered into the BRANDMAPS™ database in time to take effect with the next quarter.

Photocopy these various BRANDMAPS™ forms, as necessary, to use throughout the BRANDMAPS™ exercise. You may wish to photocopy a small supply of these various BRANDMAPS™ forms to facilitate your within-group decision making process.

Permission is hereby granted without charge, royalty, or copyright payment to anyone wishing to make photocopies of pages 126-136 for use during a BRANDMAPS™ exercise.

Since the BRANDMAPS™ participant's manual is copyrighted, you may need to show this photocopying permission statement to a commercial copy shop to facilitate photocopying of multiple copies of pages 126-136.

Reminder: All BRANDMAPS™ decisions are "permanent." That is, BRANDMAPS™ decisions stay the same from quarter to quarter until they are explicitly changed. Thus, only changes need to be entered on these decision variable change forms.

Marketing Decision Variables Change Form (A), For Firm#-Brand# [_]

	Region 1	Region 2	Region 3	Region 4	Region 5	Region 6	Region 7	Region 8
Introduce/Drop Brand?								
Manufacturer Price [$/unit]								
Dealer Rebate [$/unit]								
Advertising [$]								
Media Content [#]								
Media Mix Allocations [#s]								
Promotion [$]								
Promotional Type [#]								
Sales Forecast [units]								

General Notes and Reminders

(1) Only enter items for which changes are required.

(2) "BRANDMAPS™ numbers" may be used in this MARKETING DECISION VARIABLES CHANGE FORM (A). For example, 3,000,000 may be designated as 3M (where "M" means millions), 2,200,000 may be designated as 2.2M, and 23,000 may be designated as 23K (where "K" means thousands).

(3) When "Dropping a Brand From Active Distribution": You must also change your marketing support spending levels to zero (for advertising and promotion) and reallocate your sales force time allocation from dropped brands to actively-distributed brands.

126

Production Order [units]	
Emergency Production Limit [%]	
Research and Development Spending [$]	

Reformulation Queue Position Bid [$]	
First-Choice Reformulation Request	Formulation:
Second-Choice Reformulation Request	Formulation:
Third-Choice Reformulation Request	Formulation:

General Notes and Reminders

(1) Only enter items for which changes are required.

(2) "BRANDMAPS™ numbers" may be used in this MARKETING DECISION VARIABLES CHANGE FORM (B). For example, 3,000,000 may be designated as 3M (where "M" means millions), 2,200,000 may be designated as 2.2M, and 23,000 may be designated as 23K (where "K" means thousands).

Other Decision Variables Change Form, For Firm# [   ]

New Plant Capacity Order [units of plant capacity]	

Note: "New Plant Capacity Order" refers to the incremental amount of plant capacity that you wish to order, the amount of new plant capacity that is to be added to your current plant capacity. **Do not** enter the amount of the total capacity that you wish to have after the current plant capacity order is processed. For example, if you currently have a plant capacity of 200,000 units and you wish to increase your plant capacity to 250,000 units, enter 50,000 as your "New Plant Capacity Order."

Dividend Payment [$]	

Financial Results Statement Presentation Style [#]	

Note: The Financial Results Statement Presentation Styles include: #1, Product Operating Statement; #2, Regional Operating Statement; #3, Operating Statement; and #4, Historical Operating Statement.

Firm Name [max. of 50 characters]	

General Notes and Reminders

(1) Only enter items for which changes are required.

(2) "BRANDMAPS™ numbers" may be used in this OTHER DECISION VARIABLES CHANGE FORM. For example, 3,000,000 may be designated as 3M (where "M" means millions), 2,200,000 may be designated as 2.2M, and 23,000 may be designated as 23K (where "K" means thousands).

Sales Force Decision Variables Change Form, For Firm#

	Region 1	Region 2	Region 3	Region 4	Region 5	Region 6	Region 7	Region 8
Sales Force Salary [$ per person per month]								
Sales Force Commission Rate [% of revenues]								
Sales Force Size [# of representatives]								
Sales Force Time Allocations [%s] — Brand #1								
Brand #2								
Brand #3								
Brand #4								
	100%	100%	100%	100%	100%	100%	100%	100%

General Notes and Reminders

(1) Only enter items for which changes are required, except for sales force time allocations where numbers must be entered for all four brands in any market region in which sales force time is reallocated across brands.

(2) When changing sales force time allocations, enter time allocations for all four brands. Time allocations must sum to 100% in each market region. If any of these time allocations are 0%, be sure to enter the value 0 (zero).

(3) "BRANDMAPS™ numbers" may be used in this SALES FORCE DECISION VARIABLES CHANGE FORM. For example, 3,000,000 may be designated as 3M (where "M" means millions), 2,200,000 may be designated as 2.2M, and 23,000 may be designated as 23K (where "K" means thousands).

129

Marketing Research Pre-Order Request Form, For Firm# [ ]

1	Competitive Information - Dividends and Earnings		Firm #s:			
2	Brand Composition Analysis	Firm#s—Brand#s (max. of 4):				
3	Industry Sales Force Size					
4	Industry Advertising					
5	Industry Sales Force Compensation					
6	Industry Promotion					
7	Industry R&D					
8	Media Content Analysis					
9	Promotional Type Analysis					
10	Conjoint Analysis (*Note: A minimum of one and a maximum of four levels of each of these eight attributes must be used in this conjoint analysis. It is not necessary to use more than one level for any single attribute.*)	Region(s):				
		Attribute #1 [Syntech]:				
		Attribute #2 [Plumbo]:				
		Attribute #3 [Glomp]:				
		Attribute #4 [Trimicro]:				
		Attribute #5 [Fralange]:				
		Attribute #6 [Compatibility]:				
		Attribute #7 [Warranty]:				
		Attribute #8 [Dealer Price]:				
11	Customer Brand Awareness					
12	Concept Testing	Region(s): Formulation:				
		Region(s): Formulation:				
		Region(s): Formulation:				
		Region(s): Formulation:				
		Region(s): Formulation:				
		Region(s): Formulation:				
		Region(s): Formulation:				

		Region(s):		Formulation:
		Region(s):		Formulation:
		Region(s):		Formulation:
13	Preference Testing, Two Existing Brands	Region(s):	Price:	Firm#-Brand#:
			Price:	Firm#-Brand#:
		Region(s):	Price:	Firm#-Brand#:
			Price:	Firm#-Brand#:
	(*Note:* In this marketing research study, "price" refers to dealer price, the price at which final customers purchase vaporware brands. A dealer price must be provided for each brand, even if the dealer price is to be the same for both formulations.)	Region(s):	Price:	Firm#-Brand#:
			Price:	Firm#-Brand#:
		Region(s):	Price:	Firm#-Brand#:
			Price:	Firm#-Brand#:
		Region(s):	Price:	Firm#-Brand#:
			Price:	Firm#-Brand#:
		Region(s):	Price:	Firm#-Brand#:
			Price:	Firm#-Brand#:
		Region(s):	Price:	Firm#-Brand#:
			Price:	Firm#-Brand#:
		Region(s):	Price:	Firm#-Brand#:
			Price:	Firm#-Brand#:
		Region(s):	Price:	Firm#-Brand#:
			Price:	Firm#-Brand#:
14	Preference Testing, One Existing Brand and One Hypothetical Brand	Region(s):	Price:	Firm#-Brand#:
			Price:	Formulation:
		Region(s):	Price:	Firm#-Brand#:
			Price:	Formulation:
		Region(s):	Price:	Firm#-Brand#:
			Price:	Formulation:

(Note: In this marketing research study, "price" refers to dealer price, the price at which final customers purchase vaporware brands. A dealer price must be provided for each brand and formulation, even if the dealer price is to be the same for both formulations.)	Region(s):	Price:	Firm#-Brand#:
		Price:	Formulation:
	Region(s):	Price:	Firm#-Brand#:
		Price:	Formulation:
	Region(s):	Price:	Firm#-Brand#:
		Price:	Formulation:
	Region(s):	Price:	Firm#-Brand#:
		Price:	Formulation:
	Region(s):	Price:	Firm#-Brand#:
		Price:	Formulation:
	Region(s):	Price:	Firm#-Brand#:
		Price:	Formulation:
	Region(s):	Price:	Firm#-Brand#:
		Price:	Formulation:

15	Preference Testing, Two Hypothetical Brands	Region(s):	Price:	Formulation:
			Price:	Formulation:
		Region(s):	Price:	Formulation:
			Price:	Formulation:
	(Note: In this marketing research study, "price" refers to dealer price, the price at which final customers purchase vaporware brands. A dealer price must be provided for each formulation, even if the dealer price is to be the same for both formulations.)	Region(s):	Price:	Formulation:
			Price:	Formulation:
		Region(s):	Price:	Formulation:
			Price:	Formulation:
		Region(s):	Price:	Formulation:
			Price:	Formulation:
		Region(s):	Price:	Formulation:
			Price:	Formulation:
		Region(s):	Price:	Formulation:
			Price:	Formulation:

		Region(s):	Price:	Formulation:	
			Price:	Formulation:	
		Region(s):	Price:	Formulation:	
			Price:	Formulation:	
		Region(s):	Price:	Formulation:	
			Price:	Formulation:	

16	Operating Statistics Report	
17	Brand Quality Ratings	
18	Patent Search	Formulation:
		Formulation:
		Formulation:
		Formulation:
19	Competitive Information - Balance Sheets	Firm #s:
20	Test Marketing Experiment	Region(s): Test Market Length (max. of 3 quarters): What marketing decision variables, if any, are to be changed prior to this test marketing experiment being conducted? Be sure to specify specific firm and brand numbers for decision variable changes.
21	Brand Perceptual Ratings	
22	Aggregate Market Statistics	
23	Reformulation Activity	
24	Market Shares	
25	Dealer Prices	
26	Dealer Rebates	
27	Dealer Promotion Awareness	
28	Dealer Availability	

29	Competitive Position Audit	Firm#s—Brand#s (max. of 4):				
30	Patent Zone Search	Formulation:				
		Formulation:				
		Formulation:				
		Formulation:				
31	Industry Sales Volume Forecasts					
32	Brand Sales Volume Forecasts					
33	Reformulation Activity - Detailed					

34	Another Conjoint Analysis (*Note: A minimum of one and a maximum of four levels of each of these eight attributes must be used in this conjoint analyses. It is not necessary to use more than one level for any single attribute.*)	Region(s):				
		Attribute #1 [Syntech]:				
		Attribute #2 [Plumbo]:				
		Attribute #3 [Glomp]:				
		Attribute #4 [Trimicro]:				
		Attribute #5 [Fralange]:				
		Attribute #6 [Compatibility]:				
		Attribute #7 [Warranty]:				
		Attribute #8 [Dealer Price]:				

35	Advertising Program Experiment	Product:	Advertising ($):	
		Region:	Content [#]:	Media Mix [#s]:
		Product:	Advertising ($):	
		Region:	Content [#]:	Media Mix [#s]:
		Product:	Advertising ($):	
		Region:	Content [#]:	Media Mix [#s]:
		Product:	Advertising ($):	
		Region:	Content [#]:	Media Mix [#s]:
		Product:	Advertising ($):	
		Region:	Content [#]:	Media Mix [#s]:

		Product:	Advertising ($):	
		Region:	Content [#]:	Media Mix [#s]:
		Product:	Advertising ($):	
		Region:	Content [#]:	Media Mix [#s]:
		Product:	Advertising ($):	
		Region:	Content [#]:	Media Mix [#s]:
		Product:	Advertising ($):	
		Region:	Content [#]:	Media Mix [#s]:
		Product:	Advertising ($):	
		Region:	Content [#]:	Media Mix [#s]:
36	Competitive Information - Brand Marketing Program Profiles	Region(s):		
37	Competitive Information - Sales Force Compensation Statistics			
38	Promotion Experiment	Product:	Promotion ($):	
		Region:	Promotional Type [#]:	
		Product:	Promotion ($):	
		Region:	Promotional Type [#]:	
		Product:	Promotion ($):	
		Region:	Promotional Type [#]:	
		Product:	Promotion ($):	
		Region:	Promotional Type [#]:	
		Product:	Promotion ($):	
		Region:	Promotional Type [#]:	
		Product:	Promotion ($):	
		Region:	Promotional Type [#]:	
		Product:	Promotion ($):	
		Region:	Promotional Type [#]:	

		Product:	Promotion ($):
		Region:	Promotional Type [#]:
		Product:	Promotion ($):
		Region:	Promotional Type [#]:
		Product:	Promotion ($):
		Region:	Promotional Type [#]:

39	Competitive Information - Unfilled Sales Volume Statistics	
40	Competitive Information - Brand Margin Analysis	
41	Regional Summary Analysis	Region(s):
42	Marketing Research Ordering Statistics	
43	Marketing Support Spending Productivity	Region(s):
44	Population Forecasts	
45	Per Capita Income Forecasts	
46	Consumer Price Index Forecasts	
47	Self-Reported Attribute Preferences	Region(s):
48	Dealer Inventory Analysis — Own Brands	
49	Dealer Inventory Analysis — All Brands	
50	Price Sensitivity Analysis	Region(s):

General Notes on Pre-Ordering Marketing Research Studies

(1) To pre-order marketing research, circle the appropriate marketing research study numbers on the left side of this request form. If a marketing research study requires additional specific details, provide the specifics in the boxes to the right.

(2) Some marketing research studies may be executed simultaneously in all market regions. To order marketing research studies in all market regions simultaneously, request market region "A" when pre-ordering.

(3) "BRANDMAPS™ numbers" may be used in this MARKETING RESEARCH PRE-ORDER REQUEST FORM. For example, 3,000,000 may be designated as 3M (where "M" means millions), 2,200,000 may be designated as 2.2M, and 23,000 may be designated as 23K (where "K" means thousands).

## Chapter 8

Summary of BRANDMAPS™ Costs and Data

This chapter summarizes various costs (other than marketing research study costs) that exist in BRANDMAPS™ as of quarter 1. This summary is meant to capture all of the relevant cost and related data in one convenient place. Information on any subsequent cost changes in BRANDMAPS™ will be provided by the course instructor.

Variable Production Costs

Raw Material Costs, Per Pound:

Syntech	$25.00
Plumbo	$35.00
Glomp	$15.00
Trimicro	$10.00
Fralange	$5.00

Other Variable Production Costs, Per Unit:

Base Labor Cost	$30.00
Base Production Cost	$60.00
Packaging Cost	$10.00

Other Production-Related Costs

Production Order Charge, For Regular or Emergency Product Orders	$100,000
Emergency Production Premium Rate	25%
Finished Goods Inventory Charge (Related To Inventory Value)	5%

Plant Capacity Costs

Fixed Depreciation Rate, Per Quarter	3%
Variable Depreciation Rate, Per Quarter, At Full Capacity Usage	12%
Plant Capacity Order Cost, Fixed Cost Per Order	$250,000
Variable Plant Capacity Order Cost, Per Unit	$750

Other Costs

Reformulation Costs, Per Reformulation	$500,000
Introduction Costs, Per Market Region	$400,000
Corporate Overhead, Per Active Brand (Active In At Least One Market Region)	$100,000
Base Administrative Overhead, Per Active Brand Per Market Region	$50,000
Base Interest Rate on Loans, Per Quarter	3%
If Loans > 20% of Net Assets	4%
If Loans > 30% of Net Assets	5%
If Loans > 40% of Net Assets	6%
If Loans > 50% of Net Assets	9%

Other Overhead Costs

Sales Overhead, Based on Sales Force Compensation (Salary and Commission)	100%

## Chapter 9

Performance Evaluation in BRANDMAPS™

> *Note:* *This chapter describes topics and features that are optional within BRANDMAPS™. Your course instructor will advise you if the material in this chapter is to be used in your particular BRANDMAPS™ exercise.*

Introduction

Each team's performance in BRANDMAPS™ is evaluated on the basis of three general criteria — financial performance, market performance, and operating efficiency. The challenge facing each BRANDMAPS™ team is to maximize long-run profitability, given the initial starting situation. Overall performance evaluation in BRANDMAPS™ is based on assessing the extent to which each team fulfills this mandate. This chapter describes a quantitative performance evaluation methodology which combines measures of financial performance, market performance, and operating efficiency.

Financial Performance

Financial performance could, in principle, be measured in a number of ways. Current financial performance and trends in financial performance are both relevant. Long-term financial performance and potential are key. Attempts to achieve attractive short-term financial results at the possible expense of long-term financial performance should be viewed unfavorably.

Absolute earnings in a BRANDMAPS™ year is an obvious performance measure. More important, however, is ROI (return on investment). In BRANDMAPS™, "investment" includes both common stock and cumulative retained earnings to date, since these are the funds to which a firm has access during a BRANDMAPS™ year. Thus, as used here, ROI is a measure of return on equity. For example, suppose that a BRANDMAPS™ firm had a corporate investment of $120 million and cumulative retained earnings of $30 million at the end of year 4. For this firm, "Investment" is then $150 million. Assume that the firm pays no dividends during BRANDMAPS™ year 5. Then, new after-tax earnings of $27 million in year 5 would represent an after-tax ROI of 27/150 = 18%.

Since your vaporware firm has publicly traded stock, stock price might be viewed as a relevant measure of financial performance. Stock price presumably reflects current and recent-past financial performance, since expectations about future earnings potential presumably are based largely on current and recent-past earnings levels.

ROI is the specific financial measure used in the BRANDMAPS™ quantitative performance valuation mechanism.

Market Performance

Market performance is closely related to market share. Current market share and trends in market share through time are both relevant, however.

Market share may be reasonably interpreted as representing future earnings potential, hence its relevance in performance evaluation. Note, however, that market share may easily be manipulated in the short-run by an individual firm. For example, market share may be "bought" or "sold" at the expense or benefit of long-term profitability. Attention to trends is crucial to the successful interpretation of the strength of a market-share position.

Change in market share from year to year is the specific market performance evaluation measure used in the BRANDMAPS™ quantitative performance evaluation mechanism.

Operating Efficiency

Operating efficiency is important in any industry so that needless costs are not incurred. In general, an efficiently run firm would:

- keep minimum finished goods inventories to meet production and demand requirements
- forecast sales well
- keep its plant operating at full capacity (and not use over capacity)
- have no short-falls in finished goods inventory
- have no unfilled orders (stock outs)
- spend relatively modest amounts on support (advertising, research and development, promotion, and sales force)
- achieve a high level of profitability relative to sales revenue.

While poor performance on any of these ultimately leads to increased costs which reduces profitability, many other things affect profitability as well. Thus, it seems desirable to explicitly develop a measure of operating efficiency and to reward firms, at least partially, based on their operating efficiency.

In BRANDMAPS™, each firm is evaluated on operating efficiency as well as on financial (return on investment) and market (change in market share) performance criteria. Since operating efficiency must be gauged relative to competitors' levels, relative standing on these measures is the determinant of operating efficiency. In particular, operating efficiency is determined as follows in BRANDMAPS™:

Operating Efficiency = Inventory Management Efficiency
+ Sales Forecasting Efficiency
+ Capacity Management Efficiency
+ Emergency Premium Efficiency
+ Unfilled Orders Efficiency
+ Spending Support Efficiency
+ Profitability Efficiency.

These operating efficiency components are defined in Table 13.

Table 13

OPERATING EFFICIENCY COMPONENTS AND WEIGHTS

Component	Definition	Weight
Inventory Management	Sum finished good inventory costs and finished goods ordering costs. Divide this sum by a firm's sales revenues. [*Less is better.*]	1
Sales Forecasting	Compare sales volume forecasts to actual sales volumes. For each forecast, a forecasting score is developed based on awarding 100 points to a forecast that is within 1% of actual, 99 points to a forecast that is within 2% of actual, and so on. Thus, the average forecasting score indicates how close a firm typically forecasts sales compared to actual. For example, an average forecast score of 90 indicates that the firm typically forecasts sales volumes within 10% of actual levels. [*More is better.*]	3
Capacity Management	Fixed and variable depreciation per unit of production volume. Low values of depreciation per unit of production volume signify a firm that is managing its capacity well. [*Less is better.*]	3
Emergency Premium	Emergency production premiums divided by a firm's sales revenues. [*Less is better.*]	1
Unfilled Orders	Lost gross margin due to stockouts divided by a firm's sales revenues. [*Less is better.*]	1
Support Spending	Marketing support spending (on advertising, promotion, research and development, and sales force) across all brands and all regions to sales revenues. [*Less is better.*]	2
Profitability	After-tax profits divided by sales revenues. [*More is better.*]	3

After calculating each operating efficiency component, the number of points in "Weight" in Table 13 is awarded to each firm when its component value is less than (or more than, for measures where "more-is-better") to another firm's corresponding value. Thus, with n firms in an industry, the best-performing firm on this component receives a score of n-1 points times "Weight." The worst performing firm receives zero points. Each efficiency measure is equal to the number of points achieved in these comparisons. Thus, Operating Efficiency is an index in which higher values are better than lower values. This index has a minimum possible value of zero, if a firm is worst on all of the components of OPERATING EFFICIENCY, and a maximum value of 14(n-1) for an n-firm industry, if a firm is best on all of the components of Operating Efficiency.

In calculating Operating Efficiency, Sales Forecasting Efficiency receives a weight of three because it is a particularly pure correlate of market understanding and insight, and thus of operating efficiency. Note that good Sales Forecasting Efficiency presumably leads to efficient management of inventories and capacities. The weight of three for Capacity Management Efficiency is based on the substantial investments required in plants in the vaporware industry. Careful management of plant capacity is crucial in BRANDMAPS™. Profitability Efficiency receives a weight of three because it reflects overall profit and cost management. Note, however, that Profitability Efficiency can be influenced unduly by a firm that is "selling off" (harvesting) market share to achieve short-run profitability, even at the expense of long-run profitability. Thus, this variable is not a completely pure measure of operating efficiency. However, it has considerable relevance, hence its weight of three.

BRANDMAPS™ Quantitative Performance Evaluation

The BRANDMAPS™ quantitative performance evaluation mechanism is designed to provide a purely quantitative measure of performance in the simulation exercise. Presumably, other evaluation procedures may be used as well (written marketing plans, performance relative to specific goals, etc.).

In the first BRANDMAPS™ year, ROI, operating efficiency, and change in market share each have an overall weighting of one. After the first year, the weighting doubles. Also, after the first year, year-over-year change in each has a weighting of one.

A sample BRANDMAPS™ quantitative performance evaluation report is shown in Exhibit 14. Cumulative Points are translated automatically into a "Grade" which ranges from 70%-100% with a mean of 85%.

Exhibit 14

SAMPLE BRANDMAPS™ QUANTITATIVE PERFORMANCE EVALUATION REPORT

	Firm 1	Firm 2	Firm 3	Firm 4
Quarter 1 OE	21.0	21.0	21.0	21.0
Quarter 2 OE	31.0	25.0	6.0	22.0
Quarter 3 OE	29.5	14.0	9.0	31.5
Quarter 4 OE	29.5	8.5	14.0	32.0
Year 1, Total OE	111.0	68.5	50.0	106.5
Year 1, OE Points	3.0	1.0	.0	2.0
Year 1, ROI%	13.3	4.2	10.9	17.3
Year 1, ROI% Points	2.0	.0	1.0	3.0
Market Share Change	1.9	-2.5	-.6	1.2
Market Share Change Points	3.0	.0	1.0	2.0
Year 1, Total Points	8.0	1.0	2.0	7.0
Cumulative Points	8.0	1.0	2.0	7.0
Quarter 5 OE	13.0	23.0	25.0	23.0
Quarter 6 OE	13.0	27.0	13.0	31.0
Quarter 7 OE	5.0	26.0	24.0	29.0
Year 2, Total OE	31.0	76.0	62.0	83.0
Year 2, OE Points	.0	4.0	2.0	6.0
OE Change	-80.0	7.5	12.0	-23.5
OE Change Points	.0	2.0	3.0	1.0
Year 2, ROI%	-14.6	42.1	7.3	22.9
Year 2, ROI% Points	.0	6.0	2.0	4.0
ROI% Change	-27.9	37.9	-3.7	5.6
ROI% Change Points	.0	3.0	1.0	2.0
Market Share Change	-8.3	4.3	-7.6	11.7
Market Share Change Points	.0	4.0	2.0	6.0
Year 2, Total Points	.0	19.0	10.0	19.0
Cumulative Points	8.0	20.0	12.0	26.0
Overall Grade (Mean=85%)	77%	88%	81%	94%

## Chapter 10

Marketing Planning in BRANDMAPS™

```
Note: This chapter describes topics and features that are
optional within BRANDMAPS™. Your course instructor will advise
you if the material in this chapter is to be used in your particular
BRANDMAPS™ exercise.
```

Introduction

"When one does not know what harbor one is seeking, no wind is the right one."
● Seneca (Roman philosopher)

"Plans are nothing. Planning is everything."
● Dwight Eisenhower

"I liked having planned; I learned a lot about my business. But, I didn't like doing the planning. It was difficult."
● Anonymous BRANDMAPS™ Participant

Informal marketing planning occurs continuously within a BRANDMAPS™ exercise. Each set of decisions for each quarter requires an implicit review of a firm's on-going marketing program. In addition, however, some course instructors may require the preparation of formal written marketing plans. To aid this process, some ideas about marketing planning are raised in this chapter. A specific possible format for a marketing plan in BRANDMAPS™ is proposed.

Perspective

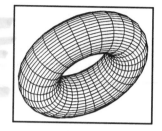

A marketing plan analyzes how you are going to achieve your profit, sales volume, and market share goals. Of course, this requires a carefully reasoned and thoughtful assessment of your current competitive market standing. The key outcome of the marketing planning process is the intricate crafting of a viable competitive marketing strategy.

In general, a bottom-up goal setting procedure will be followed in developing your marketing plan. You will formulate your plan and develop appropriate goals (financial, market share, and sales volume) within the context of your plan. Part of the evaluation of the plan will be based on the reasonableness and appropriateness of your goals. Overly optimistic or pessimistic planning and goals are to be avoided. Be realistic! Take into account your current level of financial performance, your current market position, and your management resources when you formulate your goals.

After you have developed a rough outline of your marketing plan for the next BRANDMAPS™ year, and before you start to write, it is usually desirable (and perhaps required, by some course instructors) to have a meeting with your firm's president (the course instructor) to review the scope of your goals for the next BRANDMAPS™ year. At that meeting, you will be expected to have developed appropriate pro-forma operating statements (detailed forecasts of profit and loss for each brand in each region and for the firm as a whole). The purpose of this meeting is to obtain your president's agreement as to your proposed goals for the following BRANDMAPS™ year.

With regard to financial goals, since there is a convenient hurdle ROI measure available (the interest rate on Marketable Securities), marketing plans that do not lead to forecasted earnings of at least this amount will be viewed with concern by corporate-level executives.

Short-Term Marketing Planning

The essence of a short-term annual marketing plan is the thoughtful development of answers to these six questions:
- What is happening in the market?
- How are we doing, in absolute and relative terms?
- How and what are "they" (our major competitors) doing?
- What factors are important for success in this market?
- What are we going to do? Why? With what effect? At what cost?
- Who, specifically, is to do what to make the plan work?

A Prototype Brand Marketing Plan

A prototype marketing plan for a single brand is shown below. Some parts of the plan may not be completely applicable in BRANDMAPS™, because of the structure of the vaporware industry. Some modifications will undoubtedly be required to account for the multiple-brand nature of BRANDMAPS™.

MARKETING PLAN FOR AAAAAAAA FOR 199x

Recent Market Developments: The key market developments last year included ...[major competitive development and activities, major repositionings of competitive offerings, new entrants, changes in customer values and perceptions, new trends possibly uncovered, key technological developments, major regulatory developments, ...].... The importance of these developments is that they indicate ...[What do they mean? How will they influence future marketing activities and efforts of you and your competitors? How can these market developments be exploited for maximum benefit? ...]....

Our Performance in the AAAAAAAA Market: In the last year, the market for AAAAAAAA grew by about B% to C units. Our sales of AAAAAAAA increased by D% to E units, which resulted in our profits increasing by F% to $G. Our market share grew from HH.H% to II.I% overall. By major market segment, our performance was ....

Competitive Analysis: Our major competitors in the AAAAAAAA market are J and K. We estimate that their current market position and performance is ...[market shares, sales volumes, growth rates, profitability].... Their current offerings have these major advantages and disadvantages compared to our offerings: .... Their current strategies seemed to be oriented toward .... In the near future (the 199x planning period), we believe that their marketing thrusts will be as follows: ...[expected changes (or even no changes) in product, price, ...].... Thus, the major opportunities and threats appear to be ....

Customers and Success Factors: To compete successfully in this market, we must respond to customers' concerns for: (1) ...; (2) ...; and, (3) ... when they choose a source of supply/brand/manufacturer/retailer. The importance of these particular buying factors is indicated by ...[our research, on-going discussions with key customers, ...].... Of particular note is the increasing importance of ... and ... to our customers. With regard to our major customer segments, notable variations in success factors include .... The major opportunities and threats appear to be ....

Major Assumptions: Our major assumptions for 199x include:
(1) Customers: ...
(2) Competitors: ...
(3) The Environment (Economy, Technology, Regulatory Environment): ...

Our Marketing Program For AAAAAAAA: To meet these challenges and opportunities, our marketing program will have the following major components:
(1) ...
(2) ...
(3) ...

The results of this marketing program are forecast to yield sales of L units (M% increase), revenues of $N (P% increase), an overall market share of QQ.Q% (an increase of R.R% from 199x), and profit of $S (T% increase).

To achieve these results, investments of $U will be required in support of ...[system development, facilities expansion, temporary staff addition, one-time R&D efforts, special consulting projects, ...]....

Competitor Reactions to Our Marketing Programs: Competitor reaction to our marketing program is expected to be ...[Will they notice? If they notice, is there anything they can do? If they can do something in response, will they?].... This reaction will impact on our marketing program as follows: .... This reaction, and its influence on our marketing program, has already been taken into account in our financial and market performance projects.

Implementation Issues and Procedures: To implement this plan successfully, the following implementation challenges exist: .... Our program for meeting these implementation challenges includes ...[strategies, tactics, emphasis, actions, activities, ...].... Specific responsibility assignments and time deadlines for key aspects of this marketing program include ....

Contingency Plans: Major contingencies include: .... In this event, our plan would have to be revised to ...[changes in emphasis, new initiatives, ...]....

A Possible BRANDMAPS™ Marketing Plan Format

The following style of organization is one possible format for a BRANDMAPS™ marketing plan (but lots of other formats are equally appropriate):

Cover Page: This contains the team's name, firm number, the title "Annual Marketing Plan for BRANDMAPS™ Year x (Quarters yy-zz)," and the names of the marketing team members.

Executive Summary: This contains a summary of the key features of your marketing plan. This should be written after the rest of the plan has been developed and written. This is **THE** most important part of your marketing plan.

Review of the Past Year: This contains a review of the market activities, forces and developments, competitive actions, and your team's performance (relative to goals) during the previous BRANDMAPS™ year.

Long-Run Strategy Statement: This contains a concise statement of your team's long-run marketing strategy. Your marketing strategy must take into consideration your existing market position, your financial performance in the industry, and any human resource constraints.

Major Planning Assumptions: This contains a brief discussion and justification of the major planning assumptions regarding market forces and competitive activities on which your marketing plan is based.

Brand or Region Plans: A brand or region plan must be prepared for each of your teams's brand or regions. Depending on your current team organization and brand positionings within BRANDMAPS™ regions, you may wish to format this in terms of regions (and discuss each of your active brands in a region) or in terms of brands (and discuss each region in which a brand is active). Of course, if you have only a single brand in each region, there would be no difference between these two approaches. Each brand plan should contain: a brand performance review for the previous BRANDMAPS™ year, a detailed development of brand goals (financial, market share, and sales volume) for the next BRANDMAPS™ year, and a delineation of your proposed marketing strategy (and tactics) to achieve these goals. Your brand plans should also discuss each brand's strengths and weaknesses, and consider the particular threats faced by, and opportunities available to, each brand. Note that analysis must be stressed in the brand plans; mere description of what happened is not sufficient. That is, you must emphasize why things happened the way they did, not simply describe what happened.

Marketing Research Plans: This section contains a discussion of your team's strategies and plans for marketing research activities during the next BRANDMAPS™ year. A detailed marketing research budget should also be presented in this section of your marketing plan.

A REGIONAL PRO-FORMA OPERATING STATEMENT must be completed for each active brand in each market region. In addition, each team must provide a DIVISIONAL PRO-FORMA OPERATING STATEMENT for the team as a whole. See Chapter 11 for details on the REGIONAL PRO-FORMA OPERATING STATEMENT and the DIVISIONAL PRO-FORMA OPERATING STATEMENT. Both statements should be included within a "Tables, Figures, and Charts" section at the end of the marketing plan (or in a separate document appended to the marketing plan), and not within the main text. All tables, figures, and charts must be placed in order as they are referred to in the main text, and numbered sequentially.

Some Specific Comments on BRANDMAPS™ Marketing Plans

Regardless of the specific format adopted for your marketing plan, the plan should be constructed with attention paid to the following points:

(1)   Consistency of style within the written marketing plan, and depth of analysis, are very important.

(2)   When referencing products and brands in your written marketing plan, use the BRANDMAPS™ notation "firm#-product#". Thus, for example, product 3 of firm 6 should be referenced as product (or brand) 6-3.

(3)   When referencing market shares, use percentages with a maximum of one decimal point. Thus, for example, a market share of 0.152 should be referred to as 15.2%.

(4)   Ensure that your written marketing plan is analytical rather than just being descriptive in nature. That is, your marketing plan should emphasize the "why" and the "how" rather than just describe or state what has gone on (or predict what will go on). Provide evidence for your assertions. For example, don't just say a BRANDMAPS™ market region is price-sensitive; provide the appropriate evidence to justify such a conclusion. Tables, figures, and charts may play important roles in laying out the details of your analysis procedures.

(5)   Your marketing plan should reflect the depth and breadth of your marketing strategy, planning, and analysis skills, tempered with appropriate doses of common sense and managerial acumen.

(6)   You should view the written marketing plan as an opportunity to "show your stuff." That is, your marketing plan should reflect all of your thinking, knowledge, and analysis about your firm, its products, and the BRANDMAPS™ marketplace.

A Marketing Plan Checklist

Based on previous BRANDMAPS™ participants' marketing plans and their efforts in developing marketing plans, some hints about marketing plan development have evolved over time:

✓ DO include sufficient evidence and analysis to back up your strategies and plans.

✓ DON'T view a marketing plan as a place to just say what you are going to do in the next year. You must justify your actions as being reasonable and appropriate under the circumstances. Your proposed actions should be logically and demonstrably better than other possibilities. You must try to sell your plan with analysis, insight, thoughtfulness, and evidence. Your goal is to convince others that you know what you are doing, that you understand the marketplace, and that your strategies and tactics make sense and are "do-able."

✓ DON'T just say, "We're going to follow a low price-high advertising strategy," without providing any analysis and evidence to show that this is a good and appropriate strategy.

✓ DON'T make assertions like, "This region is price-sensitive," without providing sufficient evidence to back up such a claim.

✓ DO be sure to cover all marketing decision variables in your marketing plan. These include: product policy (reformulation strategy and tactics, current preference position, research and development support), pricing policy, and promotion decisions (advertising, promotion, and sales force).

✓ DO say something about inventory and capacity management issues somewhere in your marketing plan.

✓ DO use enough numbers to allow the reader to understand what "increasing," "decreasing," "high," and "low," for example, mean.

✓ DON'T try to overwhelm the reader with numbers.

✓ DO be careful not to use a lot of vague generalities, platitudes, and buzzwords in your marketing plan. The reader can easily tell when you're trying to construct an elaborate "snow job." Specifics are important in a marketing plan.

✓ DO include competitive analysis in your plan. This should involve assessing the current situation, likely goals, and potential actions of major competitors. Assess the factors that have led to success (or lack of success) for each major competitor. After all, if you can determine such factors for your competitors, perhaps such evidence translates directly into things to which you should pay attention in formulating your own plans.

✓ DO thoroughly proofread and correct any spelling errors in your written plan.

✓ DO remember that the Executive Summary is **THE** single most important part of the marketing plan. It is to be a summary of the whole plan.

✓ DO use a tight and consistent format in each of the brand plans. Subheadings are valuable in making a marketing plan readable.

✓ DO complete your marketing plan by the scheduled time.

## Chapter 11

Budgeting in BRANDMAPS™

> *Note*: *This chapter describes topics and features that are optional within BRANDMAPS™. Your course instructor will advise you if the material in this chapter is to be used in your particular BRANDMAPS™ exercise.*

Introduction

Budgeting and budgets are facts of life in real organizations. Budgets are an integral phase of the planning process. Budgets act as constraints, especially near the end of a fiscal year. Budgets act as incentives, since "spend it or lose it" seems to be a widespread organizational axiom. Budget management, monitoring, and control dominates the lives of many marketing and non-marketing managers. Budgets are negotiated so political, emotional, and non-rational forces all come into play. Budgeting implies forced trade-offs, since resource allocation choices are a fundamental part of the process of casting a budget. Given all of these facts of organizational life, budgeting and budgets should and do play an important role in BRANDMAPS™.

Budgeting and budgets are both present in BRANDMAPS™. The budgeting process is simulated in BRANDMAPS™ with the aid of standardized budget forms. These budget forms are used in connection with the annual planning process in BRANDMAPS™. Even if you are not required to prepare formal written marketing plans within your particular BRANDMAPS™ exercise, you will find these forms of considerable use in facilitating your on-going analysis, planning, and strategy formulation efforts.

Budgets as constraints are also included within BRANDMAPS™. These constraints focus on marketing support spending. While these budget limits are negotiated with your company president (your course instructor), these constraints do affect your ability to actually spend on marketing support.

This chapter describes the budgeting and budget aspects of BRANDMAPS™.

Budgeting and Standardized Budget Forms

Standardized budgeting forms are used within BRANDMAPS™ to ensure that all firms report comparable data in an easily understood format. The standardized forms involve reporting financial and sales data in a format of the same style as that used within the BRANDMAPS™ financial and operating results reports.

Use these budgeting forms as masters and photocopy them as necessary to create as many copies as you need to complete the budgeting task. Based on experience, you should photocopy an ample supply.

Permission is hereby granted without charge, royalty, or copyright payment to anyone wishing to make photocopies of pages 152-154 for use during a BRANDMAPS™ exercise.

Since the BRANDMAPS™ participant's manual is copyrighted, you may need to show this photocopying permission statement to a commercial copy shop to facilitate photocopying of multiple copies of pages 152-154.

If you are preparing formal budgets for submission to your course instructor, your course instructor may permit you to substitute computer-generated budgets for these standardized forms, provided they are substantially identical to these BRANDMAPS™ budget forms. Given the prevalence of spreadsheets, you may wish to use one to create your budgets. The iterative nature of budgeting leads to considerable advantages to groups who use spreadsheet software to assist them in budget creation.

General Instructions

Start with the REGIONAL PRO-FORMA OPERATING STATEMENT. Complete a REGIONAL PRO-FORMA OPERATING STATEMENT for each brand in each region in which it will be active (for at least one quarter) next year. Then, complete the DIVISIONAL PRO-FORMA OPERATING STATEMENT. Finally, complete a MARKETING SUPPORT AND RESEARCH BUDGET STATEMENT.

On these budget forms, all entries should be in $000s, except for: (a) "Market Share," which is expressed in percentage terms; (b) "Brand Sales Volume," which is in 000s of units; and (c) "Manufacturer Price" and "Dealer Rebates" which are expressed in dollar per unit terms. The columns in the forms are not really wide enough to write out the full numbers, so 000s notation needs to be used.

Regional Pro-Forma Operating Statement Instructions

If a brand is actively distributed in a region for one or more quarters in a year, then a REGIONAL PRO-FORMA OPERATING STATEMENT must be completed for this brand in this market. A brand that is inactive in a region in some quarters will have zero entries in the corresponding quarterly columns.

Fill in the annual (raw) data for the "Last Year" column. These data come directly from the Cumulative Product Operating Statements for the fourth quarter of "Last Year." If data are available for the year previous to last year, fill in the annual (raw) data for the "Two Years Ago" column.

Work from the top down and fill in the quarterly forecasts. Only raw values need to be placed in the quarterly boxes. Add the four quarterly values to complete the "Next Year" column.

For "Dealer Rebates," calculate a weighted average value for the "Next Year" column (using "Brand Sales Volumes" as the weights). That is, calculate the total dollar value of the rebates over the four quarters of "Next Year," and then divided that figure by the annual "Brand Sales Volume" figure.

Annual "Manufacturer Price" is equal to the corresponding "Sales Revenues" value divided by the "Brand Sales Volume" value. Annual "Market Share" is equal to annual "Brand Sales Volume" divided by annual "Industry Sales Volume," expressed in percentage terms.

Now, calculate the index values (in parentheses) for the "Two Years Ago" and "Next Year" columns. The value for "Last Year" always has the index value 100.0, with the other values being indexed relative to the "Last Year" value. For example, if the "Next Year" value is 10.9% above the "Last Year"

Regional Pro-Forma Operating Statement

Brand	Area	Year
—		

	Annual Historical Data			Quarterly Forecasts and Budgets For Next Year			
	Two Years Ago	Last Year	Next Year	Q1	Q2	Q3	Q4
Industry Sales Volume (in 000s of units)	( )	(100.0)	( )				
Market Share (%)							
Brand Sales Volume (in 000s of units)	( )	(100.0)	( )				
Manufacturer Price (in $ per unit)	( )	(100.0)	( )				
Dealer Rebate (in $ per unit)	( )	(100.0)	( )				
Sales Revenue (in $000s)	( )	(100.0)	( )				
Cost of Goods Sold (in $000s)	( )	(100.0)	( )				
Transportation (in $000s)	( )	(100.0)	( )				
Rebates Offered (in $000s)	( )	(100.0)	( )				
Sales Commissions (in $000s)	( )	(100.0)	( )				
Gross Margin (in $000s)	( )	(100.0)	( )				
Fixed Costs							
Administrative O/H (in $000s)	( )	(100.0)	( )				
Support Spending (in $000s)	( )	(100.0)	( )				
Total Fixed Costs (in $000s)	( )	(100.0)	( )				
Operating Income (in $000s)	( )	(100.0)	( )				

Divisional Pro-Forma Operating Statement

Firm		Year		Total	Brand 1	Brand 2	Brand 3	Brand 4
Brand Sales Volume								
Manufacturer Price								
Dealer Rebate								
Sales Revenues								
Cost of Goods Sold								
Transportation								
Rebates Offered								
Sales Commissions								
Gross Margin								
Fixed Costs								
Administrative Overhead								
Advertising								
Consulting Fees								
Corporate Overhead								
Depreciation								
Disposal Sales								
Emergency Production								
Introduction Costs								
Inventory Charges [Finished Goods]								
Marketing Research								
Production Order Fixed Charges								
Promotion								
Reformulations								
Research and Development								
Sales Expenses								
Sales Salaries								
Sales Overhead								
Total Fixed Costs								
Operating Income								
Non-Operating Income								
Taxes								
Net Income								

Note: All values in this DIVISIONAL PRO-FORMA OPERATING STATEMENT (except "Manufacturer Price" and "Dealer Rebates") are expressed in $000s or 000s of units, as appropriate.

Marketing Support and Research Budget Statement

	Firm		Year	

	Proposed Spending	Approved Spending
Advertising		
Marketing Research		
Promotion		
Research and Development		
Sales Force Compensation and Overhead		

Note: All values in this MARKETING SUPPORT AND RESEARCH BUDGET STATEMENT are expressed in $000s.

value, then the index value for "Next Year" would be 110.9; if the "Two Years Ago" value was 81.6% of the "Last Year" value, then the index value for "Two Years Ago" would be 81.6.

Divisional Pro-Forma Operating Statement Instructions

The DIVISIONAL PRO-FORMA OPERATING STATEMENT is constructed from the REGIONAL PRO-FORMA OPERATING STATEMENTS.

First, for each brand, add up all the values from the REGIONAL PRO-FORMA OPERATING STATEMENTS for all regions in which a brand is to be actively marketed next year (and for which a REGIONAL PRO-FORMA OPERATING STATEMENT was prepared). Transfer the totals to the appropriate brand column on the DIVISIONAL PRO-FORMA OPERATING STATEMENT.

Then, provide the figures for the DIVISIONAL PRO-FORMA OPERATING STATEMENT that do not appear on the REGIONAL PRO-FORMA OPERATING STATEMENTS ("Consulting Fees," "Corporate Overhead," "Depreciation," "Disposal Sales," "Emergency Premiums," "Introduction Costs," "Inventory Costs [Finished Goods]," "Marketing Research," "Prod Order Fixed Charges," "Reformulations," "Research and Development," and "Sales Expenses"). Finally, sum across to complete the "Total" column, and then add and subtract down to complete the various summary rows in the "Total" column ("Total Fixed Costs," "Operating Income," etc.).

Note that "Manufacturer Price" in the total column is equal to total "Revenues" divided by total "Brand Sales Volume." "Sales Expenses" refers to the expenses associated with hiring and firing sales representatives.

The following line items will only exist for the firm as a whole, and not for any individual brand (because no unambiguous allocation of costs is possible): "Consulting Fees," "Depreciation," "Marketing Research," and "Sales Expenses."

Marketing Support and Research Budget Statement Instructions

After completing all other budgeting forms (REGIONAL PRO-FORMA OPERATING STATEMENTS for each brand in each market region and a DIVISIONAL PRO-FORMA OPERATING STATEMENT for the firm as a whole), then complete this MARKETING SUPPORT AND RESEARCH BUDGET STATEMENT. BRANDMAPS™ firms fill-in the "Proposed Spending" column. After reviewing your budget request, your firm's president (the course instructor) will fill-in the "Approved Spending" column.

Quarterly Budget Constraints

At your course instructor's discretion, quarterly marketing support spending limits may exist. These limits concern marketing support spending. Here, "marketing support spending" is the sum of the following spending items: (1) advertising, (2) promotion, (3) research and development, and (4) sales force compensation (salaries and commissions) and sales force overheads.

Note: "Marketing support spending" does not include marketing research spending. Thus, marketing research spending is not explicitly constrained by quarterly budget considerations.

Quarterly spending limits refer to the ratio of marketing support spending to "adjusted sales revenue." "Adjusted sales revenue" is defined as follows:

$$ASR_t = \begin{cases} SR_t, & \text{in quarter 1} \\ \\ (1-W_{ASR})\, ASR_{t-1} + W_{ASR}\, SR_t, & \text{after quarter 1} \end{cases}$$

where ASR_t is adjusted sales revenue in quarter t, SR_t is sales revenue, and W_{ASR} is a partial-adjustment weight for adjusted sales revenue. In BRANDMAPS™, $W_{ASR}=0.50$. Any changes in W_{ASR} will be announced by your course instructor. This definition of ASR implies that it tracks sales revenue, although with a lag. If your sales revenues increase, so too will ASR. If your sales revenues decrease, ASR will follow suit.

Note that "marketing support spending" and "sales revenue" refer to the firm as a whole, across all products and regions. These quarterly spending limits are firm-wide. It will be up to you to allocate the available spending limit across all of your brands and regions in each quarter.

The quarterly marketing support spending limit is based on the ratio of "marketing support spending" to "adjusted sales revenue." Initially, this spending ratio cannot exceed 0.40. That is, you may spend no more than 40% of your "adjusted sales revenues" on "marketing support spending" in any quarter. It may be possible to negotiate to change this maximum "marketing support spending" to "adjusted sales revenue" ratio with your company president (your course instructor).

The FINANCIAL AND OPERATING STATEMENT MESSAGES page contains a message that reports your current "adjusted sales revenue" and the maximum value of "marketing support spending" for the next quarter. A sample message is shown below:

```
QUARTERLY MARKETING SUPPORT SPENDING BUDGET REPORT
          Current quarter "adjusted sales revenue" is    89,769,280.
          Current quarter "marketing support spending" is  32,114,216.
   Maximum "marketing support spending" next quarter is    35,907,712.
```

If you inadvertently exceed your maximum permissible marketing support spending level, spending will be reduced automatically first on promotion, then on advertising, then on research and development, and finally on sales force (by firing sales representatives) to satisfy the budget limit. In all cases, pro-rata adjustments will be made, across all active products in all regions. For example, if your aggregate marketing support spending is $1,000,000 too high and your promotion spending is $5,000,000, then all promotion spending amounts will be automatically reduced 20% (1,000,000/5,000,000).

Annual Budget Constraints

At your course instructor's discretion, annual spending limits on advertising, marketing research, promotion, research and development, and sales force compensation (salaries and commissions) and overhead may exist. Such annual limits are for your firm as a whole (across all products in all regions) for the four quarters which make up each BRANDMAPS™ year. These annual spending limits are on a line-item basis. A specific budget will be established for each of advertising, marketing research, promotion, research and development, and sales force compensation and overhead.

These annual spending limits are based on your negotiated budgets, as summarized in your MARKETING SUPPORT AND RESEARCH BUDGET STATEMENT.

As a BRANDMAPS™ year unfolds, you may wish to shift some budget from one line to another (say, from promotion to advertising). Such budget adjustments will have to be negotiated with your firm's president (your course instructor) on a case-by-case basis.

If annual budget constraints are in effect, a BUDGET ANALYSIS (BUDGETED VS. ACTUAL

SPENDING) report will be included within your financial and operating reports. See Exhibit 15 for a sample BUDGET ANALYSIS (BUDGETED VS. ACTUAL SPENDING) report.

Exhibit 15

SAMPLE BUDGET ANALYSIS (BUDGETED VS. ACTUAL SPENDING)

```
*****************************************************************************
BUDGET ANALYSIS (BUDGETED VS. ACTUAL SPENDING), FIRM 9, QUARTER  5    PAGE 14
*****************************************************************************


                                                          REMAINING BUDGET
                                                          THAT STILL MAY
                          BUDGETED          YEAR-TO-DATE   BE SPENT IN THE
                          SPENDING          ACTUAL SPENDING REST OF YEAR  2
                          FOR YEAR  2       FOR YEAR  2
                       ------------------  ------------------ ------------------

                       $ AMOUNT      %     $ AMOUNT     %     $ AMOUNT     %
                       ----------  -----   ----------  -----  ----------  -----

ADVERTISING            999,999,999 100.0   10,750,000   1.1   989,249,999  98.9
MARKETING RESEARCH     999,999,999 100.0      142,848    .0   999,857,151 100.0
PROMOTION              999,999,999 100.0    4,250,000    .4   995,749,999  99.6
RESEARCH & DEVEL       999,999,999 100.0      750,000    .1   999,249,999  99.9
SALES COMPEN & O/H     999,999,999 100.0   16,364,216   1.6   983,635,783  98.4


*** NOTES ***
(1) BUDGETED SPENDING figures are absolute maximums; they may not be
    exceeded.  If exceeded inadvertently, the following actions will be taken
    automatically:
    (a) for ADVERTISING, PROMOTION, and RESEARCH & DEVELOP -- pro-rata
        reductions across all products and all market regions will be
        effected, as necessary;
    (b) for MARKETING RESEARCH -- no further marketing research requests will
        be processed; and,
    (c) for SALES COMPEN & O/H --  a phased reduction in force will occur
        (i.e., sales representatives will be fired), on a pro-rata basis
        across the market regions, as necessary.
(2) YEAR-TO-DATE ACTUAL SPENDING includes all spending up to and including
    the current quarter.
(3) All budget and actual spending figures refer to the totals across all
    products and all market regions.
(4) After the beginning of the year, BUDGETED SPENDING figures may only be
    changed (general across-the-board increases, specific line-item
    increases and re-allocations of spending across line items) with the
    approval of the President.  Such approval normally requires a completely
    new budget request proposal to be submitted for review.  Before
    seeking such adjustments, all possible re-allocations of funds across
    products and across market regions should be thoroughly examined.
```

If you inadvertently exceed your maximum permissible spending level on any line-item, spending will be reduced automatically to satisfy the annual budget spending constraint. In all cases (except marketing research), pro-rata adjustments will be made across all active products in all regions. Once you exceed your budget limit on a particular line-item, no further spending will be possible for the remainder of the current

Annual and Quarterly Budget Constraints

At your course instructor's discretion, the quarterly and annual budget constraints may both be used. If so, your actual spending must satisfy both constraints simultaneously, or else appropriate action will be taken automatically to reduce your spending to meet your budget limits.

You should keep in mind that these budget limits are negotiable. As necessary, you may wish to attempt to make a case to increase previously agreed-upon limits. You should naturally expect to make a persuasive and forceful case in support of your request. Moreover, there is no guarantee that even the most moving case will win the approval of your company president.

## Chapter 12

Using the BRANDMAPS™ Disk

> **Note:** *This chapter describes topics and features that are optional within BRANDMAPS™. Your course instructor will advise you if the material in this chapter is to be used in your particular BRANDMAPS™ exercise.*

The BRANDMAPS™ decision variable change forms on pages 126-136 are used to record your decision variable changes and marketing research pre-order requests. Someone must enter the requests on the BRANDMAPS™ forms into the BRANDMAPS™ data base. In some circumstances, the course instructor will arrange to have this data entry task handled for you. However, it is also possible to "do it yourself" using the BRANDMAPS™ software described in this chapter. By entering your own data, you take complete control over your own destiny. Data entry errors, for example, will be fully within your own control.

Note: Within BRANDMAPS™, your firm will be in a letter-designed industry — for example, industry B. Although you may refer informally to firm 2 in industry B as firm B2, the BRANDMAPS™ participant's software does not use letter codes for firms. The various data files on the BRANDMAPS™ participant's disk include information designating your industry code. Thus, when using the BRANDMAPS™ participant's disk, you never make reference to a letter-designated industry. For example, you are firm 2 not firm B2 as far as the BRANDMAPS™ participant's disk is concerned.

Introduction

All decision variable changes are entered into the BRANDMAPS™ data base via the BRANDMAP.EXE program. This program is on the BRANDMAPS™ participant's disk. Marketing research requests are also pre-ordered using the software. The course instructor may require or suggest that the usual BRANDMAPS™ decision variable change forms and marketing research request forms (i.e., those contained on pages 126-136 in the BRANDMAPS™ participant's manual) be submitted along with the BRANDMAPS™ participant's disk.

The BRANDMAPS™ input program (used for changing decision variables and pre-ordering marketing research studies) is split into two programs: B_DV.EXE (to change decision variables) and B_PREMRS.EXE (to pre-order marketing research studies). To provide convenient access to these programs and to other useful functions, a front-end driver — BRANDMAP.EXE — exists. Please use program BRANDMAP.EXE to access the BRANDMAPS™ participant's disk.

> *Note: If you do not have sufficient RAM available on your personal computer to run BRANDMAP.EXE, you may also access the individual BRANDMAPS™ programs directly. Programs B_DV.EXE and B_PREMRS.EXE may be run directly from the DOS prompt.*

Pre-ordered marketing research studies are not executed at the time of pre-ordering. Rather, all necessary marketing research study parameters and specifications are recorded by the B_PREMRS.EXE program. Later, after the next BRANDMAPS™ game run, these parameters and specifications are used to execute the pre-ordered marketing research studies.

The BRANDMAPS™ participant's disk contains the BRANDMAPS™ input programs, all data files used by the input programs, and all updated financial and marketing research results files after each BRANDMAPS™ game run. Due to the size of these files, there will be little or no room for any other "personal" (not generated by the BRANDMAPS™ software) files on this disk.

Only this single disk is needed for all BRANDMAPS™ activities. To use this disk, a PC/XT/AT/386/486 or "100%"-compatible clone, running under PC- or MS-DOS (Versions 2.10 or later), is required. This machine must have at least 500K of free RAM after loading DOS and at least one disk drive.

General Instructions For Program BRANDMAP.EXE

In what follows, things that are typed at the keyboard are **bolded and italicized**. As with all DOS-based personal computer programs, after typing any numerical entry, you will need to press the <*Enter*> key to have the program process your entry.

Menus in program BRANDMAP.EXE (and in sub-programs B_DV.EXE and B_PREMRS.EXE) require you to use the cursor keys to select a menu element, and then press <*Enter*> to execute your actual choice. If you press <*Esc*> while at a menu, you will immediately terminate your current activities and branch to the next higher menu level.

At some points within BRANDMAP.EXE, you will be prompted to enter a number. For example, you may be asked to input the number of a particular product or market region. To terminate processing of any program command part-way through this input process, press <*Esc*>. Processing of the current command then terminates immediately and program control passes to the next higher level of the program.

When inputing numerical values in these programs, BRANDMAPS™ numbers may be used. For example, input of *2M* will be interpreted as the value 2,000,000. Similarly, the input of *2.7K* will be interpreted by the BRANDMAPS™ programs as the value 2,700.

When entering numerical values, do not use commas. That is, enter *2000000* not 2,000,000. Of course, a shorter, faster, and less error-prone way to enter *2000000* is by entering this value as *2M*. Small or capital letter versions of "K" and "M" may both be used.

When You Receive the BRANDMAPS™ Disk

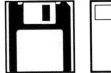

When you receive the BRANDMAPS™ participant's disk, certain files (described below) must always be on the disk. Other files will be created along the way by the program. The contents of these files are described later in this documentation. If these files are not on your disk, contact your course instructor immediately to obtain a replacement disk.

If your BRANDMAPS™ firm disk is a 360K disk, then the following 11 files are always present on your firm's BRANDMAPS™ disk (where "i" is your industry code and "n" is your firm number):

```
BRANDMAP.EXE
B_DV.EXE
B_MENU.EXE
B_PREMRS.EXE
DVn.B_i
DVPARAMn.B_i
FINRECn.B_i
INDUSTRY
LIBRARY.B00
PREMRSn.B_i
REBEEP.COM
```

If your BRANDMAPS™ firm disk is a 720K (or more) disk, then the following 18 files are always present on your firm's BRANDMAPS™ disk (where "i" is your industry code and "n" is your firm number):

```
ALERT.EXE
AMAZE.TXT
BRANDMAP.EXE
B_DV.EXE
B_MENU.EXE
B_PREMRS.EXE
DVn.B_i
DVPARAMn.B_i
FINRECn.B_i
FPICK.DOC
FPICK.EXE
INDUSTRY
LIBRARY.B00
PREMRSn.B_i
READ.ME
REBEEP.COM
SEE.EXE
SIREN.EXE
```

Given the sizes of these and other BRANDMAPS™-related files, you should not add any other files to the BRANDMAPS™ disk. You may freely copy files from the BRANDMAPS™ disk to another disk or sub-directory.

Starting and Running Program BRANDMAP.EXE

To start program BRANDMAP.EXE:

[1] Boot-up your personal computer. If you are using a hard disk machine, turn the machine on. If you are using a two-disk drive machine with no hard disk, place a copy of a disk which contains the operating system in the A: drive and then turn on the machine. During the boot-up phase, the operating system may ask for the date and the time. Just hit the *<Enter>* key twice; it isn't necessary to enter a date and time. You should now be at the A> prompt.

[2] Put the BRANDMAPS™ participant's disk in the A: drive. If you are using a hard disk machine, make the A: drive the default drive by typing *A:* .

[3] Type *BRANDMAP* to initiate the execution of the BRANDMAPS™ driver program. Press the *<Enter>* key or any other key to continue on from the BRANDMAPS™ introductory identification screen.

The BRANDMAP.EXE program's main menu, shown below, then appears:

Main Menu [v3.00 06/01/93]
Run Program B_DV.EXE To Change Marketing and Operations Decision Variables Run Program B_PREMRS.EXE To Pre-Order Marketing Research Studies
Print Any ASCII-Text File To Printer Port LPT1 With DOS COPY Command Print Any ASCII-Text File To Printer Port LPT1 With DOS PRINT Command
See Any File on the Screen With Program SEE.EXE
Exit This Program and Return to the DOS Prompt

Press the cursor keys, <Up> or <Down>, to position the highlight bar on a
menu selection option and then press <Enter> to execute the highlighted menu
selection option. Press the <Esc> key at any time to exit this menu.

The current menu item is always shown in reverse video. Use the cursor keys to identify the desired menu item, and then press *<Enter>* to select it.

Changing Decision Variables With Program B_DV.EXE

The first menu item on the BRANDMAP.EXE program main menu, **Run Program B_DV.EXE To Change Marketing and Operations Decision Variables**, leads you to sub-program B_DV.EXE, which permits you to change your marketing and operations decision variables.

Note: If you do not have sufficient RAM available on your personal computer to run BRANDMAP.EXE, you may also access the individual BRANDMAPS™ programs directly. Program B_DV.EXE may be run directly from the DOS prompt.

Only changes in decision variables must be entered via program B_DV.EXE. Decision variables which do not change from one quarter to the next do not have to be entered. Unless changed, all decision variables from the previous quarter will still be in effect in, and carry over to, the next quarter.

The B_DV.EXE program main menu appears when beginning program B_DV.EXE:

```
┌─────────────────────────────────────────────────────────────────┐
│                                                                   │
│  ┌─────────────────────────────────────────────────────────────┐ │
│  │              Program B_DV:  Main Menu                        │ │
│  ├─────────────────────────────────────────────────────────────┤ │
│  │ Change Decision Variables                                   │ │
│  │ Change Decision Variables For Test Marketing Experiment (MR Study #20) │ │
│  ├─────────────────────────────────────────────────────────────┤ │
│  │ Save Files and The Exit Program B_DV (Normal Exit)          │ │
│  └─────────────────────────────────────────────────────────────┘ │
│     Select an Option Using the Cursor Keys and Then Press the <Enter> Key, │
│       or Press <Esc> To Quit (Which Automatically Saves All Files) │
│                                                                   │
└─────────────────────────────────────────────────────────────────┘
```

The current menu item is always shown in reverse video. Use the cursor keys to identify the desired menu item, and then press **<Enter>** to select it.

In the main menu shown above:

- **Change Decision Variables** leads to a series of screens that permit you to change your current decisions variables. When you complete your decision variables changes, all current decision variables are "checked" for logical consistency. Unusual situations will be flagged and displayed on the screen and also written to an ASCII-text file, MESSAGES.D_i (where "i" refers to your industry), on the BRANDMAPS™ disk. After "checking" decision variables, you should review any things flagged to ensure that the flagged entries are as you really want them to be. "Checking" does not check all possible logical relationships, nor can it read your mind with regard to what you meant to input. However, it will identify some obvious problem areas, if they exist.

- **Change Decision Variables For Test Marketing Experiment (MR Study #20)** leads to a series of screens that permit you to change your current decision variables for use within the test marketing experiment in BRANDMAPS™, Marketing Research Study #20. Only make these changes after completing all of your changes to your regular decision variables.

- **Save Files and Exit Program B_DV (Normal Exit)** exits program B_DV.EXE. All relevant files are automatically updated and saved to disk during this exit procedure. You may also exit B_DV.EXE by pressing **<Esc>**.

Spreadsheet-style inputing exists in BRANDMAPS™ program B_DV.EXE. This includes screens that display the current values of decision variables, permit you to use the cursor keys to move around a screen, and select a specific decision variable to change. When you have located the cursor on the particular data element you wish to change, you just start typing in the new value. By pressing *<Enter>* or any other cursor control key after typing the last digit of your entry, the new value will be recorded in the BRANDMAPS™ data base. As the new value is recorded in the BRANDMAPS™ data base, it will also be displayed in the appropriate field displayed on your screen.

Follow the instructions on the decision variable change screens. For ease of reference, current decision variable values are shown on the various spreadsheets. You do not have to re-enter these values.

With the cursor in a particular spreadsheet cell (highlighted in reverse video):

- If you press a number (0-9), it is presumed that you wish to update this cell's value. Continue to type the rest of the number's digits, concluding with a cursor control key (such as *<Enter>* or *<Cursor-Down>*). When a cursor control key is encountered, B_DV.EXE will process your update (and check to see that you have entered a valid number, within the appropriate BRANDMAPS™ upper and lower bounds) and then move to the cell indicated by your cursor control key. Concluding your entry with *<Enter>* automatically moves you one cell to the right. To move down the spreadsheet, conclude your data entry with *<Cursor-Down>*.

- If you press a cursor control key (such as *<PgUp>*, *<PgDn>*, *<Enter>*, *<Cursor-Up>*, *<Cursor-Right>*, *<Cursor-Left>*, or *<Cursor-Down>*), it is presumed that you wish to move to another spreadsheet cell. Note that cursor control keys *<Home>* and *<End>* result in immediate movement to the upper-right and lower-left cells on the spreadsheet, respectively.

When using BRANDMAPS™ program B_DV.EXE, a signalling feature permits users to quickly identify which decision variables have been changed. Flashing symbols after decision variables are associated with changed values. Here, "changed" means a value different from the value which existed immediately after the last game run. In particular:

- A flashing "+" after an entry denotes that this decision variable has been changed and increased from the value that existed immediately after the last game run.

- A flashing "-" after an entry denotes that this decision variable has been changed and decreased from the value that existed immediately after the last game run.

- A flashing "c" after an entry denotes that this decision variable has been changed from the value that existed immediately after the last game run. This symbol is used for decision variables where "increases" and "decreases" are not meaningful (e.g., product activity status, media content, media mix allocations, and promotional type).

In addition:

- An "a" after an entry denotes a decision variable that is automatically controlled. Such a decision variable may not be changed from its current value.

- An "f" after an entry denotes a decision variable that is fixed at the present time. Such a decision variable may not be changed from its current value.

- An "n" denotes a vaporware brand that is not currently available for use. The decision variables associated with this vaporware brand may not be changed.

Enter all of your changes in BRANDMAPS™ decision variables, as required. All decision variable changes are entered via the B_DV.EXE program.

It is possible to reset decision variables to their "original" values. Here, "original" refers to the values that existed immediately after the last game run. To reset a decision variable, move the cursor to the desired spreadsheet element (corresponding to the decision variable that you wish to reset) in B_DV.EXE and immediately strike the *<BackSpace>* key. Follow the subsequent on-screen instructions to complete the reset operation. (Incidentally, if the cursor is on any position but the first within a cell in the various B_DV.EXE spreadsheets, the *<BackSpace>* key does not perform a reset operation. Rather, *<BackSpace>* just deletes the character immediately to the left of the current cursor position.)

The decision variable change screens consist of two general instruction screens and a series of decision variable change screens. These decision variable change screens mimic the standard BRANDMAPS™ decision change forms. By pressing the *<PgUp>* or *<PgDn>* keys, you can move from one screen to the next.

The BRANDMAPS™ spreadsheet screens in program B_DV.EXE display only four market regions at a time on a single screen. If your BRANDMAPS™ industry includes more than four market regions, another screen — accessed by pressing *<PgDn>* key — will follow for market regions 5+.

By pressing *<Enter>* or any other cursor control key, you automatically move to the next data element on the screen. By pressing *<Esc>*, you will leave the decision variables change operation and return to the main menu.

After exiting B_DV.EXE, current values of decision variables are automatically written to file DVn.D_i (where "n" is your firm number and "i" is your industry). This ASCII-text file may be printed or displayed on your screen.

Pre-Ordering Marketing Research With Program B_PREMRS.EXE

Marketing research studies may be pre-ordered using program B_PREMRS.EXE. Pre-ordering means that you request a marketing research study at the same time that you use B_DV.EXE to record your decision variable changes. Pre-ordered marketing research studies are executed immediately after the subsequent game run, so they will reflect the current quarter situation at the time the pre-ordered marketing research studies are executed. (Marketing research studies reflect the market conditions existing at the end of the just-completed game run.) When pre-ordering marketing research studies, all necessary marketing research study parameters and specifications are recorded by the B_PREMRS.EXE program. These are used later during the actual execution of the marketing research studies.

The second menu item on the BRANDMAP.EXE program main menu, **Run Program B_PREMRS.EXE To Pre-Order Marketing Research Studies**, leads you to program B_PREMRS.EXE, which permits you to pre-order marketing research studies.

Note: If you do not have sufficient RAM available on your personal computer to run BRANDMAP.EXE, you may also access the individual BRANDMAPS™ programs directly. Program B_PREMRS.EXE may be run directly from the DOS prompt.

The B_PREMRS.EXE program main menu appears when beginning program B_PREMRS.EXE:

Program B_PREMRS: Main Menu

Process Marketing Research Pre-Order Requests
Set Current MR Study Pre-Orders To Equal Previous MR Study Pre-Orders
Cancel All Pre-Ordered Marketing Research Studies

Save Files and The Exit Program B_PREMRS (Normal Exit)

Select an Option Using the Cursor Keys and Then Press the <Enter> Key,
or Press <Esc> To Quit (Which Automatically Saves All Files)

The current menu item is always shown in reverse video. Use the cursor keys to identify the desired menu item, and then press *<Enter>* to select it.

In the main menu shown above:

- **Process Marketing Research Study Pre-Order Requests** leads to a sub-menu that has options allowing you to execute, cancel, or display the status of marketing research study pre-orders.

- **Set Current MR Study Pre-Orders To Equal Previous MR Study Pre-Orders** results in the current marketing research study pre-orders being set equal to their values as of the previous quarter.

- **Cancel All Pre-Ordered Marketing Research Studies** results in all marketing research study pre-orders being canceled.

- **Save Files and Then Exit Program B_PREMRS (Normal Exit)** exits program B_PREMRS.EXE. All relevant files are automatically updated and saved to disk during this exit procedure. You may also exit B_PREMRS.EXE by pressing *<Esc>*.

Marketing research studies may be "temporarily" or "permanently" pre-ordered. A "temporary" marketing research request will be executed only once, after the next quarter. Then, such "temporary" marketing research requests will be automatically "canceled" (turned-off). A "permanent" marketing research request will be executed repeatedly (after each subsequent quarter), until it is formally "canceled." Be careful with the use of "permanent" marketing research study pre-orders.

After selecting **Process Marketing Research Study Pre-Order Requests** from the B_PREMRS.EXE main menu, the marketing research sub-menu will appear. To select a particular marketing research study, use the cursor keys to locate the study of interest. Then, by pressing one of the keys indicated at the bottom of this screen, the appropriate pre-order activity will be processed:

- *<A>* for **Display All** results in the current status of all marketing research study pre-orders being displayed on the screen.

- *<C>* for **Cancel** results in this marketing research study pre-order being canceled.

- *<D>* for **Display** results in the current status of this marketing research study pre-order being displayed on the screen.

- *<P>* for **Permanent** results in the marketing research study being "permanently" pre-ordered.

- *<T>* for **Temporary** results in the marketing research study being "temporarily" pre-ordered.

- *<Esc>* results in marketing research study pre-orders being terminated. Program control passes back to the main B_PREMRS.EXE program menu.

Some marketing research selections will lead you to "infinite loops" where you will be continually prompted to input more marketing research requests. To terminate such "infinite loops," press *<Esc>* at the prompt.

Program B_PREMRS.EXE produces two DOS files, one that is viewable through normal DOS commands and one that is not. File PREMRSn.D_i (where "n" refers to a firm number and "i" refers to an industry) — e.g., file PREMRS4.D_T for firm 4 in industry T — is an ASCII-text file that records the current status of all marketing research study pre-orders.

Pre-Ordering Test Marketing Experiments

To pre-order Marketing Research Study #20 using the disk-based input option in BRANDMAPS™, you must normally complete both of the following steps:

(1) Pre-order Marketing Research Study #20 for the desired market region(s) from within the "Process Marketing Research Study Pre-Order Requests" sub-menu in program B_PREMRS.EXE. When entering your test marketing pre-order requests, you will be asked to provide the length (the number of quarters) of each test marketing experiment. You may pre-order test marketing experiments at any time, before or after Step (2) below.

(2) From the main menu in B_DV, select item "Change Decision Variables For Test Marketing Experiment" and then make any decision variable changes that are to be in effect throughout the test marketing period. Decision variable changes made within the "Change Decision Variables For Test Marketing Experiment" sub-menu are only relevant for test marketing experiments; these changes have nothing to do with your normal BRANDMAPS™ decision variables.

> *Note: Make these test marketing decision variable changes ONLY AFTER you have made all of your normal decision variable changes. If you subsequently make normal BRANDMAPS™ decision variable changes, you MUST RE-ENTER ALL of your test marketing decision variable changes.*

The test marketing decision variables are stored in a separate file (DVTESTn.B_i, for industry "i" and firm "n"). These test marketing decision variables are only processed by the BRANDMAPS™ software when test marketing experiments are conducted.

If you only complete Step (1) above, BRANDMAPS™ assumes that no changes in decision variables are required during test marketing experiments. If that is your intention, be sure to erase any existing BRANDMAPS™ test marketing decision variables file (issue the command **ERASE DVTESTn.B_i**, for industry "i" and firm "n" at the DOS prompt). If you only complete Step (2) and do not execute Step (1), no test marketing experiment is conducted.

Managing Space on the BRANDMAPS™ Disk

The BRANDMAPS™ participant's disk may contain 340K-350K in BRANDMAPS™-related files. This is fairly close to the limit of 360K on a double-sided, double-density 5-1/4" disk.

Given the limited space on the BRANDMAPS™ disk for other files, do not place any non-BRANDMAPS™ files on this disk. As necessary, you may copy any BRANDMAPS™ files from the BRANDMAPS™ participant's disk to another disk for further processing, storage, or any other reason.

Contents of the BRANDMAPS™ Disk

The files on the BRANDMAPS™ disk have the contents and uses (where "n" refers to your firm number) shown in the following table:

File Name	Description of File Contents	File Type
ALERT.EXE	A beeping utility program used by the BRANDMAPS™ programs. *Note: This file will not be on the BRANDMAPS™ participant's disk if the disk is only a 360K disk.*	Executable

AMAZE.TXT	A documentation file associated with SEE.EXE. *Note: This file will not be on the BRANDMAPS™ participant's disk if the disk is only a 360K disk.*	ASCII-Text
BRANDMAP.EXE	The main driver program for the BRANDMAPS™ participant's disk.	Executable
B_DV.EXE	The decision variables change program.	Executable
B_MENU.EXE	A menuing program.	Executable
B_PREMRS.EXE	The marketing research pre-order program.	Executable
DVn.B_i	A binary file containing the current values of all decision variables (for firm "n" and industry "i"). This file is used by the BRANDMAPS™ programs.	Binary
DVn.D_i	Current values of all decision variables (for firm "n" and industry "i").	ASCII-Text
DVPARAMn.B_i	A binary file containing some decision variable parameters and limits (for firm "n" and industry "i"). This file is used by the BRANDMAPS™ programs.	Binary
FPICK.DOC	A documentation file associated with FPICK.EXE.	ASCII-Text
FPICK.EXE	An alphabetical file picking utility program used by the BRANDMAPS™ programs. *Note: This file will not be on the BRANDMAPS™ participant's disk if the disk is only a 360K disk.*	Executable
FRESn.D_i	Financial and operating results for the just-completed quarter (for firm "n" and industry "i").	ASCII-Text
INDUSTRY	Industry parameters. This file is used by the BRANDMAPS™ programs.	ASCII-Text
LIBRARY.B00	Main menu file for program BRANDMAP.EXE.	ASCII-Text
MESSAGES.D_i	A message file written out by program B_DV.EXE (for this firm in industry "i").	ASCII-Text
MRSTUDYn.DAT	Marketing research results, other than "Test Marketing," for the just-completed quarter.	ASCII-Text
PREMRSn.B_i	A binary file containing the pre-ordered marketing research requests (for firm "n" and industry "i"). This file is used by BRANDMAPS™ program B_PREMRS.EXE.	Binary
PREMRSn.D_i	Current pre-ordered marketing research requests (for firm "n" and industry "i").	ASCII-Text
READ.ME	A "read me" file. *Note: This file will not be on the BRANDMAPS™ participant's disk if the disk is only a 360K disk.*	ASCII-Text

REBEEP.COM	A beeping utility program used by the BRANDMAPS™ programs.	Executable
SEE.EXE	A file display utility program used by the BRANDMAPS™ programs. *Note: This file will not be on the BRANDMAPS™ participant's disk if the disk is only a 360K disk.*	Executable
SIREN.EXE	A beeping utility program used by the BRANDMAPS™ programs. *Note: This file will not be on the BRANDMAPS™ participant's disk if the disk is only a 360K disk.*	Executable

Note that binary files cannot be printed, listed, or edited. However, ASCII-text files may be printed or listed. Executable files are binary in format, so they may not be printed, listed, or edited.

Questions, Problems, Difficulties

Any questions, problems, or difficulties that arise when using the BRANDMAPS™ participant's disk should be referred to your course instructor.

If major problems arise, complete the standard BRANDMAPS™ decision variable change forms and marketing research pre-order request forms and turn these into your course instructor at the appropriate time. Your course instructor will then arrange to have your data entered into the BRANDMAPS™ data base prior to the next game run.

Final Reminders

Some final instructions and reminders regarding the use of the BRANDMAPS™ programs are provided below:

✓ Only enter items for which changes are required. If no changes are required, then it is not necessary to re-enter already existing decision variables.

✓ "BRANDMAPS™ numbers" may be used when making decision variable changes. For example, 3,000,000 may be designated as 3M (where "M" means millions), 2,200,000 may be designated as 2.2M, and 23,000 may be designated as 23K (where "K" means thousands).

✓ WHEN DROPPING A BRAND: You must also change your Advertising and Promotion expenditures to zero and reallocate your Sales Force Time Allocation from dropped brands to actively-distributed brands.

✓ Decision variable changes are only physically changed on your disk when you exit the program. Until that time, the changes only reside within the active software.

✓ When changing the sales force time allocations, be sure to change allocations for all brands in a region. Time allocations must sum to 100% in each region. Regional time allocation totals will flash when they do not sum to 100%.

Index